Christmas 2000

To Nathan
Have a G
Love
Jacqueline
& U. George

D0343954

THE
UNIQUE
TREBLE

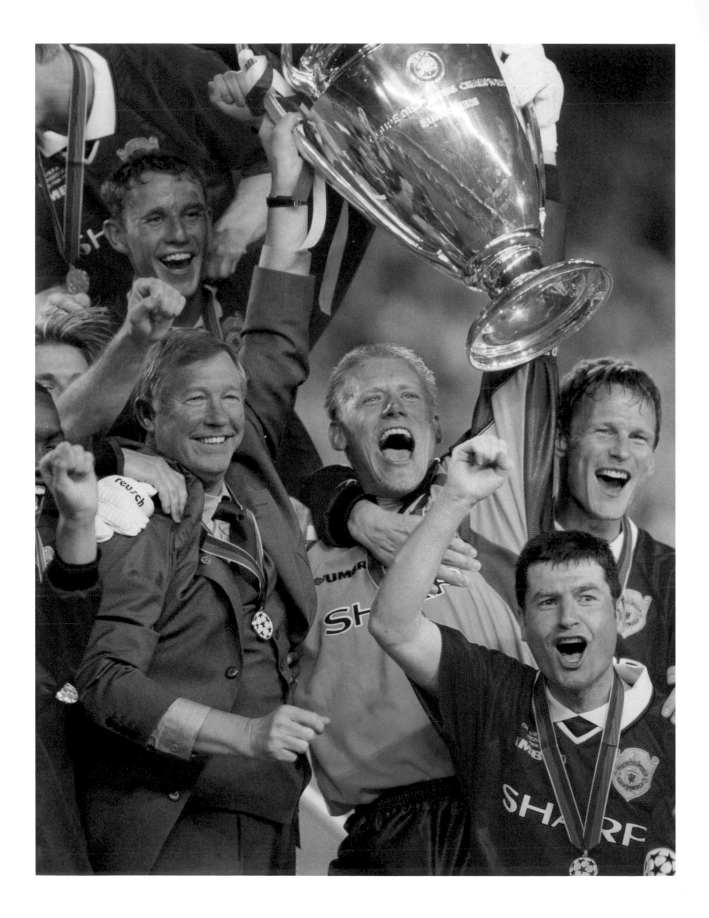

THE UNIQUE TREBLE

Sir Alex Ferguson

with David Meek

tells the inside story – match by match

Hodder & Stoughton

Also by Alex Ferguson

Managing My Life

Copyright © 2000 Sir Alex Ferguson

First published in Great Britain in 2000 by Hodder & Stoughton
A division of Hodder Headline PLC

The right of Sir Alex Ferguson to be identified
as the Author of the Work has been asserted by him in accordance
with the Copyright, Designs and Patents Act 1988.

10 9 8 7 6 5 4 3 2 1

A CIP catalogue record for this title
is available from the British Library

ISBN 0 340 79261 2

Printed and bound in Great Britain by
Butler & Tanner Ltd, Frome, England

Hodder and Stoughton
A division of Hodder Headline PLC
338 Euston Road
London NW1 3BH

Contents

Tuesday 29 December	**Chelsea** (A)	84
Sunday 3 January	**Middlesbrough** (H)	86
Sunday 10 January	**West Ham United** (H)	90
Saturday 16 January	**Leicester City** (A)	92
Sunday 24 January	**Liverpool** (H)	94
Sunday 31 January	**Charlton Athletic** (A)	96
Wednesday 3 February	**Derby County** (H)	98
Saturday 6 February	**Nottingham Forest** (A)	100
Sunday 14 February	**Fulham** (H)	102
Wednesday 17 February	**Arsenal** (H)	104
Saturday 20 February	**Coventry City** (A)	106
Saturday 27 February	**Southampton** (H)	108
Wednesday 3 March	**Inter Milan** (H)	110
Sunday 7 March	**Chelsea** (H)	112
Wednesday 10 March	**Chelsea** (A)	114
Saturday 13 March	**Newcastle** (A)	116
Wednesday 17 March	**Inter Milan** (A)	118
Sunday 21 March	**Everton** (H)	120
Saturday 3 April	**Wimbledon** (A)	122
Wednesday 7 April	**Juventus** (H)	124
Sunday 11 April	**Arsenal** (Villa Park)	126
Wednesday 14 April	**Arsenal** (Villa Park)	128
Saturday 17 April	**Sheffield Wednesday** (H)	130
Wednesday 21 April	**Juventus** (A)	134
Sunday 25 April	**Leeds** (A)	138
Saturday 1 May	**Aston Villa** (H)	140
Wednesday 5 May	**Liverpool** (A)	142
Sunday 9 May	**Middlesbrough** (A)	144
Wednesday 12 May	**Blackburn Rovers** (A)	146
Sunday 16 May	**Tottenham Hotspur** (H)	148
Saturday 22 May	**Newcastle** (Wembley)	152
Wednesday 26 May	**Bayern Munich** (Nou Camp)	156

They say when people write books there is a compulsion to write and write, a sort of magnetism that draws you to the pen. By the time my autobiography was completed we were preparing to play the final game of that memorable season in Barcelona, so possibly we missed the opportunity or the moment to capture it all. The idea of a photographic book and analyses of that incredible achievement was just too important to put to one side. I hope you will share with me, game by game, the unfolding of a unique period in the history of Manchester United Football Club.

To aid me in this delving into the depths of each game, I asked David Meek to team up with me again. We had been successful in two other ventures and David, the former *Manchester Evening News* reporter, is without question an authority on the history of Manchester United after writing about the club for over 40 years. He is also a man in whom I have complete trust and for whom I have great admiration, so I just had to force him off his old rocking chair one more time.

Other notable assistants were David Browne who did a great job with all the sketches, John and Matthew Peters, our likeable and capable photographers, my son Jason and his partners Kieran Toal and Ann-Marie Duffy for their attention to the negotiations with Roddy Bloomfield, my Editor. But at the end of the day, it really is the story of a great bunch of lads, the players. No manager could ask for a more loyal, talented and determined bunch of men. Their achievements mark them down as a team of distinction. I am proud of every one of them.

Lastly, thanks must go to my staff, all of whom work tirelessly in the preparation of the players, especially my chief coach, Steve McClaren, and Jim Ryan. I am blessed by first-rate people who work at our Carrington training ground like Albert Morgan, our kit man, and his assistant Alec Wylie; also my secretary Lyn Laffin and her staff, Kath Phipps on Reception, and of course Diana Law who has the unenviable job of trying to keep me onside with the press under the guidance of Ken Ramsden.

Then we have top-class coaches like Tony Coton, Mike Phelan, Dave Williams and Neil Bailey supported by the medical expertise of Dr Mike Stone, Robert Swire, and their medical back-up.

My chief scout is Mick Brown along with Martin Ferguson in that department, while much appreciated is the work being achieved by an excellent Academy staff headed by Les Kershaw.

Last but not least are our laundry girls, where would we be without them?

I cannot begin to acknowledge the work done at Old Trafford by our secretary, Ken Merrett, and the numerous departments of our great club, except perhaps to single out the man who can make or break us every match day with his pitch at Old Trafford, Keith Kent, our groundsman, and his hard-working staff who also prepare our pitches at Carrington and at my first training home at The Cliff. I would also like to make special mention of the late Alan Tomlinson for his service to Manchester United.

They and many others are all part of the team behind the team, and I gladly acknowledge them all in what we achieved in our treble season.

‘I don't think it will ever happen again. I believe Manchester United's unique treble will remain exactly that for all time. So many things have to come together, and the odds of this happening a second time with today's increasingly intensive demands seem to me to be stacked so high against as to make it well nigh impossible.

When we were inching towards the end of the season and it was actually happening, something told me we had a real chance. I had this gut feeling that we could pull it off. It was strange because my outlook is usually pragmatic.

I'm a realist and I have never been one to shout the odds that we are going to win this, that and the other.

We all have our pipe dreams of course. One of my great ambitions has always been to go through an entire season without being beaten. I almost achieved it as a player with Rangers when we needed to avoid defeat in the last match of the season to remain unbeaten. We lost and for good measure it meant we also lost the League.

That was a reminder of how easy it is in football to have the prize almost within your grasp but to end up with nothing. So when Manchester United arrived in March of season 1998–99 with a treble beckoning, my experience told me it would be one hell of a task to land all three prizes. We would need so many things to work out right for us.

In that situation you certainly need an element of luck, and I would be the first to acknowledge that we got our fair share. You also need players who can get through game after game after game, and to a certain extent this was an unknown quantity with the players I had around me at the time. I was fairly certain, knowing the characters of Roy Keane, David Beckham and Gary Neville, that they would be blessed by great endurance, but I was worried about Ryan Giggs. I just didn't know how many games he would make because of his susceptibility to injury. Of course, I didn't know whether injury would rob me of other players, either. This is where you definitely need good fortune and I'm happy to say that fate smiled down on us. If you analyse the latter part of the season, Henning Berg was the only player ruled out for any length of time. Roy Keane missed two or three games on the run-in but overall the squad remained fit and this gave me the freedom to juggle players about and keep everyone fresh.

My twitchy moments came with the two away fixtures before entertaining Spurs at Old Trafford for the final match of the season. We had to play first at Middlesbrough and then at Blackburn, on paper not the most difficult of fixtures, but to me they seemed loaded with danger. I knew if we could win those games, we were home and dry for the League. I certainly fancied us against Spurs at Old Trafford.

It was a difficult situation for Bryan Robson at Middlesbrough. We had won the League there before and I knew the last thing our former skipper would want would be a thrashing from his old team. We scrambled through with a 1–0 win, but I was still fearful about the next fixture, away to Blackburn. Again a former player was ranged against us in Brian Kidd, my coach until he left to become a manager himself. Blackburn were fighting relegation while we were going for the Premiership title, a contrast ripe for a shock result. Indeed, we had to

Going into the season, Ryan Giggs was a worry because of his susceptibility to injury, but fate looked down kindly on the team, and there was nothing more thrilling than seeing our left winger in full flight.

settle for a 0–0 draw, which took us to the wire needing to beat Spurs to win not only the championship but, in my view, the other two prizes as well. I was convinced that winning the League was the key to winning the FA Cup and the Champions League. I felt that if we could make it as champions then everything else would fall into place.

I remembered all too clearly losing the League in the last game of the 1994–95 season when we could only draw 1–1 against West Ham at Upton Park, and how difficult it was preparing for the FA Cup final against Everton the following weekend. I made a lot of noise about having six days to recover and that the disappointment would be a great incentive to win the Cup. I stressed that Wembley always brings out the best in Manchester United, but come the day, we got a very flat performance which I put down to losing the League.

It works the other way if you can finish the League successfully, as we saw the following season when we wrapped up the championship and were still flying when we beat Liverpool to clinch a League and FA Cup double.

It's the momentum that's important. Working on the back of a league success, you don't have to boost the players and you don't have to analyse quite so deeply whether you are picking the right team. You know you will be selecting successful and confident players. There is relaxation in the camp and everything seems to fall into place.

As I prepared for the Spurs match, the one thing I had to work out was how many chances I could afford to take with my team, bearing in mind the FA Cup final to come and then the game of all games against Bayern Munich.

No matter how much I tried to play down the Champions League final in Barcelona, as far as I was concerned Europe had become a personal crusade. I knew I would never be judged a great manager until I won the European Cup, and so I had to make sure we were ready and fresh for the big one in the Nou Camp.

In the end I left Andy Cole out of the starting line-up for the Tottenham match, with Teddy Sheringham coming back in. I put Andy Cole on at half-time and he promptly scored for a 2–1 win. With the League safely in the bag, I knew we were in with a real chance. I made one early decision, telling Jesper Blomqvist that he wouldn't be playing at Wembley but that he would definitely be in the side for the European final. Jesper is not the most confident of players and I thought this was the best way of preparing him for Barcelona. I didn't play Nicky Butt at Wembley, either, because with Roy Keane and Paul Scholes both out of the European match through suspension he was going to be my main midfield engine. I didn't risk Jaap Stam in order to protect his Achilles injury and I left Dwight Yorke on the bench with him because I felt he needed a little break and I wanted him in top condition against the Germans. I felt he could be a key player.

These decisions are much easier to make set against a background of achievement. We kept the momentum going, disposing of Newcastle really quite effortlessly, and flew out to Spain in style aboard Concorde.

Every time I close my eyes I can still see our extra-time goals against Bayern Munich. The memory will last for ever, not just because they

A trio with a great deal to celebrate – Andy Cole, Dwight Yorke and Gary Neville.

completed our fabulous treble, but because of the late drama of our victory. Never in the history of 44 European finals has there been one to compare and I doubt whether there will be one like it again. Bayern were convinced they were the victors until Teddy Sheringham and Ole Gunnar Solskjaer stunned them with those two injury-time goals. It was a brilliant climax for players, coaches, fans and everyone involved in the huge operation that makes up Manchester United Football Club.

As I say, I doubt that the treble will be won again, but even if it is, nothing can take away the fact that Manchester United were the first. I am particularly proud to have contributed to this piece of history, in keeping with all the other pioneering achievements of our innovative club. United were the first to enter European competition and the first to realise the vast potential of commercial development. Now we are treble-winners and I am delighted to have played a part in this tremendous achievement.

Planning the way forward with my new coach, Steve McClaren.

Now I begin to wonder what the future holds for me. My prime objective is to make sure that, despite our success, nothing slips and that we maintain our standards. The fact that we won the Premiership the following season by a record margin suggests that our ambition remains as keen as ever. The hunger still burns and I certainly don't see my final seasons before retirement in 2002 as a matter of simply marking time. I am determined I shall hand over to my successor with Manchester United still at the forefront of football.

People say to me, why retire? The team are doing well, but there comes a time when you have to take a family point of view. I am conscious that if I wait too long in this most demanding and time-consuming job as manager of Manchester United, I will not have the health and fitness to do the other things that excite me. For instance, there is another kind of momentum at Old Trafford which requires to be kept going and expanded. The club are looking globally to more distant horizons these days and someone is going to have to consolidate this work abroad. I am not thinking so much commercially as developing the football alliances that we have already started to create in South Africa and Belgium. The relationship with the Royal Antwerp Club is prospering and Fortune FC in Cape Town is also coming along promisingly. In the next few years I can see Manchester United fostering partnerships in China, the Far East, Australia and America. There are difficulties inherent with projects such as these – communication problems and assessment of how the operation is doing, for instance – and this is the kind of work I think I could help with.

Ole Gunnar Solskjaer didn't start in every game, but he never lost his way to goal.

I certainly wouldn't want to stay hovering on the edge of the first team. I wouldn't be happy, nor would my successor!

Decisions about my future are not entirely in my own hands of course, but I do hope there will be a role for me. In the meantime, I shall strive to keep Manchester United on the winning track with the unique treble our inspiration pointing to many more winning moments.

I have talked in this introduction mainly about the final exciting matches, but of course our treble was much more than that. It involved a total of 62 matches and they all counted. Let me take you on a journey through that incredible season. ❥

Ryan Giggs set United on the way in the Champions League with a great display against Lodz.

Manchester United: Schmeichel, G. Neville, Irwin, Keane, Johnsen, Stam, Beckham, Butt, Cole, Scholes (Solskjaer 82), Giggs

LKS Lodz: Wyparlo, Omodiagbe (Jakubowski 85), Kos, Bendkowski, Cebula, Krysiak, Pawlak, Zuberek (Paszulewicz 72), Niznik (Carbone 57), Wieszcycki, Wyciszkiewicz

Match Report

Manchester United came into the European Champions League by the back door, courtesy of an expanded competition which allowed for selected clubs who had been runners-up in their domestic leagues to play in a qualifying round.

United weren't in the mood to complain after conceding an FA Cup and league double to Arsenal and suffering a European knock-out against Monaco. Even though it meant playing in Europe before opening their Premiership campaign, they were simply thankful to get another crack at Europe.

They had also been given a shock to the system when they crashed 3–0 to Arsenal in the FA Charity Shield the previous weekend so there was a determined air about them as they welcomed the Polish team from Lodz to Old Trafford.

Happily, one player in particular hit top gear right from the start with Ryan Giggs clearly anxious to make up for lost time after missing key games last season with a hamstring problem.

The manager has for some time been toying with the idea of playing Giggs through the middle in order to utilise his great ability to run hard at defenders. The Welshman certainly seems to relish the idea because right from the start he was getting in strikes on goal. He had goalkeeper Boguslaw Wyparlo in action several times before slotting United into a 16th minute lead after being set up by Paul Scholes.

With their authority established, United dominated the rest of the match, though it wasn't until the 81st minute that Andy Cole was able to make it 2–0 for a healthy lead to take to Poland for the second leg.

Roy Keane, who had taken over the captaincy from Peter Schmeichel, looked good, especially considering his long lay-off with injury. New signing Jaap Stam was solid on his Old Trafford debut after uncertain moments in the Charity Shield at Wembley, though it's true Lodz did not do a great deal of attacking.

In fact, when United goalkeeper Peter Schmeichel was asked for his comments at the end of the match, he said it would be more appropriate if the media asked someone who had actually played in the game!

Manager's Report

❝I had thought about turning down the invitation to play in this season's Champions League on principle because I had always felt that the competition should be for what it said – champions! But it was only a fleeting thought which lasted a millisecond. Europe figures so high in the priorities of both the club and the fans that we simply had to take part, however ironic from my point of view.

It was a worry, of course, starting in Europe before playing in the Premiership and it was something of a step in the dark. Mick Brown had gone to Poland to scout them out but the match was postponed at the last minute and he spent the afternoon sitting in a car.

So we had little information about Lodz and I told the players that the game would be about us rather than them, and that we should make

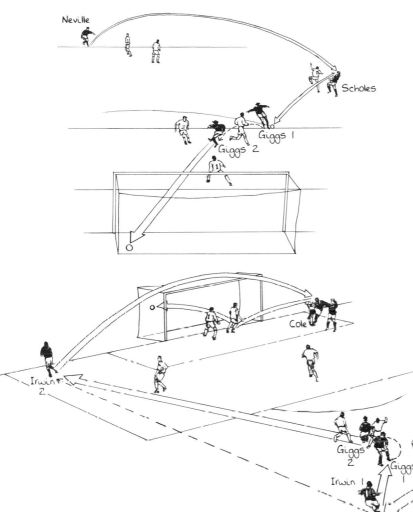

GOAL NO.1
Ryan Giggs 16 minutes

Gary Neville launched an attack from his right-back position with a crossfield ball to Paul Scholes who had moved to the left. Scholes headed the ball down into the path of Ryan Giggs who raced up to take the ball in his stride, jink around a defender and score with a shot wide of the goalkeeper. It was a good example of third-man running with Giggs showing great awareness.

GOAL NO.2
Andy Cole 81 minutes

David Beckham started the scoring move from midfield with a square pass to Denis Irwin on his left. The full-back drew an opponent before passing inside to Ryan Giggs who rolled round his marker to find Irwin with a return ball, again demonstrating excellent vision to pick out Irwin on his overlap. Irwin kept running to reach the by-line and cross for Andy Cole to score with a header at the far post. It was a marvellous move.

Andy Cole in action.

sure we played with a good tempo. It's important for our style that our passing should be quick and precise. I also stressed that they should try to get the feel of the ball early in the game. It's one of the reasons that we rarely score early. I believe it is more important to establish the pattern than go gung-ho in attack. Some fans may be mystified by our failure to take a quick lead, and that's the explanation. We have had some cruel lessons, such as losing early goals to the counterattack against the likes of Fenerbahce, Monaco, Dortmund and Juventus.

As it turned out, we had a smooth ride and I was pleased with a 2–0 result to take to Poland. My particular satisfaction was to see Roy Keane playing again. I have always felt that Roy is the heartbeat of our team and I fancy last season would not have been without a trophy if we had had Roy in certain games.

I am also pleased with Jaap Stam, my £10.75 million signing from PSV Eindhoven. He has a daunting task to follow in the footsteps of Gary Pallister and build the kind of partnership Gary enjoyed with Steve Bruce, but I like the look of him.

It was good, too, to see Ryan running freely and scoring a particularly good goal. I think we will get through this qualifying round now. ❥

Match Report

United were staring defeat in the face against a team who quickly reminded them of Premier League reality. Three days earlier in their European tie against Lodz, the pace and passion had been relaxed but Leicester had different ideas.

Right from the start they shrugged off any fears of the Old Trafford big stage and attacked with a zip that unsettled the home side. After just seven minutes Muzzy Izzet got past Gary Neville to pull Ronny Johnsen out of the middle. With Jaap Stam also adrift, Izzet found Emile Heskey for the big Leicester striker to score with a shot which clipped the bar as it went in.

The new defensive partnership of Stam and Johnsen had to be broken up at the interval with Stam troubled by a thigh muscle injury. Henning Berg took over but United still struggled to contain the fierce Foxes with Tony Cottee letting them off the hook with two missed chances. The little striker made no mistake in the 76th minute, though, when he gave Peter Schmeichel no chance with a header from a centre delivered by Robbie Savage, the one-time United junior.

It looked as though United were on a loser but they staged a magnificent revival with the help of two players who had suffered with England at the World Cup in France during the summer. A minute after Cottee's goal, the manager stepped up his attacking force by putting on Teddy Sheringham to replace full-back Gary Neville. It was a bold gamble which quickly paid off. Leicester started to wobble in the face of Sheringham's knack of being able to turn a game on its head. He hates the term 'super-sub' but it's exactly what he is. In this

		P	W	D	L	F	A	Pts
1	Wimbledon	1	1	0	0	3	1	3
2	Coventry City	1	1	0	0	2	1	3
3	Liverpool	1	1	0	0	2	1	3
4	West Ham Utd	1	1	0	0	1	0	3
5	Leicester City	1	0	1	0	2	2	1
6	Manchester Utd	1	0	1	0	2	2	1
7	Aston Villa	1	0	1	0	0	0	1
8	Blackburn Rovers	1	0	1	0	0	0	1
9	Charlton Athletic	1	0	1	0	0	0	1
10	Derby County	1	0	1	0	0	0	1
11	Everton	1	0	1	0	0	0	1
12	Leeds Utd	1	0	1	0	0	0	1
13	Middlesbrough	1	0	1	0	0	0	1
14	Newcastle Utd	1	0	1	0	0	0	1
15	Arsenal	0	0	0	0	0	0	0
16	Nottingham Forest	0	0	0	0	0	0	0
17	Chelsea	1	0	0	1	1	2	0
18	Southampton	1	0	0	1	1	2	0
19	Sheffield Wednesday	1	0	0	1	0	1	0
20	Tottenham Hotspur	1	0	0	1	1	3	0

16 August 1998

Teddy Sheringham came on as a substitute to inspire a fight-back and score United's first goal of the game. Sheringham gets support from Henning Berg in this raid.

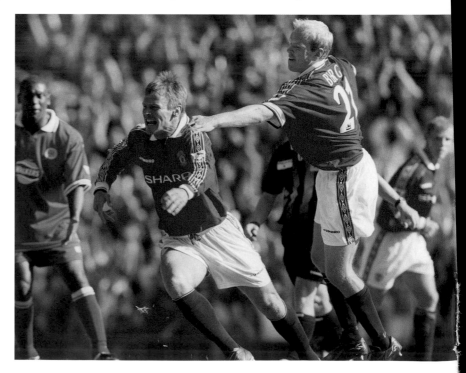

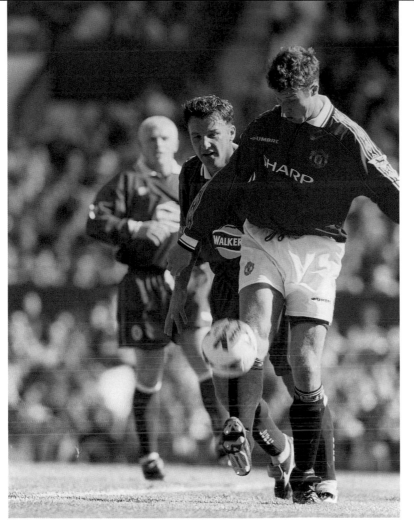

Left: *Ronny Johnsen had a hard time against Leicester, trying to make his new partnership with Jaap Stam work, and the Reds were soon two goals down.*

Below: *Peter Schmeichel does his best to organise his under fire defence.*

instance he had been on the field for just a couple of minutes when he got in a headed flick to divert a rocket of a shot from David Beckham past substitute goalkeeper Pegguy Arphexad.

It was a sweet moment for both the United players with bitter World Cup memories still fresh in their minds. Sheringham had been squeezed out of the England team by Michael Owen and Beckham, of course, was still having nightmares following his dismissal in St Etienne.

Beckham had an even more satisfying moment three minutes into injury time when he scored direct from a free kick, one of his trademark specialities and a repeat of his effort against Colombia in Lens. It reminded everyone that his World Cup had not been solely about that sending off!

Manager's Report

❝ English football is unique. I watch the game abroad and the team playing away just has no culture of attack. They plan what I can only describe as a "bedding-in" type of game and it is an attitude that runs right through European football. It is in such contrast to what we knew we could expect from Leicester City. We knew they would want to

make an early impact and in Martin O'Neill they have a manager with the courage to follow that course at Old Trafford. They say teams reflect their managers, and it's as if he is saying, "We may be small but we are as big as you."

His players didn't let him down in this match. They rose to the challenge and before we knew it we were a goal down. Gary Neville got caught on the by-line by Izzet for Emile Heskey to score what for us was a slack goal.

Leicester have good ammunition for the bold way they play, getting the ball forward to Heskey who has got the pace to run behind defenders and the strength to carry him through against challenges. I wouldn't call him a battering ram, but he has a formidable physique and power, and in Tony Cottee an admirable foil, quick to react to any crumbs from a Heskey thrust.

Our defence was all over the place for the first ten minutes but maybe it's too early to expect our new central partnership of Jaap Stam and Ronny Johnsen to come in on cue every time. The Leicester approach was new to them and we had a battle to stem the tide coming at us.

In that kind of situation I cannot wait to get the players in at half-time and earn my money sorting out the tactics necessary to rescue the situation. We improved in the second half and we started to get about

David Beckham capped the revival with one of his free-kick specials, ensuring that United earned a point from a difficult match.

them. Pressing forward can at times prove suicidal and with quarter of an hour to go we went another goal behind.

I immediately brought on Teddy Sheringham for Gary Neville to get an extra forward into the team, asking David Beckham to cover by playing right wing-back. The boy can get up and down and run for ever, so it was a risk worth taking. At any rate it took just two minutes for Sheringham to glance in David Beckham's free kick. Old Trafford came alive because there is no better theatre than Manchester United chasing a goal with a serious chance of rescuing the game.

Leicester hung on until they were undone by another Beckham free kick. To draw our first home game to Leicester is no doubt unsatisfactory to many supporters, but to steal a point from a game after being two goals down with just 14 minutes to go is what champions are made of.

I believe the identity of the new team was revealed to-day. People at the match watched unfolding before them the kind of resilience and refusal to accept defeat that we will need. It revealed a quality best summed up by Vincent Lombardi, the great coach of the Green Bay Packers, who once memorably said: "We didn't lose, we just ran out of time." **❯**

GOAL NO.1
Teddy Sheringham 79 minutes
A Ryan Giggs corner from the left was headed out of the Leicester goalmouth but only as far as David Beckham who was in the left midfield area. The England player steadied himself and then let rip with one of his famed rocket benders which Pegguy Arphexad probably had covered but he was wrong footed by Teddy Sheringham who bravely put his head to the shot, deflecting it wide of the goalkeeper.

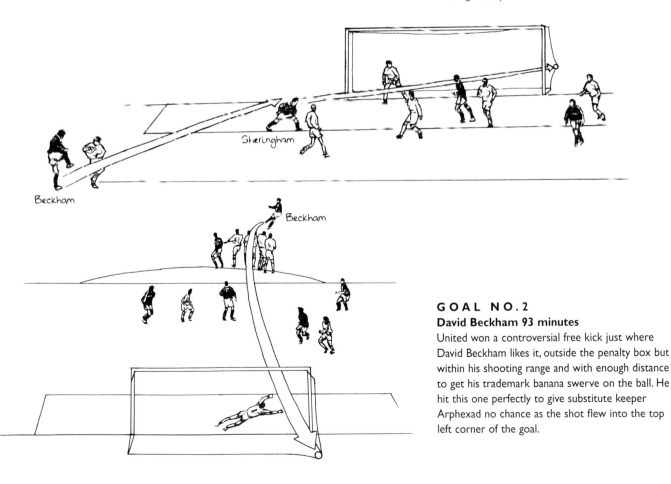

GOAL NO.2
David Beckham 93 minutes
United won a controversial free kick just where David Beckham likes it, outside the penalty box but within his shooting range and with enough distance to get his trademark banana swerve on the ball. He hit this one perfectly to give substitute keeper Arphexad no chance as the shot flew into the top left corner of the goal.

		P	W	D	L	F	A	Pts
1	Charlton Athletic	2	1	1	0	5	0	4
2	Leicester City	2	1	1	0	4	2	4
3	Aston Villa	2	1	1	0	3	1	4
4	Wimbledon	2	1	1	0	3	1	4
5	Arsenal	2	1	1	0	2	1	4
6	Liverpool	2	1	1	0	2	1	4
7	West Ham Utd	2	1	1	0	1	0	4
8	Sheffield Wednesday	2	1	0	1	3	1	3
9	Coventry City	2	1	0	1	2	2	3
10	Nottingham Forest	2	1	0	1	2	2	3
11	Manchester Utd	2	0	2	0	2	2	2
12	Newcastle Utd	2	0	2	0	1	1	2
13	Derby County	2	0	2	0	0	0	2
14	Blackburn Rovers	1	0	1	0	0	0	1
15	Leeds Utd	1	0	1	0	0	0	1
16	Chelsea	2	0	1	1	2	3	1
17	Middlesbrough	2	0	1	1	1	3	1
18	Everton	2	0	1	1	0	2	1
19	Tottenham Hotspur	2	0	0	2	1	6	0
20	Southampton	2	0	0	2	1	7	0

23 August 1998

Match Report

In this match, United gave Dwight Yorke his debut following his £12.6 million transfer from Aston Villa, launching him into action with Andy Cole as his partner but with Teddy Sheringham given a chance for the last 20 minutes.

The dream-ticket strike force failed to find the net, though there was one encouraging combination of passes after an hour culminating in a smart shot from Yorke which was blocked by Neil Ruddock. Indeed the defences dominated at both ends.

The West Ham fans seemed to spend most of their energy booing David Beckham for his World Cup dismissal. It was a trying ordeal for the United Londoner but he kept his cool and played well enough to answer those who felt he might have to move abroad to escape his persecutors.

The Hammers had the edge in the first half but with Jaap Stam still missing through injury, Henning Berg and Ronny Johnsen stood firm. The home defence were equally effective after the interval when United seized more of the initiative and Roy Keane became an increasing influence in midfield.

Yorke would have loved a goal to mark his much-heralded arrival but Shaka Hislop in the West Ham goal had other ideas. Certainly he has every reason to know Yorke's scoring secrets after playing with him for Trinidad and Tobago from the age of ten. Shaka is confident that Yorke will soon be among the goals: 'He's an accomplished finisher who keeps a cool head in front of goal and who usually manages to find the perfect finish. He will not only reproduce his Aston Villa form but improve on it with United.'

Manager's Report

❛ If ever there was to be a test for David Beckham following his dismissal at the World Cup in France, this was it! The build-up in the

Andy Cole battled for a breakthrough against West Ham, but found himself well marked.

West Ham: Hislop, Impey, Lazaridis, Pearce, Ferdinand, Ruddock, Lampard, Sinclair, Berkovic (Abou 72), Hartson, Lomas

Manchester United: Schmeichel, G. Neville (P. Neville 52), Irwin, Keane, Johnsen, Berg, Beckham, Butt, Cole (Sheringham 70), Yorke, Giggs

Left: *Dwight Yorke, on his debut for United, here struggles to get free of Frank Lampard.*

Below: *David Beckham had a hostile reception at West Ham and came through with flying colours.*

media for our visit to West Ham was intense and uncalled for, quite over the top.

David has, in fact, held up well following his ordeal. It can't be easy when you are vilified by a nation but once back in the fold at Old Trafford where he's safe and concentrating on his football again, he has revealed the strength of character that I believe is the hallmark of a Manchester United player. United players have to be stronger than most because they are subjected to more criticism than most. Other players get sent off but don't get the kind of abuse heaped on Beckham.

A match at Upton Park, never a place known for its tolerance or appreciation of visitors, was the last thing he needed so soon after the World Cup, but even in the atmosphere of hostility that greeted the arrival of our coach as we manoeuvred our way into the car park there were comical moments. With the West Ham fans giving us all kinds of vitriol and mouthing obscenities, the coach eased forward and one screaming maniac fell backwards over a box. That provided some light relief and reminded us that it was a game after all!

The game turned out to be a non-event. We should have had a penalty in the first minute when Neil Ruddock handled but the referee didn't spot it and in the end I was happy with a point.

The main problem exercising my mind was figuring out the best front partnership. I knew the combinations involving Sheringham, Solskjaer and Cole, but now I needed to find out as quickly as I could how each of the three would fit in with our new arrival, Dwight Yorke.

I started this match with Yorke and Cole, but they didn't show a great understanding and I brought on Sheringham. There was an improvement, so I have some serious thinking to do while also reminding myself that the championship is more of a marathon than a sprint. ❥

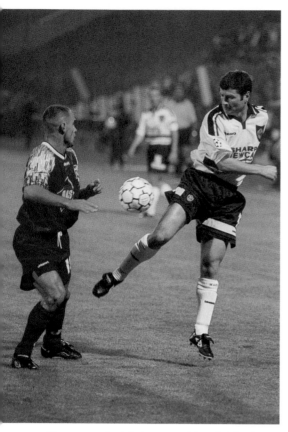

The evergreen Denis Irwin was a rock in a disciplined defensive display.

LKS Lodz: Wyparlo, Jakubowski (Bugaj 85), Kos, Bendkowski, Lenart (Pluciennik 82), Krysiak, Pawlak, Zuberek (Matys 52), Niznik, Wieszcycki, Wyciszkiewicz

Manchester United: Schmeichel, P. Neville, Irwin, Keane, Johnsen, Stam, Beckham, Butt, Scholes, Sheringham, Giggs (Solskjaer 65)

Match Report

Jaap Stam returned after his thigh injury for the trip to Poland to help protect the two-goal lead from the first leg. It proved to be a busy night for the giant defender as Lodz shook off the caution they had showed at Old Trafford and attacked with zest.

Rafal Niznik gave United an early warning of their intentions by trying to rush the visitors off their feet with a shot after only 20 seconds. It flew just inches wide of Peter Schmeichel's goal. Stam did well to halt Zbigniew Wyciszkiewicz on a breakaway, a tackle which seemed to take the steam out of the Polish team and enabled United to take more possession of the game.

It was a cautious team selection. With Dwight Yorke ineligible and Andy Cole on the substitutes' bench, Teddy Sheringham was the sole orthodox striker up front. Sheringham came close to celebrating his first senior start of the season with a goal when he got on the end of a corner from Ryan Giggs only to head wide.

David Beckham, Nicky Butt, Roy Keane and substitute Ole Gunnar Solskjaer, coming on for Giggs, all got in useful strikes, but the main purpose was to play with patience and safeguard the first-leg lead. It was a sound and disciplined performance which qualified United to go through to the competition proper.

Manager's Report

❝We laboured, and in fact we have not been at our best in these opening games. I think we have missed our normal pre-season preparation which we started late because so many of our players had been involved in the World Cup and then we had to cut everything short because of needing to play in the early qualifying round of the Champions League.

I have been particularly worried about Gary Neville and I left him out of this match in favour of his brother Phil. Gary has not been quite right since coming back from the World Cup, and he is now away on a month's holiday. I would rather be without him for a break than see him struggle all season.

In fact, right at the start of the season I sat down with all the international players who had been away and told them that they would all be given rests at different stages. Taking part in a World Cup takes a lot out of a player.

But we survived this match. We were not beaten. We were comfortable in our lead and Lodz did not do enough to turn it round. Naturally, I am delighted to get through to the full competition with an exciting opener to come against Barcelona at Old Trafford. It would have been nice to have scored one or two goals rather than come away with a goalless draw. Nevertheless it was a steady performance revealing good discipline and patience. Overall I can detect signs of improvement as we settle down and I was pleased to see the measure of control we displayed in Lodz and, for that matter, in the previous game at West Ham, even though we were again goalless.

We should make more of an impact next month after we come back from a short break. We entertain Charlton Athletic at Old Trafford and by that time I hope we will be more into our stride and expressing our real selves.

So far I have not been able to give Ole Gunnar Solskjaer a senior game and I am conscious of the fact that during the summer he had the chance to go to Tottenham but elected to stay with us. I have got to be fair to all of our strikers.

Above: *Teddy Sheringham goes to ground. Sheringham tried desperately to break the deadlock on his first appearance of the season in the starting line-up.*

Left: *Paul Scholes flat out with Rafal Pawlak*

9 September 1998	P	W	D	L	F	A	Pts
1 Liverpool	4	3	1	0	8	2	10
2 Aston Villa	4	3	1	0	5	1	10
3 Leeds Utd	4	2	2	1	5	1	8
4 Wimbledon	4	2	2	0	8	5	8
5 Arsenal	4	1	3	0	2	1	6
6 Derby County	4	1	3	0	2	1	6
7 Nottingham Forest	4	2	0	2	4	5	6
8 Tottenham Hotspur	4	2	0	2	4	7	6
9 Manchester United	3	1	2	0	6	3	5
10 Charlton Athletic	4	1	2	1	6	4	5
11 West Ham Utd	4	1	2	1	4	4	5
12 Middlesbrough	4	1	2	1	3	4	5
13 Leicester City	4	1	1	2	4	4	4
14 Blackburn Rovers	4	1	1	2	2	3	4
15 Everton	4	1	1	2	2	3	4
16 Coventry	4	1	1	2	2	3	4
17 Sheffield Wednesday	4	1	0	3	3	3	3
18 Chelsea	3	0	2	1	2	3	2
19 Newcastle Utd	4	0	2	2	2	6	2
20 Southampton	4	0	0	4	2	12	0

Match Report

This was a timely win following the furore that has greeted the sale of Manchester United to Rupert Murdoch's BSkyB television for £623 million. Most fans are still trying to make up their minds whether it is a good or bad move for the club and there will undoubtedly be more controversy to come.

Chairman Martin Edwards, under fire from groups of supporters who are banding together to oppose the sale, was certainly glad to see the emphasis put back on to the game with the 4–1 victory and two goals apiece for Dwight Yorke and Ole Gunnar Solskjaer.

A bright performance kept the minds of the spectators firmly on the game, though not before Charlton had taken a shock 32nd minute lead. A shot from skipper Mark Kinsella took a deflection to beat Peter Schmeichel and United knew it wasn't going to be the canter they perhaps expected.

They responded quickly and effectively. Solskjaer, making his first start of the season, took a return from Yorke to equalise seven minutes later, and then it was the turn of Yorke to mark his home debut on the stroke of half-time by heading in David Beckham's free kick. Three minutes after the interval, Yorke met a Beckham cross to head the Reds

Ole Gunnar Solskjaer wheels away in delight after scoring against Charlton.

in front while Solskjaer got his second of the match after 63 minutes with the help of Henning Berg.

Jesper Blomqvist, another new player to Old Trafford, made his debut in this game, following his recovery from a foot injury. A Swedish international who played against United for Gothenburg before moving into Italian football with AC Milan, Blomqvist was signed from Parma for £4.5 million as an experienced understudy for Ryan Giggs. His opening performance was modest but with Giggs injured he maintained the team's balance as a natural left-sided player.

Manager's Report

❝I was pleased with this performance because, as our four goals suggest, there was a cutting edge lacking in recent performances. The pace and angles of our passing were also top-class, a useful quality against a team which has a high work ethic.

The fact that Dwight Yorke scored twice playing in front of the Old Trafford fans for the first time will help him enormously. No matter how confident a striker may feel coming to Old Trafford, the reality is

Manchester United: Schmeichel, P. Neville, Irwin (Berg 57), Keane, Johnsen, Stam, Beckham, Scholes, Solskjaer (Cole 68), Yorke (Sheringham 68), Blomqvist

Charlton Athletic: Ilic, Mills, Powell, Redfearn, Brown, Youds, Newton (Mortimer 56), Kinsella (Jones 76), Hunt, Mendonca (Jones 71), Robinson

GOAL NO.1
Ole Gunnar Solskjaer 39 minutes
Paul Scholes picked out Ole Gunnar Solskjaer from the right side and the Norwegian immediately started off for goal. He played a one-two with Dwight Yorke standing in front of him, though some would say he got a lucky bounce off his team-mate, but he kept going and burst through the Charlton defence to plant a shot past Sasa Ilic.

GOAL NO.2
Dwight Yorke 45 minutes
David Beckham used his crossing skills to find Dwight Yorke just outside the penalty box, and taking the pass neatly in his stride, Yorke burst through the last line of the visitors' defence for a clinical finish and powerful header.

Dwight Yorke netted twice.

that he needs an early strike to confirm that he made the right decision and that he is in the right place.

I brought Dwight to our club because I felt we had reached a stage where we needed a forward player capable of changing a game on his own, someone with the ability and confidence to take on an opponent and beat him. I looked around and the two best players in that area in my view are Ronaldo and Dwight Yorke. We investigated the Ronaldo situation and financially it was impossible so we paid a record fee for Dwight. He is two-footed, has pace, good balance, and he is strong and brave, as well as possessing the talent I mentioned of being able to create something out of nothing. I also felt he needed the kind of platform we can give him at Old Trafford and that once here he would blossom. This was certainly a great night for him, scoring two and being involved in the other two.

We have had some good partnerships up front. First I had Mark Hughes and Brian McClair. They were both powerful, never injured and prolific scorers. Then Eric Cantona arrived and I don't have to explain what he did for us, except to say that he was so good that teams started to read us and sit deeper. We needed another type of player which is why I went for the quickness of Andy Cole in the box. Then I had to find a replacement for Cantona which

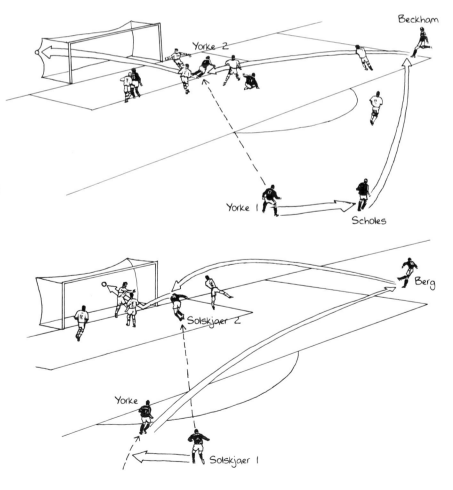

GOAL NO.3
Dwight Yorke 48 minutes
Dwight Yorke started the move with a square ball to Paul Scholes before sprinting towards goal. Scholes quickly moved the ball on to David Beckham at outside-right and Yorke arrived in the six-yard box at just the right moment to meet the winger's perfectly flighted cross and sidefoot the ball into the net.

GOAL NO.4
Ole Gunnar Solskjaer 63 minutes
United's fourth goal followed a similar pattern with a short pass to Dwight Yorke from Ole Gunnar Solskjaer who also immediately hared forward. Yorke ran a few yards before finding Henning Berg who had overlapped down the right wing. The defender centred for Solskjaer to score from close in with a diving header.

brought Teddy Sheringham to the club followed by Ole Gunnar Solskjaer who came from obscurity to overnight success, a fantastic goalscorer.

There is always a progression with strikers and, as I say, I needed a player like Dwight to keep us ahead of the field, and I think he is going to be a big success here.

I was also pleased to see Solskjaer indicating that he has retained his eye for goal on his first chance of action. I took him and Dwight off in the second half in order to give Andy Cole and Teddy Sheringham a run. It is always difficult to leave out good players but it's a squad game these days and I have to continue to experiment with the different partnerships I have on hand. I have four super strikers, five if you include Ryan Giggs playing through the middle, an option which interests me. They give me good guarantees against injury and will also enable me to keep freshening up the team as the season progresses. In terms of a long and busy season, it could be our trump card.

I was also happy to give Jesper Blomqvist his first senior game. He has had an unlucky start to his career here with a foot injury but he was tenacious and kept going despite coming in on the back of three games in seven days in a rush to get him match fit. ❯

Ole Gunnar Solskjaer scores the first of his two goals to put United level following Charlton's shock early lead.

13 September 1998							
	P	W	D	L	F	A	Pts
1 Aston Villa	5	4	1	0	7	1	13
2 Liverpool	5	3	1	1	9	4	10
3 Leeds Utd	5	2	3	0	5	1	9
4 Derby County	5	2	3	0	4	2	9
5 Manchester Utd	4	2	2	0	8	3	8
6 Middlesbrough	5	2	2	1	6	4	8
7 Wimbledon	5	2	2	1	8	7	8
8 West Ham Utd	5	2	2	1	6	5	8
9 Arsenal	5	1	4	0	3	2	7
10 Sheffield Wednesday	5	2	0	3	6	3	6
11 Nottingham Forest	5	2	0	3	5	7	6
12 Tottenham Hotspur	5	2	0	3	4	10	6
13 Charlton Athletic	5	1	2	2	7	6	5
14 Newcastle Utd	5	1	2	2	6	6	5
15 Leicester City	5	1	2	2	5	5	5
16 Chelsea	4	1	2	1	4	4	5
17 Everton	5	1	2	2	2	3	5
18 Blackburn Rovers	5	1	1	3	2	6	4
19 Coventry City	5	1	1	3	2	6	4
20 Southampton	5	0	0	5	2	16	0

Paul Scholes

Match Report

United could not have produced a better display more calculated to disturb the peace of mind of mighty Barcelona, the team they meet in the Champions League in four days' time. Coming on top of their scoring spree against Charlton, their comprehensive 2–0 win against Coventry City at Old Trafford is further evidence that they have got their act together following a modest start to the season.

Dwight Yorke was on the scoresheet again to emphasise that the Old Trafford stage is a comfortable one for him, while at the back, the defensive partnership of Jaap Stam and Ronny Johnsen looks more than capable of maintaining the solid foundation established for so many years by Gary Pallister and Steve Bruce.

Barcelona are likely to provide a stiffer test but certainly United were too strong for Coventry. They took a 20th minute lead through Yorke for his third goal in two games, with the second scored in the 48th minute by Johnsen. Coventry, as expected, worked hard but Stam and Johnsen, before his unfortunate last-minute ankle injury, dealt comfortably with everything thrown at them by the lively Dion Dublin and Darren Huckerby.

Indeed, the manager felt so confident of cruising home for the points after the second goal that he replaced his two ace wingers, Ryan Giggs and David Beckham with Nicky Butt and Jesper Blomqvist, to keep them fresh for next Wednesday's tie in the Champions League.

The picture that the fans took home with them, though, was the smile that Yorke has brought to Old Trafford. It's a smile that never leaves his face and the joy is reflected in his football.

United are looking good, and as Gordon Strachan, the Coventry manager who also graced Old Trafford with distinction in his playing days, summed up: 'United's hunger for the game is exceptional and it comes from the manager. From our point of view, we approached the game like a patient going to the dentist knowing the pain was soon to come.'

Manager's Report

‘When you play as we did against Charlton, the next match can't come quickly enough, though I always knew that the game against Coventry was going to be more difficult. Gordon Strachan is like a Jack-in-the-box, never away from the touchline and insistently demanding of his players. All credit to them, they run as hard as he shouts and you have to match their effort or you cannot get into the game. This is the hard part, and this 2–0 win was probably harder than it looked. It was comfortable in the end but initially we had to work very hard.

It was good to welcome Gary Neville back after his holiday and with a good tan to show for it. I hope the break will see him fully recovered now from the World Cup and set up for the season ahead.

Dwight Yorke took the eye again by scoring, which followed the two he got against Charlton, but I didn't like it at the press conference after the match when a reporter wanted me to compare Dwight with Eric Cantona. It would be unfair to saddle him with that comparison, even if Dwight does produce similar moments of magic and wear his shirt with an upturned collar, something he adopted, incidentally, because of his admiration for the Frenchman.

But I do have to admit that Dwight is already well on the way to enjoying the kind of popularity with the fans enjoyed by Eric. Our supporters are the best in the country when it comes to recognising real talent and they are not slow to take really good players to their hearts, especially one as laid back as our Trinidad and Tobago international. He plays with great confidence. Some have found Old Trafford daunting but Dwight has taken to the big stage like a duck to water. He is so relaxed with that beautiful smile of his. I think we have signed a winner from Aston Villa.

Jaap Stam and Ronny Johnsen were superb in this match. They were completely in control and we are in good shape for our first really big match in the European Champions League next week. **,**

Dwight Yorke scored the opening goal.

Manchester United: Schmeichel, G. Neville, P. Neville, Keane, Johnsen, Stam, Beckham (Butt 78), Scholes, Solskjaer, Yorke, Giggs (Blomqvist 78)

Coventry City: Hedman, Wallemme, Burrows, Quinn, Shaw, Breen, Huckerby (Hall 73), Edworthy, Dublin, Telfer, Boateng

GOAL NO.1
Dwight Yorke 20 minutes
Ole Gunnar Solskjaer pushed the ball wide on the left to Ryan Giggs for the winger to centre on the run. Magnus Hedman came for the cross but could only palm it out to Paul Scholes who promptly returned the ball low back across the face of goal. Dwight Yorke, lurking at the far post, turned it in with a nimble sidefoot flick to give United the lead.

GOAL NO.2
Ronny Johnsen 48 minutes
A corner from Ryan Giggs had Coventry in trouble with a couple of shots blocked as the ball ran loose. The final rebound reached Paul Scholes on the edge of the box. The midfield man shot low for Ronny Johnsen, standing just wide of the goal, to guide the ball inside the post and make the game safe.

Group D	
Brondby 2	Bayern Munich 1
Manchester Utd 3	Barcelona 3

David Beckham is swamped by team-mates after scoring another free-kick special.

Match Report

This was one of those heart-stopping matches that conjure up all the magic that United supporters have associated with European football from the early days with Sir Matt Busby. Drawn with Barcelona, Bayern Munich and Brondby in the popularly labelled 'group of death', United were plunged right into the deep end with an opening game at Old Trafford against the Spanish giants.

The first half suggested that United have absolutely nothing to fear, however mighty the opposition. A superb strike from Ryan Giggs in the 17th minute followed by an even more dazzling move finished off by Paul Scholes after 25 minutes with no reply from the visitors meant that United led by two goals at half-time.

This was United flying at their finest, but after the interval Barcelona revealed their true worth, hauling themselves up off the floor and turning in their own sparkling display. Rivaldo, demonstrating the power and pace that have made him a world star, stormed through a United defence slow to react. The ball ran loose for his fellow Brazilian, Anderson, to score with a fierce shot. Rivaldo forced a penalty out of Jaap Stam for Giovanni to level the score, but David Beckham delighted the home fans when he scored one of his speciality free kicks after Dwight Yorke had been fouled.

More drama was to follow with Butt sent off for hand-ball on the line, stopping what otherwise would have been a goal. Luis Enrique fired home the spot-kick and United had to be content with a 3–3 draw.

Manager's Report

❝For me this was the perfect football match – both teams trying to win with scant regard for the consequences. That's how football should be played and in a sense this match was a throw-back to the days before detailed organisation of teams. It's a concept you seldom find in Italian football and I can only think Louis van Gaal has the same belief as Manchester United that we can score more goals than you!

He has this attacking ideal and he is a straight shooter. He says what he means and means what he says. I like that. He is younger than me and I just hope my Dutch friend serves as long as me to keep his ideas flourishing! Playing against his teams poses a particular problem. You have to choose between a gradual build-up to try to cope with their attacking play, or going for it.

We are no good at stifling teams anyway and we have players who like to attack and score, especially in big games. So we went for the throat and the first half was absolutely fantastic for us. We tried to make sure we got defenders on to Rivaldo and Figo while at the same time playing the ball forward quickly using our wide players and having our midfield men running through the middle.

I just didn't want the first half to finish. It was such a good performance, though I did worry at half-time about how much we had left in us after playing at such a pace because we had been the team making all the running.

Nevertheless, that first half showed the heights this team is capable of reaching. Players do emerge at new levels and I think this was a significant display. Yes, we lost our way in the second half, but when you consider that two of their goals were penalties and that we had a man sent off, a draw wasn't too bad a result. Certainly we know for sure now that if we can hit that early level on a consistent basis, we need fear nobody in the competition. **,**

Manchester United: Schmeichel, G. Neville, Irwin (P. Neville 79), Keane, Berg, Stam, Beckham, Scholes Solskjaer (Butt 55), Yorke, Giggs (Blomqvist 84)

Barcelona: Hesp, Reiziger, Sergi, Luis Enrique, Abelardo, Cocu, Figo, Zenden, Anderson, Giovanni (Xavi 68), Rivaldo

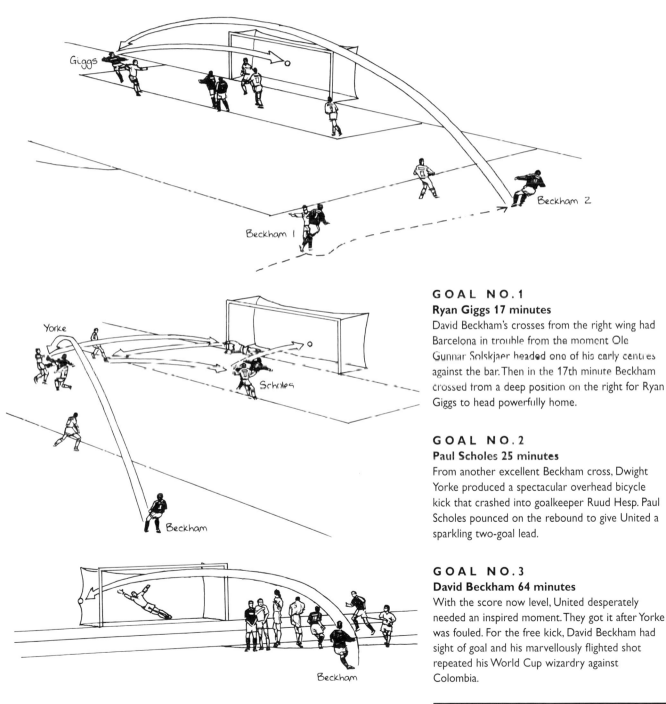

GOAL NO.1
Ryan Giggs 17 minutes
David Beckham's crosses from the right wing had Barcelona in trouble from the moment Ole Gunnar Solskjaer headed one of his early centres against the bar. Then in the 17th minute Beckham crossed from a deep position on the right for Ryan Giggs to head powerfully home.

GOAL NO.2
Paul Scholes 25 minutes
From another excellent Beckham cross, Dwight Yorke produced a spectacular overhead bicycle kick that crashed into goalkeeper Ruud Hesp. Paul Scholes pounced on the rebound to give United a sparkling two-goal lead.

GOAL NO.3
David Beckham 64 minutes
With the score now level, United desperately needed an inspired moment. They got it after Yorke was fouled. For the free kick, David Beckham had sight of goal and his marvellously flighted shot repeated his World Cup wizardry against Colombia.

20 September 1998							
	P	W	D	L	F	A	Pts
1 Aston Villa	6	4	2	0	7	1	14
2 Derby County	6	3	3	0	6	2	12
3 Liverpool	6	3	2	1	12	7	11
4 Wimbledon	6	3	2	1	10	8	11
5 Arsenal	6	2	4	0	6	2	10
6 Leeds Utd	6	2	4	0	5	1	10
7 Middlesbrough	6	2	3	1	8	6	9
8 West Ham Utd	6	2	3	1	6	5	9
9 Newcastle Utd	6	2	2	2	11	7	8
10 Manchester Utd	5	2	2	1	8	6	8
11 Nottingham Forest	6	2	1	3	5	7	7
12 Tottenham Hotspur	6	2	1	3	5	11	7
13 Sheffield Wednesday	6	2	0	4	7	5	6
14 Charlton Athletic	6	1	3	2	10	9	6
15 Everton	6	1	3	2	4	5	6
16 Chelsea	4	1	2	1	4	4	5
17 Leicester City	6	1	2	3	5	7	5
18 Blackburn Rovers	5	1	1	3	2	6	4
19 Coventry City	6	1	1	4	3	11	4
20 Southampton	6	0	1	5	3	17	1

Match Report

United were reminded in the FA Charity Shield that losing out to Arsenal for the championship last season was no fluke, and this match confirmed that the Gunners are once again a force in football. Playing in an all-black strip seemed to add a funereal air to an abject showing as United went steadily downhill to a 3–0 defeat.

An early trademark swerving free kick from David Beckham suggested United might be capable of repeating the fine football they had served up against Barcelona in the first half but Arsenal's dominant midfield, with Patrick Vieira turning in an outstanding display, had other ideas.

Tony Adams gave Arsenal a 14th minute lead when he climbed above Jaap Stam to head in a free kick from Stephen Hughes. Beckham hit the Arsenal post but the home side roared back with Marc Overmars always a threat. Such was their pressure that although Peter Schmeichel stopped Nicolas Anelka's shot with an outstretched leg, the striker beat him with a second attempt for a two-goal interval lead. The dismissal of Nicky Butt for tripping Vieira didn't help and Arsenal got their third in the 80th minute through substitute Fredrik Ljungberg.

Manager's Report

❛Our performance was so disappointing, even depressing, and in London, too! It's urgent I find a few answers to what went wrong.

I was amazed to see us deflate so quickly after playing such marvellous football in the first half against Barcelona in midweek and I must examine the reasons why Arsenal looked more determined to

Roy Keane tussles with Stephen Hughes.

Arsenal: Seaman, Dixon, Winterburn, Vieira, Keown, Adams, Parlour, Hughes, Anelka (Ljungberg 80), Bergkamp, Overmars

Manchester United: Schmeichel, G. Neville, Irwin, Keane, Berg, Stam, Beckham, Butt, Blomqvist, Yorke, Giggs

win the game than us. I am not in the business of kneejerk reactions, but I was not happy with the way we surrendered so much of the game to the opposition, and as well as myself, the players must ask themselves some questions about attitude and standards.

Of course, there are certain factors to take into consideration. This is the fifth team I have managed in my time at Old Trafford, starting with the one I more or less inherited. Then there was the side that won the FA Cup and the European Cup Winners' Cup as we turned into the nineties, followed by the team that brought the league championship back to Old Trafford in 1993, and the double-winning side which has now evolved into the present squad. It's still at something of an experimental stage and one must expect disappointments during development. I tried playing Ryan Giggs through the middle up front and I know it can work. He has played there for both ourselves and Wales and has been sensational, but it may need time for the rest of the team to adapt.

We have also brought in three new players, Jaap Stam, Dwight Yorke and Jesper Blomqvist, while saying farewell to a couple of great servants in Gary Pallister and Brian McClair who are being missed perhaps more than one would imagine.

Set against that background, I feel our younger players have to take on more responsibility, but it's something that does not happen overnight. We'll get there, though, and in the meantime I shall examine the reasons why we were up against opposition more determined and hungrier than ourselves. It's quite unusual and it's something that will always register with me. Even so, we'll handle it. We have been the baton carriers for the past eight years and that position has never daunted us. We are not afraid of challenges and I am just glad that we are in action again so quickly after Sunday with the chance to put things right against Liverpool at Old Trafford. That will be a demanding game and I know we will play with much more determination than was on offer in London at the weekend. ❞

Left: Jesper Blomqvist races for the ball in the all-black strip that gave United's poor performance an even more sombre look.

27 September 1998

		P	W	D	L	F	A	Pts
1	Aston Villa	7	5	2	0	8	1	17
2	Derby County	7	3	3	1	6	3	12
3	Wimbledon	7	3	3	1	11	9	12
4	Newcastle Utd	7	3	2	2	13	7	11
5	Manchester Utd	6	3	2	1	10	6	11
6	Leeds Utd	7	2	5	0	8	4	11
7	Liverpool	7	3	2	2	12	9	11
8	Chelsea	6	3	2	1	10	7	11
9	Arsenal	7	2	4	1	6	3	10
10	Sheffield Wednesday	7	3	0	4	8	5	9
11	West Ham Utd	6	2	3	1	6	5	9
12	Middlesbrough	7	2	3	2	8	8	9
13	Tottenham Hotspur	7	2	2	3	8	14	8
14	Charlton Athletic	7	1	4	2	11	10	7
15	Everton	7	1	4	2	4	5	7
16	Nottingham Forest	7	2	1	4	5	9	7
17	Leicester City	7	1	3	3	6	8	6
18	Blackburn Rovers	7	1	2	4	5	10	5
19	Coventry City	7	1	2	4	4	12	5
20	Southampton	6	0	1	5	3	17	1

Andy Cole was in the thick of the action as United bounced back from the Arsenal disaster to win against Liverpool.

Manchester United: Schmeichel, G. Neville, Irwin, Keane, P. Neville, Stam, Beckham, Scholes (Butt 88), Solskjaer (Cole 70), Yorke, Giggs

Liverpool: Friedel, Berger, Bjornebye, McAteer, Carragher, Babb, McManaman, Ince, Riedle (Fowler 75), Owen, Redknapp

Match Report

United made amends for their Highbury flop with a 2–0 winning display against a Liverpool team of no little ability. United were clearly up for it and had taken their manager's questions on board in a big way because the improvement ran right through the team.

Their first goal in the 19th minute was admittedly a penalty but it was the result of pressure on the goalkeeper. First Brad Friedel nervously let a shot from Ole Gunnar Solskjaer squitter through his hands for a corner and then his punched clearance of David Beckham's corner kick fell short. Jason McAteer was left tussling with Paul Scholes as he attempted to get the ball away but it hit his arm and the referee ruled hand-ball. Denis Irwin, the immaculate penalty taker who so rarely misses, sent the American goalkeeper diving the wrong way.

The penalty award seemed to enrage Liverpool who stepped up a gear, testing a reshuffled United defence that had Gary Neville at centre-back alongside Jaap Stam. Neville played in central defence in his junior days and he played a key role in restoring the team's shattered morale, even though it took a linesman's flag to disallow a strike from Karlheinz Riedle.

Substitute Andy Cole, replacing Solskjaer, eased the worries of the home fans with a centre that had the visitors in trouble, and Scholes swerved a shot past Friedel for a goal that put the game beyond Liverpool.

As Gary Neville summed up afterwards: 'We all worked hard for each other, and we showed a lot more commitment and desire compared with our performance against Arsenal when we let everyone down.'

Manager's Report

❛ I think we saw the real Manchester United in this match with every-one responding in the right way after a bad defeat.

We were worth our 2–0 win in a game that predictably was full of passion, commitment and incident. Whichever side scored first was going to have a huge advantage because the level of concentration when we play Liverpool is so high. We got the first break with a penalty and after that I felt it was just a matter of time before we scored a second goal. They had their moments in the second half for 15 min-utes but we finished strongly.

Jaap Stam and Gary Neville played well together at the back. I switched Gary alongside Stam for this match because of his quickness of thought and movement to counter the pace of Michael Owen. Gary knows more about Owen than Henning Berg does because they came up together as youth players and are both in the England squad.

They subdued Owen brilliantly. It's always good to get a solid centre-back partnership because it relaxes the rest of the team who can then concentrate on expressing themselves. If they trust the people behind, they can go and enjoy their football.

It was certainly a welcome performance and answered the question vexing me after Arsenal. Very few teams outfight United and I think the Highbury non-performance was a one-off.

I was impressed by Andy Cole when he came on as a substitute. He was lively and keen to get started, an attitude which underlined the number of options I enjoy up front, a situation which over the season is going to be of immense importance to us. ❜

David Beckham

GOAL NO.1
Denis Irwin 19 minutes penalty
Liverpool manager Roy Evans described referee Steve Lodge's penalty award as 'diabolical' when he ruled that Jason McAteer had deliberately handled in a tussle with Paul Scholes. But Denis Irwin shrugged off the controversy to send goalkeeper Brad Friedel diving the wrong way as he crashed his kick into the net.

GOAL NO.2
Paul Scholes 80 minutes
Andy Cole found Dwight Yorke with a centre which his pal and partner flicked on to Paul Scholes who cleverly worked himself some space and got a bend on a shot which beat Brad Friedel.

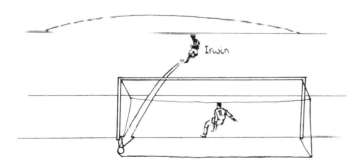

Group D	
Barcelona 2	Brondby 0
Bayern Munich 2	Manchester Utd 2

Match Report

Another drawn game for United means Barcelona lead the group on four points with Bayern Munich on three, United next on two and Brondby last with one. Things are not looking good on the European front; Group D has not been dubbed the group of death for nothing!

United were disappointed in this match because right until the very last minute they were leading 2–1 and it was only a rare error by Peter Schmeichel that forced them to accept a 2–2 result.

United were disappointed in this match because right until the very last minute they were leading 2–1 and it was only a rare error by Peter Schmeichel that forced them to accept a 2–2 result.

United started badly with their defence collapsing in the face of a bewildering exchange of passes by the German forwards which led to a goal from Elber after only 11 minutes. The Brazilian, lively all night in his partnership with the menacing Carsten Jancker, looked suspiciously offside but United kept their cool and really opened up in attack in reply. David Beckham led the way with an inspiring display and in the 30th minute he crossed for Dwight Yorke to head in an equaliser.

Paul Scholes put United ahead early in the second half when he steamed through the Bayern defence to force the ball past Oliver Kahn. It was a stinging fight-back but like most German sides, Bayern were certainly not ready to concede. They roared back into the game with both Stefan Effenberg and Elber going close and giving Schmeichel a hectic time.

The United defence seemed to have weathered the storm and they were just seconds away from a remarkable victory when Schmeichel suffered his rush of blood. The big Dane came hurtling out of goal to collect a long throw-in but missed and Elber had an easy job knocking the ball into an empty net despite Teddy Sheringham's efforts to clear.

Skipper Roy Keane stoutly defended his goalkeeper: 'Nobody is blaming him. Just minutes before, he had made two great saves to keep us in the game.'

Manager's Report

❝ We were very disappointed to let the game slip in the closing minute. It was a real kick in the teeth because I felt we were worth a 2–1 win after great goals from Dwight Yorke and Paul Scholes.

Above: *Paul Scholes scores after sweeping right through the German defence.*

Right: *David Beckham gave an inspiring display.*

Bayern Munich: Kahn, Babbel, Lizarazu, Jeremies (Fink 82), Linke, Salihamidzic (Goktan 63), Jancker (Daei 63), Strunz, Elber, Matthaus, Effenberg

Manchester United: Schmeichel, G. Neville, Irwin, Keane, P. Neville, Stam, Beckham, Scholes, Yorke, Sheringham, Blomqvist (Cruyff 69)

The draw has put us on the back foot in Europe and makes the next fixture with Brondby a win at all costs occasion. I am confident we will handle it, though, because in terms of overall performance there was little wrong with us in Munich. We conceded an early goal but recovered well and I was pleased with the way we played because it was a big occasion for us against a good side.

I planned carefully and made a change up front to bring in Teddy Sheringham. My reasoning was twofold. I wanted his experience on the big European stage and at the same time I thought his height would be useful in defensive set pieces in face of a physically big side. When you saw them coming down the tunnel, they are one ruddy big side with several at 6ft 2ins and over.

Teddy's performance duly justified his selection and at 2–1 up we looked comfortable. Then Peter Schmeichel had his kamikazi moment but his goalkeeping has been faultless in so many games that you have to write off the occasional error as just one of those things. Even in this match he gave a magnificent display and didn't deserve to be punished for one mistake. He is a frustrated centre-forward really and always delights in reminding me that he once scored from open play in a league game in Denmark.

At the end of the day I was pleased we came back so determinedly after going an early goal down. It's a good sign. My only concern now is simply to get us through the group.

The plane due to take us home has developed a fault and we have an unscheduled stop-over in Germany. I may have to revise our week-end travel plans. ❞

Dwight Yorke

GOAL NO.1
Dwight Yorke 30 minutes
David Beckham picked up a poor clearance from the normally impeccable Lothar Matthaus and nodded it square to Teddy Sheringham. He ran forward to take the return and knock the ball in for Dwight Yorke to score with a diving header, his first European goal for United. It was the club's 150th goal in European competition.

GOAL NO.2
Paul Scholes 49 minutes
Dwight Yorke played a part in the second goal when he headed Phil Neville's free kick down for Paul Scholes to come in at speed and bulldoze his way through two defenders attempting to stop him. It was a combination of a fortunate bounce and sheer determination as he forced the ball past the goalkeeper.

		P	W	D	L	F	A	Pts
	4 October 1998							
1	Aston Villa	8	6	2	0	10	2	20
2	Manchester Utd	7	4	2	1	13	6	14
3	Arsenal	8	3	4	1	9	3	13
4	Middlesbrough	8	3	3	2	12	8	12
5	Liverpool	8	3	3	2	13	10	12
6	Chelsea	7	3	3	1	11	8	12
7	Derby County	8	3	3	2	6	4	12
8	Wimbledon	8	3	3	2	12	11	12
9	West Ham Utd	8	3	3	2	7	8	12
10	Newcastle Utd	8	3	2	3	13	10	11
11	Leeds Utd	8	2	5	1	8	5	11
12	Tottenham Hotspur	8	3	2	3	9	14	11
13	Charlton Athletic	8	2	4	2	12	10	10
14	Everton	8	2	4	2	6	6	10
15	Sheffield Wednesday	8	3	0	5	8	9	9
16	Leicester City	8	2	3	3	7	8	9
17	Blackburn Rovers	8	2	2	4	8	10	8
18	Nottingham Forest	8	2	1	5	5	10	7
19	Coventry City	8	1	2	5	5	14	5
20	Southampton	8	0	1	7	3	21	1

Dwight Yorke in action.

Match Report

After trying various permutations of his four strikers, the manager paired Dwight Yorke and Andy Cole for only the second time since Yorke's £12.6 million arrival from Aston Villa. It was an instant success with each striker scoring in a 3–0 win after defeats on their previous three visits.

Things had not looked good before the game with Peter Schmeichel, Ryan Giggs and Paul Scholes – three goals in four games – all missing through injury. The delayed return journey from Germany had not helped. It meant they had to forego training on the Friday in order to catch up with their rest.

But apart from David Howells letting them off the hook at the start of the game with a glaring miss, United readily clicked into gear and went in front after only 12 minutes when Dwight Yorke poked in a cross from Andy Cole for his fifth goal of the season.

Cole went through on his own from Jesper Blomqvist, deputising for Giggs, to put United further ahead on the hour before Jordi Cruyff, a player many thought might have departed Old Trafford in the summer, started and finished a 75th minute move which completed a good afternoon for United.

It was United's first away win of the season and moved them up to second place in the Premiership.

Manager's Report

❝ I have given all the strikers a go alongside Dwight Yorke now, and before his arrival I also had Paul Scholes and Ryan Giggs playing through the middle. Dwight has looked the part, whomever he has had up front with him. Good players can play with anyone and Dwight has so many different aspects to his game.

They have all had a crack but I must say I liked the look of Andy Cole with him this afternoon and I think it's a combination I shall pursue. They seem to have struck up a friendship, and are developing an understanding. When they have had the opportunity to play together in matches they have started to show decent form. I am still giving the pairing of Ole Gunnar Solskjaer and Dwight a fair show, which has meant Teddy Sheringham taking something of a back seat, but I know what he can do. He has a different way of playing and he brings different qualities to the game, not least an ability to change things.

At this point I have no hard and fast thoughts on my best combination. My main preoccupation is the balancing act of trying to keep all four happy and getting them to understand the reasons for changing the strikers around.

We had a good record at the Dell until recently. It's a tight ground and normally you have to work very hard for your goals. Today, though, we got them quite easily. We are in a good vein of form with a good purpose about us. We are playing without Ryan Giggs at the moment but Jesper Blomqvist is proving his worth in his place. It was our first away win and it lifted us into second place in the Premiership.

Roy Keane is getting better all the time. I never really had any doubts about him making a successful return after his knee and cruciate injuries but there is always a niggle in the back of your mind when a player has been out for such a long time. There must have been a doubt in Roy's own mind, too, but he is such a strong character that, as I expected, he put it right out of his thoughts. 🍂

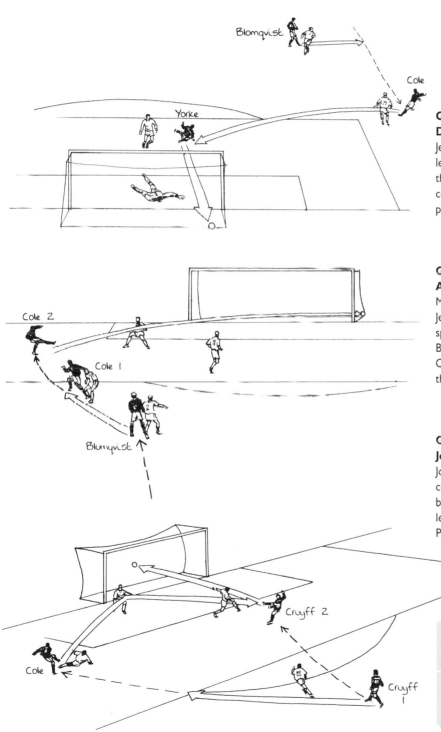

GOAL NO.1
Dwight Yorke 12 minutes

Jesper Blomqvist got Andy Cole moving down the left wing and the striker's cross was prodded in at the near post by Dwight Yorke. He didn't get real contact on the ball as he slid in, but enough to propel it past Paul Jones in the Southampton goal.

GOAL NO.2
Andy Cole 60 minutes

Making the most of the absence of Ryan Giggs, Jesper Blomqvist ran through from midfield and spotted Andy Cole's shrewd run behind his marker. Blomqvist pushed the ball forward into space and Cole collected, checked and curled a shot into the net.

GOAL NO.3
Jordi Cruyff 75 minutes

Jordi Cruyff made all the running for this goal, coming through the midfield from his own half before sending Andy Cole scampering away to the left. Cole swung a cross into the goalmouth which Paul Jones palmed away only to find that Cruyff had kept running. He collected the ball and gave Jones no chance with a first-time volley.

Southampton: Jones, Warner, Benali, Palmer, Lundekvam (Gibbens 56), Monkou, Le Tissier, Ripley (Beattie 64), Bridge, Ostenstad, Howells

Manchester United: Van der Gouw, G. Neville, Irwin (Brown 79), Keane, P. Neville, Stam, Beckham, Butt, Cole, Yorke (Sheringham 73), Blomqvist (Cruyff 73)

		P	W	D	L	F	A	Pts
1	Aston Villa	9	6	3	0	10	2	21
2	Manchester Utd	8	5	2	1	18	7	17
3	Middlesbrough	9	4	3	2	14	9	15
4	Chelsea	8	4	3	1	13	9	15
5	Arsenal	9	3	5	1	10	4	14
6	Newcastle Utd	9	4	2	3	15	11	14
7	Liverpool	9	3	4	2	13	10	13
8	West Ham Utd	9	3	4	2	7	8	13
9	Leeds Utd	9	2	6	1	9	6	12
10	Derby County	9	3	3	3	7	6	12
11	Wimbledon	9	3	3	3	13	16	12
12	Everton	9	2	5	2	6	6	11
13	Tottenham Hotspur	8	3	2	3	9	14	11
14	Charlton Athletic	9	2	4	3	13	12	10
15	Leicester City	8	2	3	3	7	8	9
16	Sheffield Wednesday	9	3	0	6	8	10	9
17	Blackburn Rovers	9	2	2	5	9	12	8
18	Nottingham Forest	9	2	2	5	6	11	8
19	Coventry City	9	2	2	5	6	14	8
20	Southampton	9	0	2	7	4	22	2

18 October 1998

Dwight Yorke congratulated by Andy Cole.

GOAL NO. 1
Andy Cole 19 minutes
Wimbledon were caught square by a pass down the middle from David Beckham. Andy Cole raced clear to score with a well-placed shot.

Match Report

Manchester United simply carried on where they had left off at Southampton with the goals flowing even more extravagantly. Two for Andy Cole and another for Dwight Yorke confirmed that this is the most lethal pairing of strikers. Ryan Giggs and David Beckham also got in on the scoring act.

It must have been a sobering experience for the Brondby coach who watched the match at Old Trafford in readiness for his team's European Champions League tie against the Reds in Denmark next week. Indeed, as Ebbe Skovdahl admitted: 'I can't shut my eyes without seeing United score goals! I was very impressed. United have quality in all areas. The only surprise for me was that they didn't score four or five more goals. I know it is going to be very difficult for us in Copenhagen on Wednesday and then again at Old Trafford. I am not writing us off but I have to be realistic and say that the qualification in our group is between the big three of United, Barcelona and Bayern Munich.'

There was certainly no stopping United in this match with Cole opening the scoring in the 19th minute after bursting through onto a Beckham pass. Wimbledon equalised after 39 minutes when a shot from Jason Euell took a deflection off Jaap Stam, giving Raimond Van der Gouw no chance. Just before the interval, Giggs restored the lead, coming in at the far post to meet a centre from Jesper Blomqvist. Almost as quickly after the break, Beckham scored with a free kick.

The Wimbledon defence had the shakes by now, especially when they were confronted by Cole and Yorke. Neil Sullivan did his best in goal, and it was an impressive best to mark his Scotland international call-up, but he couldn't prevent Yorke and Cole taking the score to 5–1.

Joe Kinnear, the Dons' manager, said simply at the end: 'There is no shame in being beaten by a great team.'

Manager's Report

❝ I am sure a lot of drama lies ahead for us in the Premiership, but we are back in business and getting better. Beating Liverpool, drawing in Munich, winning at Southampton and then hitting five against Wimbledon in this match is a fair return and a great response after that dark day at Arsenal!

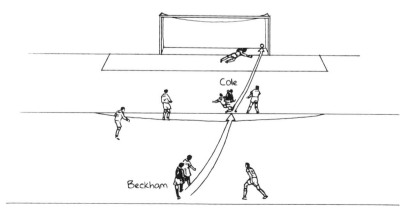

Our form for several weeks suggested that someone was going to get a battering and this was it. The rhythm and tempo of our passing was superb. The conditions were perfect for us with a morning drizzle giving the pitch a real zing, which suited us.

Wimbledon are a club carved out of attitude and they have survived at the top level because they have not changed their beliefs. Every manjack works his tail off to get into the team and to stay there. It makes for a great unit. Every season the pundits say they will be relegated and they use this "them against us" to motivate themselves. It's a lovely club. I admire Sam Hammam, and their chairman, Stan Reed, is a terrific guy. It would be a sad day if they were ever relegated. You can never underestimate a victory against Wimbledon. You have to earn it and we did with this performance.

It was particularly satisfying because injuries put me in the position of being able to give young Wes Brown a full league debut after playing him as a substitute against Leeds at the end of last season, and he came through to confirm the promise he has shown. We believe he will develop into an outstanding player, definitely one for the Manchester United first-team. It is often a risk playing youngsters in defence because they haven't had the experience to get everything sorted out, but I don't feel it with Wes, which is a testament to his potential. Ironically, Wimbledon asked about him during the summer and Joe Kinnear saw for himself today just why his inquiry was turned down so emphatically! ➙

Manchester United: Van der Gouw, G. Neville, P. Neville (Curtis 74), Keane, Brown, Stam, Beckham (Cruyff 57), Blomqvist, Cole, Yorke, Giggs (Scholes 66)

Wimbledon: Sullivan, Cunningham, Kimble (Ardley 45), Perry, Blackwell, Thatcher, Euell, Earle, Leaburn (Gayle 45), Roberts, Hughes

GOAL NO.2
Ryan Giggs 45 minutes
Dwight Yorke saw his shot cleared off the line but United were soon back with Jesper Blomqvist crossing from the left for Ryan Giggs to head home at the far post.

GOAL NO.3
David Beckham 47 minutes
David Beckham picked up a forward pass from Phil Neville and accelerated through the visitors' defence to score with a fierce low drive from 25 yards out.

GOAL NO.4
Dwight Yorke 52 minutes
A long goal kick from Raimond Van der Gouw was controlled brilliantly by Dwight Yorke as he turned past his marker. The striker ran for goal, checked inside a defender and then picked his spot to beat Neil Sullivan.

GOAL NO.5
Andy Cole 88 minutes
Wimbledon were repeatedly opened up down the middle. This time David Beckham released Andy Cole who ended a long run by twisting inside the last defender to score across the face of goal.

Group D	
Bayern Munich 1	Barcelona 0
Brondby 2	Manchester Utd 6

Brondby: Krogh, Bjur, Bo Jensen (Vragel 27), Nielsen (Mikkel Jensen 31), Rasmussen, Ravn, Colding, Daugaard, Sand, Hansen (Bagger 67), Lindrup

Manchester United: Schmeichel, G. Neville, P. Neville, Keane, Brown, Stam, Blomqvist, Scholes, Cole (Solskjaer 61), Yorke (Wilson 66), Giggs (Cruyff 61)

Match Report

It was wonderful, wonderful Copenhagen as far as United were concerned with this storming 6–2 win over Peter Schmeichel's old club.

Draws in their two opening Champions League games had posed a question mark against United's chances of qualifying in a hotly contested group of big guns, but their response was dramatic and decisive. Even though Brondby were perceived as the weakest of the teams, they had nevertheless beaten Bayern Munich 2–1 in their opening game and Barcelona had beaten them only 2–0 at the Nou Camp.

United wasted no time getting down to business in the wet conditions with Ryan Giggs scoring twice in the first 21 minutes quickly followed by a goal from Andy Cole. Schmeichel allowed a free kick from Kim Daugaard to squirm through his hands for the Danes to go off at the interval 3–1 down and still in the game, but not for long. Roy Keane, Dwight Yorke and substitute Ole Gunnar Solskjaer piled in three more goals in a blistering seven-minute spell in the second half.

Ebbe Sand scored a late consolation goal for Brondby, but with the help of Bayern Munich beating Barcelona, United topped the group.

Manager's Report

❝Ignoring the shocking weather we could not have had a better night in Copenhagen. To win 6–2 was a real morale booster after our draws against Barcelona and Bayern, a result which suddenly became hugely significant as the news came through of the German victory over Barcelona.

We gave away the ball too often for my liking with sloppy passing and careless moments, though I must acknowledge the manner of our goals. For me the scoring was the big feature of our game and you cannot dismiss that aspect. To score six goals away from home is a record in the Champions League and it sends out good messages to our rivals. It's no bad thing to establish a reputation for scoring goals.

At the same time we must not allow ourselves to be carried away because it must be acknowledged that we got a real break with a goal gifted to us after just a minute and a half. There was a mix-up between their goalkeeper and a defender which put us in front. With Ryan Giggs scoring again after 20 minutes we had Brondby on the back foot. The suddenness of the goals unsettled them and sent us on our way. When we hit form we are very difficult to play against, as I think the Danes discovered.

Certainly, we couldn't be in a better position. I fancied Bayern to beat Barcelona because the Germans knew after losing to Brondby that they had to do something and they did. They are a very good side and overall I rate our performance in Munich, although only a draw, as our best in the Champions League so far.

We still have a lot to do of course. Our group might not be decided until the very last round of matches and it could well be that losing in Barcelona could put us out. Definitely we must go for the points when we meet Brondby at Old Trafford in the return and remember that their best results have come away from home. We must not think it will be easy. When we get complacent, we just don't perform.

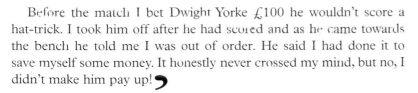

GOAL NO.1
Ryan Giggs 2 minutes

Wes Brown marked his European debut with a surge down the right and a centre which Mogens Krogh dropped for Ryan Giggs to notch an early score.

GOAL NO.2
Ryan Giggs 21 minutes

Ryan Giggs was on hand again to head in Jesper Blomqvist's left-wing cross and rock Brondby.

Before the match I bet Dwight Yorke £100 he wouldn't score a hat-trick. I took him off after he had scored and as he came towards the bench he told me I was out of order. He said I had done it to save myself some money. It honestly never crossed my mind, but no, I didn't make him pay up! 🗭

GOAL NO.3
Andy Cole 28 minutes

Dwight Yorke chested down a ball from the dynamic Ryan Giggs to put Andy Cole clear and his partner scored with a crisp shot.

GOAL NO.4
Roy Keane 55 minutes

Roy Keane beat two men on a typically powerful run, exchanged passes with Dwight Yorke and scored with a shot that went in off the post.

GOAL NO.5
Dwight Yorke 60 minutes

Full-back Phil Neville advanced to swing over a centre and Dwight Yorke, meeting it perfectly, scored with a header.

GOAL NO.6
Ole Gunnar Solskjaer 62 minutes

With Brondby still reeling, Dwight Yorke played a ball from Roy Keane to Ole Gunnar Solskjaer for the substitute to run clear and sweep in the sixth goal.

Far left: Ryan Giggs scored after just two minutes and gets a deserved well done from skipper Roy Keane.

Left: Ryan Giggs was in fine form and soon grabbed a second goal.

25 October 1998							
	P	W	D	L	F	A	Pts
1 Aston Villa	10	6	4	0	11	3	22
2 Manchester Utd	9	5	3	1	19	8	18
3 Arsenal	10	4	5	1	12	5	17
4 Liverpool	10	4	4	2	18	11	16
5 Middlesbrough	10	4	4	2	16	11	16
6 Chelsea	9	4	4	1	13	9	16
7 Newcastle Utd	10	4	2	4	15	13	14
8 Tottenham Hotspur	10	4	2	4	12	16	14
9 Charlton Athletic	10	3	4	3	17	14	13
10 Leeds Utd	10	2	7	1	9	6	13
11 Derby County	10	3	4	3	8	7	13
12 Leicester City	10	3	4	3	10	10	13
13 Wimbledon	10	3	4	3	15	18	13
14 West Ham Utd	10	3	4	3	9	12	13
15 Everton	10	2	6	2	6	6	12
16 Sheffield Wednesday	10	3	1	6	8	10	10
17 Blackburn Rovers	10	2	2	6	10	14	8
18 Coventry City	10	2	2	6	7	16	8
19 Nottingham Forest	10	2	2	6	7	16	8
20 Southampton	10	1	2	7	6	23	5

Andy Cole tries hard to find a way to goal.

Jordi Cruyff about to shoot through a ruck of players for the goal that earned a point.

Derby County: Hoult, Laursen (Dorigo 45), Schnoor, Powell, Prior, Stimac, Carsley, Sturridge, Wanchope, Delap, Burton

Manchester United: Schmeichel, G. Neville (Scholes 82), P. Neville, Keane, Brown, Stam, Beckham, Butt (Cruyff 82), Cole, Yorke, Giggs (Blomqvist 82)

Match Report

The fireworks United produced in Brondby were reduced to a damp squib at Derby with a curiously low-key performance producing a lacklustre 1–1 draw. But the game was not without its redeeming features, notably United's refusal to accept defeat and their knack of being able to pull off the unexpected.

For most of this game Derby were in charge. Despite going into the game on the back of three successive defeats, Jim Smith went boldly to the attack by selecting three front runners in Paulo Wanchope, Dean Sturridge and Dean Burton. His tactics kept United tied up at the back and it was no big surprise when Darryl Powell swept a centre across the face of goal for Burton to give the home team the lead with just quarter of an hour to go.

United's renowned response to that kind of potential disaster kicked in and they stepped up a gear with the manager contributing his own tactical master stroke by taking off Ryan Giggs, Nicky Butt and Gary Neville in favour of Jesper Blomqvist, Paul Scholes and Jordi Cruyff for the final eight minutes.

Cruyff, not always the most dynamic of players, became the United hero with a display Derby just couldn't pin down. The Dutchman was in the thick of the action and after only four minutes of pitch time, he fired in a goal which earned United a valuable point.

Manager's Report

❝ I wish Derby had scored earlier because it woke us up and we would have had longer than quarter of an hour in which to have got something more than a point. There was no aggression about our game. We just went into it nice and easy and nothing exciting was happening at either end.

Was it a reaction to hitting the heights in Brondby earlier in the week? We mustn't get into the habit of using that as an excuse. We have been playing in Europe a lot now and I am just not prepared to accept that kind of thinking.

The positive aspects that came out of this game were, firstly, our reaction to going a goal down and, secondly, my good fortune in having quality players on the bench. For though we pulled ourselves together a bit after Derby had scored, we still didn't look like real winners, which is why I put on three substitute forwards all together. I knew I had three players of quality, each of them capable of scoring. I didn't see it as some desperate last throw of the dice but a move to try something different and snap us out of a rut with fresh legs and fresh ideas. Jim Smith said afterwards that it was like the Alamo and asked me if I had sent on the three subs without taking anyone off!

At least it got us a point with Jordi Cruyff making the most of his chance. He wasn't on for long but he packed a lot in. Jordi is a lovely lad who has been unfortunate with injuries holding him back and then when he has recovered we have been playing well and he has been unable to get into the team.

One day he will be a major player, hopefully with United, but I have a feeling that to achieve his true potential he will have to go where the football is more suited to his style. He has adapted quite well to the English game, but perhaps he will be better able to express himself in the Spanish game. He has a lovely talent but living in his father's shadow cannot have been easy. He is maturing now, though, and he is his own man, which I think will see his real emergence. ❞

Jordi Cruyff is buried with congratulations from relieved team-mates.

GOAL NO. 1
Jordi Cruyff 86 minutes
Jordi Cruyff, on for the last eight minutes in place of Nicky Butt, immediately had Derby in trouble with his roaming role. Four minutes from the end he took a short pass from Dwight Yorke and scored with a low shot just inside the post. It beat the goalkeeper with its direction rather than its pace.

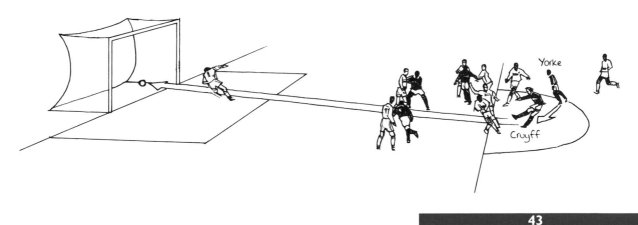

Third round	
Barnsley 2	Bournemouth 1
Charlton Athletic 1	Leicester City 2
Liverpool 3	Fulham 1
Luton Town 2	Coventry City 0
Northampton Town 1	Tottenham Hotspur 3
Norwich City 1 (Bolton won 3–1 pens)	Bolton Wanderers 1
Nottingham Forest 3 (Forest won 4–3 pens)	Cambridge Utd 3
Sunderland 2	Grimsby Town 1
Tranmere Rovers 0	Newcastle utd 1
Birmingham City 1	Wimbledon 2
Chelsea 4	Aston Villa 1
Crewe Alexandra 0	Blackburn Rovers 1
Derby County 1	Arsenal 2
Leeds Utd 1	Bradford City 0
Manchester Utd 2	Bury 0
Middlesbrough 2	Everton 3

Manchester United: Van der Gouw, Clegg (Brown 70), Curtis, May, P. Neville, Berg, Wilson (Scholes 70), Mulryne (Nevland 45), Solskjaer, Cruyff, Greening

Bury: Kiely, Woodward, Barrick, Daws, Lucketti, Redmond, Swailes, Patterson, D'Jaffo (Preece 58), Johnrose, Ellis (James 63)

Erik Nevland slides in at the far post to score.

Match Report

United's opening line-up against Bury featured just one player who had started at the weekend against Derby, but it was hardly a novice side. The manager took the opportunity to advance the careers of youngsters such as Michael Clegg, John Curtis, Mark Wilson, Philip Mulryne and Jonathan Greening, but there was also considerable experience in the team with David May, Henning Berg, Phil Neville, Ole Gunnar Solskjaer, Jordi Cruyff and Raimond Van der Gouw.

The game almost developed into a personal duel between Solskjaer and Dean Kiely, the Bury goalkeeper, who had every reason to feel an upset was a possibility after keeping goal for the York City side which had dispatched United from the League Cup three seasons previously. The Republic of Ireland international repeatedly denied Solskjaer with a string of super saves which took the game into extra time. Chris Lucketti, Andy Woodward and substitute Andy Preece all went close for Bury, but Solskjaer looked the biggest scoring threat.

As the game swung into the second period of extra time and Bury found it difficult to maintain their concentration, it was the Norwegian striker who finally got the better of Kiely by sweeping in a cross from Greening which went in off a post. United pressed their advantage and five minutes from the end their other Norwegian, Erik Nevland, who had replaced Mulryne, slid in at the far post to touch in a centre from Wes Brown who had taken over from Clegg.

Bury fought bravely and had the consolation of a good revenue day. A crowd of over 52,000 turned up for a game for which they knew Alex Ferguson would ring the selection changes!

Manager's Report

'It annoys me when people talk about Manchester United fielding a weakened team. Football these days is a squad game, at least it is for a successful and ambitious club like ourselves.

The media and supporters are beginning to understand, but it has been a slow process getting them to appreciate that we are asked to play so much football that it is essential to have a pool of quality players available. In a successful season at Old Trafford, we compete on four

fronts and you just can't expect the same players to play in so many games, at least you can't if you want them to keep winning.

I set out some time ago to create a squad with real quality in depth and the Worthington Cup gives me the opportunity to select those players who have not been in the first team lately, as well as to give some of my younger players the chance to step up a level.

I never pick a side that I don't think can cope and I had every confidence that the mixture of experience and youth could handle Bury. This was my opportunity to freshen up the team and at the same time play fair with the full range of my squad. If we achieve what I expect this season, I know I shall need every one of them. They will all get plenty of games.

I was glad the draw for this third round gave Bury a trip to Old Trafford because we have a special relationship with Gigg Lane and this will bring them welcome revenue. At one point we had an agreement to play our reserve fixtures on the Bury ground and a number of our players have also been on loan there. Neville Neville, their commercial manager, is a frequent visitor to Old Trafford, at least for midweek games, because he is the father of Gary and Philip.

Bury did well and took us to extra time before we got the goals we needed, but I was pleased with our youngsters. I am proud of the players we produce at Old Trafford, and not just the ones who are in our first-team squad. The reserve team of three years ago has contributed importantly to our senior pool but it has also spread far and wide. Michael Appleton, Colin Murdock and Jonathan Macken are all excelling at Preston. Simon Davies, Pat McGibbon and John O'Kane have all moved on to better themselves.

They are only the tip of the iceberg because we have developed many more players who have gone on to good careers with other clubs. It gives me a lot of pleasure to see our system working in this way and I am proud of them all. ❩

Jonathan Greening

GOAL NO.1
Ole Gunnar Solskjaer 106 minutes
Jonathan Greening showed his dribbling skills by cutting in from the right and pulling defenders out of position to set up a chance for Ole Gunnar Solskjaer. The Norwegian international shot low and this time diving Dean Kiely could only fingertip the ball and it went in off the post.

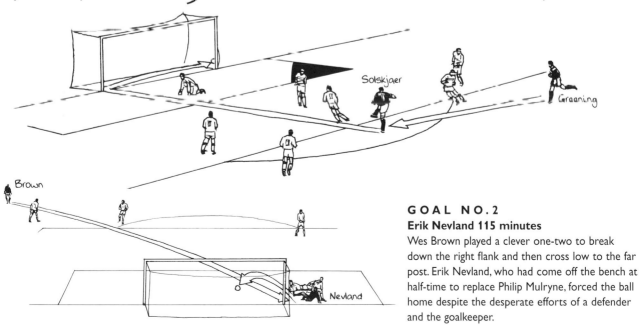

GOAL NO.2
Erik Nevland 115 minutes
Wes Brown played a clever one-two to break down the right flank and then cross low to the far post. Erik Nevland, who had come off the bench at half-time to replace Philip Mulryne, forced the ball home despite the desperate efforts of a defender and the goalkeeper.

1st November 1998							
	P	W	D	L	F	A	Pts
1 Aston Villa	10	6	4	0	11	3	22
2 Manchester Utd	10	6	3	1	23	9	21
3 Arsenal	11	5	5	1	13	5	20
4 Middlesbrough	11	4	5	2	17	12	17
5 Liverpool	11	4	4	3	18	12	16
6 Chelsea	9	4	4	1	13	9	16
7 Leicester City	11	4	4	3	11	10	16
8 West Ham Utd	11	4	4	3	12	12	16
9 Leeds Utd	11	2	8	1	11	8	14
10 Derby County	11	3	5	3	10	9	14
11 Newcastle Utd	11	4	2	5	15	16	14
12 Wimbledon	11	3	5	3	16	19	14
13 Tottenham Hotspur	10	4	2	4	12	16	14
14 Charlton Athletic	10	3	4	3	17	14	13
15 Everton	11	2	6	3	7	10	12
16 Sheffield Wednesday	11	3	2	6	8	10	11
17 Blackburn Rovers	11	2	3	6	11	15	9
18 Nottingham Forest	11	2	3	6	8	17	9
19 Coventry City	11	2	2	7	7	17	8
20 Southampton	11	1	3	7	6	23	6

Match Report

United made nonsense of Everton's run of ten matches without defeat by beating them 4–1.

The powerful Duncan Ferguson had Jaap Stam at full stretch in the early stages and the Goodison Park team, now under the management of Walter Smith, were clearly up for it. Almost from the kick-off, the Scottish striker had Peter Schmeichel in action and the home team were still pressing hard in the 14th minute when Paul Scholes engineered the opening which gave Dwight Yorke his eighth goal of the season in 12 appearances, a marvellous scoring rate.

The goal steadied United down in face of fierce home support and the crowd were further quietened after 23 minutes when a right-wing cross from David Beckham had the goalkeeper and two defenders in such a mix-up at the far post that Craig Short headed into his own net.

Duncan Ferguson surged through a crowded goalmouth to chalk up his first goal for Walter Smith but United rose to the challenge with two goals in five minutes from Andy Cole and Jesper Blomqvist to emerge with a slightly flattering scoreline.

No, they're not dancing, just celebrating Jesper Blomqvist's first goal for Manchester United.

Dwight Yorke is chased by John Collins. Yorke scored the opener to give him the brilliant scoring return of eight goals in 12 appearances and send United on their way to a 4–1 win.

United's performance must certainly have been another frightener for Ebbe Skovdahl, Brondby's coach taking a final look at the opposition before entertaining United in Denmark on Wednesday. Skovdahl had seen United put six goals past his team in a pre-season friendly, five past Wimbledon in a Premier League game and then score another six in the first Champions League encounter at Old Trafford. Now this was further evidence of United's mean scoring machine!

Manager's Report

❝Everton showed their capabilities in the early stages when Duncan Ferguson was a menace but by the end, as the score suggests, we were in control.

I am pleased with our form now. The players are clearly enjoying their game and playing with the kind of enthusiasm and hunger that suggests we could well have something to show for our efforts at the end of the season.

You can never afford to be complacent but it is helping that the new signings have settled in much quicker than one can always count on. I recall only too clearly my struggle ten years ago when I signed too many players at the same time and then had to watch them take their time to come together.

Some come to Old Trafford and take it in their stride. Eric Cantona, for instance, marched into Old Trafford and immediately took centre stage as if he had been there all his life. I am delighted to say that Dwight Yorke has done pretty much the same, playing with an infectious smile and zest that is good to see. I am pleased, too, with the way Jesper Blomqvist is now emerging from his shell. He arrived at the

Everton: Myhre, Short (Dunne 67), Ball, Dacourt, Watson, Unsworth, Collins, Materazzi, Ferguson, Bakayoko, Cadamarteri

Manchester United: Schmeichel, G. Neville, P. Neville (Irwin 67), Keane, Brown, Stam, Beckham, Scholes, Cole, Yorke, Blomqvist

GOAL NO.1
Dwight Yorke 14 minutes

Andy Cole on the left found Paul Scholes with a great crossfield ball. The midfielder chipped into the goalmouth for Dwight Yorke who hit the goalkeeper with his first shot and then snapped on to the rebound to run in his eighth goal of the season.

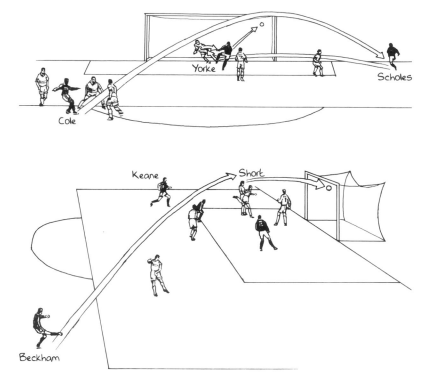

GOAL NO.2
Craig Short (own-goal) 23 minutes

A tantalising cross by David Beckham on the right to the far post found Thomas Myhre rooted on his line while Dave Watson and Craig Short tried to decide which one of them would meet the challenge from Roy Keane. In the end, Short tamely headed past his own keeper.

club with a foot injury which took longer to mend than we had expected, but now he is fit, he has done very well. His presence means that we are much better equipped to deal with the loss of key players like Ryan Giggs. Indeed, I believe if we had had Jesper available to play on the left side last season when Ryan was injured, we would have won the championship.

Jaap Stam has also been impressive, especially considering that he had a long and busy World Cup, playing for Holland all the way to the match to decide third and fourth places. Playing at that level always has a draining effect which, with the kind of limited summer break that Jaap had after the tournament, can reach into the new season. Jaap has shrugged off the problem and he is going to get even better as we build a new central defensive partnership, at the moment with Gary Neville alongside him. They are doing very well.

I think being able to ring the changes has also helped us lately. After the Derby match, I was able to put out a side against Bury that was fresh and included senior players itching for a big game alongside youngsters keen to play at senior level. Then with several players enjoying a rest in midweek, I was able to bring them back today with a refreshing look about their game, as the score indicated. It seemed to me to make all the difference. Everton had had a tough tie against Middlesbrough involving extra time.

Too many changes can be difficult for players to handle, but they have got to learn that this is the way forward these days at a club where we plan to progress in all competitions.

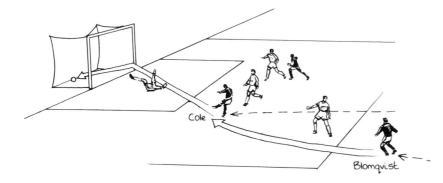

GOAL NO.3
Andy Cole 59 minutes

A typically bright run by Andy Cole was well read by Jesper Blomqvist who prodded the ball forward for Cole to collect and score with a low shot across the face of goal. It went in off the far post.

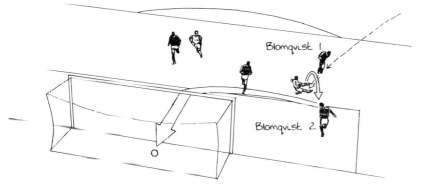

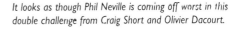

GOAL NO.4
Jesper Blomqvist 64 minutes

Jesper Blomqvist burst through on to David Beckham's pass and closed in on the Everton goal. Thomas Myhre blocked Blomqvist's first attempt to knock a shot past him, but the ball flew up and the Swede was able to head in his first goal for United, completing a fine display.

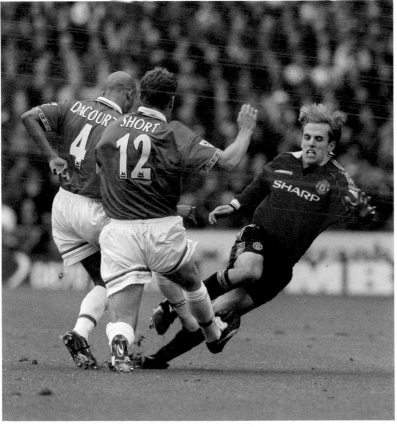

It looks as though Phil Neville is coming off worst in this double challenge from Craig Short and Olivier Dacourt.

Group D	
Barcelona 1	Bayern Munich 2
Manchester Utd 5	Brondby 0

Dwight Yorke powers in a header to score in United's five-goal romp.

Manchester United: Schmeichel, G. Neville, Irwin, Keane, P. Neville (Brown 32), Stam, Beckham, Scholes, Cole (Solskjaer 53), Yorke, Blomqvist (Cruyff 45)

Brondby: Andersen, Bjur (S. Krogh 74), Skarbalius, Nielsen, Rasmussen, Ravn, Faxe, Daugaard, Sand (Hansen 77), Colding, Bagger (Thygesen)

Match Report

A bewildered Brondby reeled under another heavy scoring onslaught as United roared to a five-goal victory and finished up as the bookmakers' favourites to become champions of Europe.

It would be easy to dismiss the Danes as the Group D chopping block but with their earlier win over Bayern Munich in mind perhaps it would be more appropriate to give United credit for their super-charged form. Certainly after opening in the group with two drawn games, the high-scoring wins over Brondby are a dramatic signal of a more focused intent. United now top the group and need to win just one of their remaining two fixtures to go through to the knock-out stage in the second half of the season.

Brondby had hardly drawn breath before David Beckham hit them with a goal from a free kick. Two more from Andy Cole and Phil Neville meant Brondby were three goals down in the first 16 minutes. Dwight Yorke also got into the scoring act before the interval, and even though United eased their foot off the accelerator slightly, Paul Scholes struck just after the hour to make it five without reply.

Brondby had changed their goalkeeper since their first game against United, but Emeka Andersen fared little better than Mogens Krogh except to savour an even higher quality of goal put past him.

Peter Schmeichel nominated Andy Cole's almost telepathic link-up with Dwight Yorke before chipping the goalkeeper as the best goal he had seen at Old Trafford.

Manager's Report

‘This victory was stunning, probably the best performance in the first half that I have seen in my time at Old Trafford. The goals were superb, well created and brilliantly executed with a movement and imagination that was fantastic to see. If we maintain this form we can beat anyone and go all the way. We have definitely got the ability to win our group now. We have scored 27 goals in our last seven league and European games, which by anyone's standards is mighty good going. Dwight Yorke and Andy Cole between them have scored 11 in just seven games.

The speed of our play, the sheer imagination and the goals, it was all such stunning stuff. The goals by Andy Cole and Phil Neville, in particular, were excellent. The build-up which sent Andy through must have been bewildering for their defenders and Phil Neville, through on goal with the help of Cole, finished as if he had been playing up front all his life. After that, I thought our game might fall away but it didn't and we continued to score and maintain our rich vein of form. The front players are looking so sharp and they are producing fantastic goals.

Quite naturally there is an optimistic mood in the camp, though we still have a lot to do. We go to Barcelona at the end of the month but the really big night could well be in December when Bayern Munich come to Old Trafford for our final group game. It could all rest on the outcome and if Bayern beat us we could still end up going out.

Winning 2–1 in Spain was an outstanding result for them and with so much experience in their side it could be a tough one. Still, things are going well and the fact that the bookmakers are now making us favourites suggests it is not just my dreams running away with me! ✎

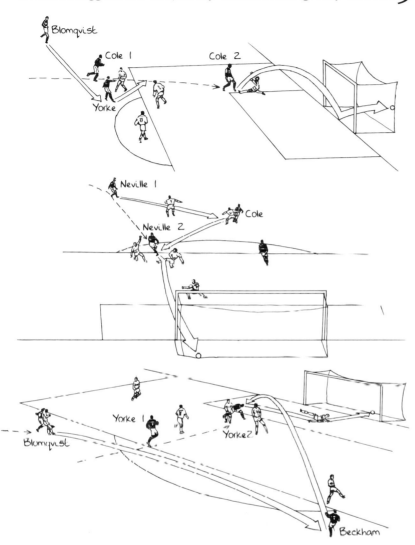

GOAL NO.1
David Beckham 7 minutes
David Beckham caught Brondby cold with a free kick from his favourite position, about 30 yards out and slightly to the left of goal. He curled this one round a three-man wall. It dipped low just inside the post and gave the goalkeeper no chance.

GOAL NO.2
Andy Cole 13 minutes
Certainly the goal of the night. Andy Cole stepped over a cross from Jesper Blomqvist, letting the ball run through to Dwight Yorke. Yorke promptly gave him the return and he finished with an immaculate chip over the goalkeeper's head.

GOAL NO.3
Phil Neville 16 minutes
Urged forward by David Beckham, Phil Neville kept going and cut in to play a one two with Andy Cole. The return was perfect and he burst through the last line of Brondby's defence to blaze the ball past the goalkeeper for his first goal in Europe.

GOAL NO.4
Dwight Yorke 28 minutes
Jesper Blomqvist set this one up with a brilliant dribble from deep in his own half. He found David Beckham whose cross from the right was met with such a forceful, close-range header by Dwight Yorke that the ball squeezed underneath the goalkeeper.

GOAL NO.5
Paul Scholes 62 minutes
A typically tenacious thrust from Paul Scholes took him past two attempted tackles and, as other defenders closed in, he finished with a piledriver for a well-executed solo goal.

Wes Brown made a big impression with an increasing number of first-team appearances.

	8 November 1998	P	W	D	L	F	A	Pts
1	Aston Villa	11	7	4	0	14	5	25
2	Arsenal	12	6	5	1	14	5	23
3	Manchester Utd	11	6	4	1	23	9	22
4	Middlesbrough	12	4	6	2	20	15	18
5	Chelsea	10	4	5	1	14	10	17
6	Leeds Utd	12	3	8	1	13	9	17
7	Derby County	12	4	5	3	12	10	17
8	Leicester City	12	4	5	3	11	10	17
9	West Ham Utd	12	4	5	3	13	13	17
10	Wimbledon	12	4	5	3	17	19	17
11	Liverpool	12	4	4	4	19	14	16
12	Charlton Athletic	12	3	6	3	19	16	15
13	Newcastle Utd	12	4	3	5	15	16	15
14	Tottenham Hotspur	12	4	3	5	16	21	15
15	Everton	12	2	6	4	7	11	12
16	Sheffield Wednesday	12	3	2	7	9	12	11
17	Coventry City	12	3	2	7	9	18	11
18	Blackburn Rovers	12	2	3	7	12	17	9
19	Nottingham Forest	12	2	3	7	8	18	9
20	Southampton	12	1	4	7	9	26	7

Paul Scholes in determined mood.

Match Report

Newcastle rubbed the shine off United's highly polished scoring feats – 30 goals in nine games – with this goalless home draw. It proved to be one of Ruud Gullit's better moments of the season so far with bold selection and tactics that finally brought United's fast-rolling bandwagon to a shuddering halt. Gullit packed his midfield, even sacrificing the experienced Stuart Pearce in order to match United's pace, and Alex Ferguson's team struggled to get into their usual dominating position.

The Old Trafford pitch has started to cut up, a factor of great concern to the manager who considers that his team's ball-playing, passing style needs the best possible surface. The problem was first noticeable in the previous match against Brondby and with more rain huge divots have been churned up. The turf, relaid just last summer, is coming away from the sub-soil. This is a revolutionary new system, imported from Australia and used at the famous Melbourne Cricket Ground, involving a mesh for the roots to bind into, but it seems that at Old Trafford this has just not happened.

Certainly the game against Newcastle was a below par display which came as all the more of a shock following United's outstanding form of the previous few weeks. Perhaps there is a European hangover, too, after the intoxicating goals against Brondby, another issue which concerns the manager.

It could easily have been worse with the visitors convinced they should have had a penalty when Denis Irwin knocked over Paul Dalglish five minutes before the interval. The referee ruled that the challenge had been a fair shoulder charge. There was another let-off for the Reds early in the second half when Dalglish found himself one-on-one with the goalkeeper only to discover, like many strikers before him, that the huge Peter Schmeichel was too good to beat.

United might also have snatched full points with their best chance falling to David Beckham just after the hour. The England man was face to face with Shay Given following Gary Neville's defence-splitting pass, but he pulled his shot wide. In that situation Beckham would normally have scored.

Manager's Report

❝ Ruud Gullit is a colourful character with a lot of experience as a player at the highest of levels and he certainly came up with the unexpected with the team he sent out against us in this match.

I would never have picked it. He filled his side with as many quick players as he could find. In fact I didn't even know two of them, which for me is saying something. It was an enterprising selection aimed at getting among us with speed, and in terms of teams coming to Old Trafford and holding us to a draw, it worked!

Their tactics forced us on to the back foot and we were very flat. We improved in the second half and when you create four good scoring chances in a tight match you hope that you will take at least one of them. It wasn't to be and we had to settle for a disappointing goalless draw.

I have got to say, though, that there are a couple of other factors on my mind which might have had a bearing on the result. I certainly wasn't happy about the pitch. It has suddenly started to cut up. Perhaps the poor autumn weather and a tremendous amount of rain finally proved too much, despite all the hard work put in by our groundsman, Keith Kent, and his staff. I will be looking into the problem. Our players need a surface to match their abilities.

I am also wondering to what extent the midweek match against Brondby in the Champions League had an effect. We won well and played some marvellous football, so it was quite a let-down to watch us struggle to come to terms with Newcastle. ❞

Manchester United 0
Newcastle United 0

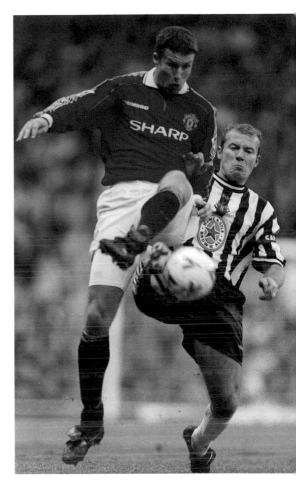

Above: *Ronny Johnsen battles with Alan Shearer.*

Left: *Andy Cole gets up high but not high enough for a goal.*

Manchester United: Schmeichel, G. Neville, Irwin, Keane, Brown (Johnsen 58; Butt 83), Stam, Beckham, Scholes, Cole, Yorke, Blomqvist

Newcastle United: Given, Charvet, Griffin, Batty, Hughes, Dabizas, Georgiadis, Hamann (Speed 67), Dalglish, Glass

Worthington Cup

Fourth round
11 November 1998

Fourth round	
Bolton wanderers 1	Wimbledon 2
Liverpool 1	Tottenham Hotspur 3
Luton Townn 1	Barnsley 0
Arsenal 0	Chelsea 5
Everton 1 *(Sunderland won 5–4 pens)*	Sunderland 1
Leicester City 2	Leeds Utd 1
Manchester Utd 2	Nottingham Forest 1
Newcastle Utd 1 *(Blackburn won 4–2 pens)*	Blackburn Rovers 1

Manchester United: Van der Gouw, Clegg, Curtis, May (Wallwork 45), Berg, Wilson, Greening, Butt, Solskjaer, Cruyff, Mulryne

Nottingham Forest: Beasant, Louis-Jean, Rogers, Armstrong, Chettle, Gray, Stone, Gemmill, Harewood (Hooijdonk 63), Freedman, Bart-Williams

Ole Gunnar Solskjaer

Match Report

The manager again made no bones about his policy in the Worthington Cup with a selection which, as before, combined those members of his first-team squad who had had a thin time getting picked with his up-and-coming youngsters. The result was an opportunity for Ole Gunnar Solskjaer, Henning Berg, Jordi Cruyff and David May to show their paces alongside the promising Jonathan Greening, John Curtis, Michael Clegg, Mark Wilson and Philip Mulryne.

Solskjaer, ably supported by Cruyff, certainly seized his chance to remind Alex Ferguson of his undoubted scoring prowess. Prompted on both occasions by the Dutchman, Solskjaer scored twice in three minutes in the second half to reinforce the manager's claim that he always picks a team he considers capable of winning.

Steve Stone replied with a thundering goal from 30 yards but United came home 2–1 winners with the 25-year-old Solskjaer clearly regarding the Worthington Cup as a lifeline and emphasising that he wants to go all the way to Wembley.

An envious Dave Bassett, the Forest manager, said later that if his team had had the Norwegian they would have been two goals up by the interval.

Manager's Report

❝ I am inclined to freeze whenever the topic of the Worthington Cup crops up because I inevitably find myself becoming apologetic. I respect sponsors who put money into football and the Worthington people are entitled to get a proper return on their investment.

I am sure they look at the teams I put into the competition and question why one or two of the more familiar names are missing. I have a lot of sympathy with that view, but at the same time I have to consider my requirements and use my own judgement of the English game to determine my selections.

I firmly believe that if Manchester United are going to be successful, I must prioritise what I am trying to do. Anyone in tune with the desires of the club would want us to win the championship and do well in Europe. They would also consider the FA Cup to be very important, all of which means that the Worthington Cup comes fourth in our rankings.

That is obviously unfortunate for the Worthington Cup but it is a fact of football life. So I pick my teams to use my full group of players, especially the younger ones who have to be given the opportunity to show how they stand up in more senior football in terms of not just their ability, but their character and temperament. I have got to be honest and say that over the years it has worked well for Manchester United in this way, even though we have not won the League Cup for some years.

I believe it is correct for me to persist with my policy of utilising my extensive pool, and it must also be borne in mind that I am still putting out teams of a very high standard. In this match against Nottingham Forest for instance, we had six full internationals in the squad, compared with Nottingham Forest's two in Steve Stone and Scot Gemmill.

So are we really denigrating the competition as I juggle with my squad to preserve our hopes for the season? I think not.

The further problem with the League Cup is that it comes so early in the season and puts you under pressure because so much lies ahead. If the competition fell into the calendar at the time of the FA Cup it would be a different matter. As it is, it starts early and has to be treated that way.

But whatever the arguments, my team did not let us down. They played well and it was a good result for us. Ole Gunnar Solskjaer and Jordi Cruyff were excellent, though I must concede that Steve Stone's great 30 yard goal was the highlight of the night. It reminded me of the lad's capability before he had his terrible injury but scoring like that will have done him a power of good. Injuries have a big influence on careers of course. In our team for instance, Jordi Cruyff is without doubt one of the most talented players I have handled and I just regret that he did not stay clear of injuries in his early days with us so that he could have bedded in better. ❥

A rare first-team chance for David May.

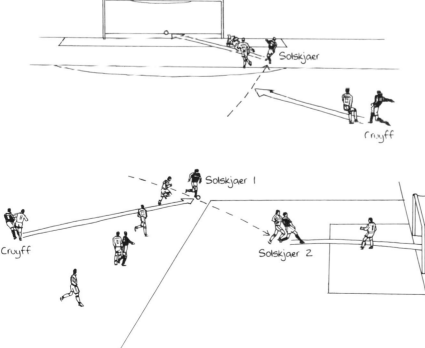

GOAL NO.1
Ole Gunnar Solskjaer 57 minutes
Jordi Cruyff split a square defence with a fine ball down the middle which was so well executed that most spectators probably thought Ole Gunnar Solskjaer was offside, but the Norwegian had in fact beaten the trap as he raced clear to rifle the ball past Dave Beasant.

GOAL NO.2
**Ole Gunnar Solskjaer
60 minutes**
Jordi Cruyff launched into a midfield meander before catching the Forest defence on the hop again with a pass behind their last line for Ole Gunnar Solskjaer to beat the 39-year-old Beasant.

15 November 1998							
	P	W	D	L	F	A	Pts
1 Aston Villa	12	8	4	0	18	6	28
2 Manchester Utd	12	7	4	1	26	11	25
3 Arsenal	13	6	6	1	14	5	24
4 Chelsea	11	5	5	1	17	10	20
5 Leeds Utd	13	4	8	1	16	10	20
6 West Ham Utd	13	5	5	3	16	15	20
7 Middlesbrough	13	4	7	2	21	16	19
8 Derby County	12	4	5	3	12	10	17
9 Leicester City	13	4	5	4	13	13	17
10 Wimbledon	13	4	5	4	17	22	17
11 Charlton Athletic	13	3	7	3	20	17	16
12 Liverpool	13	4	4	5	20	17	16
13 Newcastle Utd	13	4	4	5	16	17	16
14 Tottenham Hotspur	13	4	4	5	16	21	16
15 Coventry City	13	4	2	7	12	18	14
16 Sheffield Wednesday	13	3	3	7	10	13	12
17 Everton	13	2	6	5	7	14	12
18 Blackburn Rovers	13	2	3	8	14	20	9
19 Nottingham Forest	12	2	3	7	8	18	9
20 Southampton	13	1	4	8	10	30	7

Match Report

Blackburn opened brightly with Kevin Davies close to giving the visitors a shock lead. He chipped cleverly and got the ball over Peter Schmeichel only to find he had cleared the bar as well.

United also had an early culprit in front of goal with Andy Cole hitting the post as if confirming the wisdom of Glenn Hoddle's decision to leave him out of the England squad he had named for a friendly against the Czech Republic.

After half an hour Dwight Yorke got Paul Scholes away for the midfielder to put United in front and shortly before the interval Yorke himself scored, becoming the first United player to reach double scoring figures this season.

Not long after the restart, Rovers put themselves at a disadvantage when Tim Sherwood, their influential captain, perhaps excited by a few stormy moments as the tempo hotted up, was sent off for elbowing David Beckham. Scholes immediately punished the ten-men visitors by scoring United's third goal and the stage seemed set for an easy canter home, but the ending proved far different. Blackburn, incensed by the dismissal, roared back at United. Dario Marcolin scored in the 66th minute followed by a 74th minute goal from Nathan Blake.

Suddenly United were fighting desperately to hold on to their lead – and against a depleted side, too – but they hung on to take full points.

Full-back Phil Neville is always striving to get forward down his wing.

Dwight Yorke was the first United player to take his goal tally into double figures in the treble-winning season.

Manager's Report

❝ I saw it as a careless performance. We took the foot off the pedal to find ourselves desperately defending a three-goal lead against ten men. We managed it in the end but we should never have let it slip in the first place.

My irritation was nothing compared with the distress suffered by Roy Hodgson. He was visibly hurt by his players' performance, especially their discipline, because the last thing he needed was to be playing Manchester United with ten men. I felt sorry for him, and now, a week later, he's been sacked. Football is such a strange game. A few weeks ago Jack Walker was warning other clubs to keep their hands off his manager but now he is booting him out.

We have had this kind of scenario before with managers sacked after being beaten by Manchester United. It happened to Howard Wilkinson soon after Leeds lost 4–0 to us and David Pleat lost his job at Sheffield Wednesday after a defeat against United.

I wonder about it. Surely if there is one team to lose to without feeling disgraced it's Manchester United. It's the one game most clubs don't expect to win. Yet we have this kneejerk reaction and you wonder if there is a jealousy that gets through to people like Jack Walker and makes them react illogically in the aftermath of a defeat against us. I certainly feel for Roy, even though a lot of my thoughts this weekend are centred on the announcement by Peter Schmeichel that he intends to retire from English football at the end of the season.

Manchester United: Schmeichel, G. Neville, Curtis, Scholes (Cruyff 63; Keane 81), P. Neville, Stam, Beckham, Butt, Cole, Yorke, Blomqvist (Solskjaer 67)

Blackburn Rovers: Filan, Kenna, Davidson (Croft 56), Sherwood, Peacock, Henchoz, Johnson, Dailly, Blake, Davies (Gallacher 78), Duff (Marcolin 52)

Peter, a truly great Manchester United player, is a remarkable character who has shared in so much of our success. Indeed, he has been one of the key factors in achieving it and it goes without saying that he will be missed.

I vividly remember my first sighting of him. We were in Spain one January on a winter break and Brondby were staying in the same hotel. We shared the same training pitch and because we had been told about this goalkeeper breaking through in Danish football I stayed behind one day to watch him. His enthusiasm and fanaticism in training, as well as his obvious competence, immediately impressed me and so we started to have him watched. You always wonder how a goalkeeper from the Continent will cope with the more physical English game and I had Alan Hodgkinson, our goalkeeper coach, watch him over a period of six matches.

Alan had no reservations, saying that he thought he would be ideal in our League, so we went in for him. Brondby turned down our first approach but we went back as his contract was coming to an end and

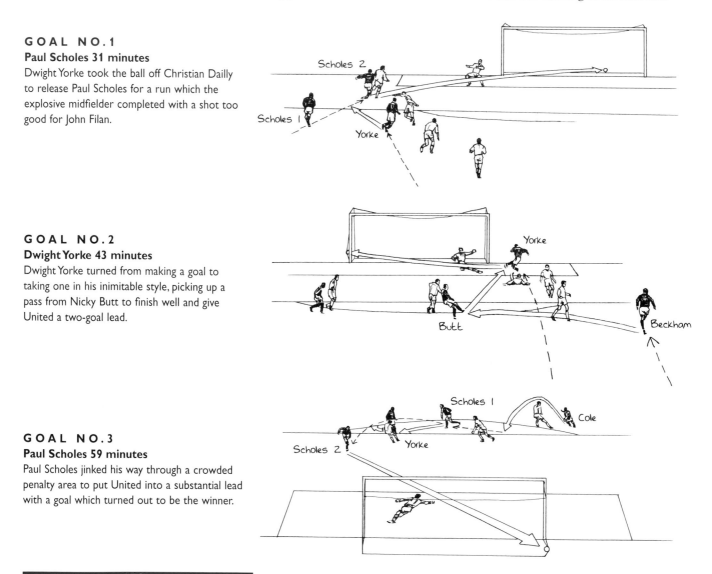

GOAL NO.1
Paul Scholes 31 minutes
Dwight Yorke took the ball off Christian Dailly to release Paul Scholes for a run which the explosive midfielder completed with a shot too good for John Filan.

GOAL NO.2
Dwight Yorke 43 minutes
Dwight Yorke turned from making a goal to taking one in his inimitable style, picking up a pass from Nicky Butt to finish well and give United a two-goal lead.

GOAL NO.3
Paul Scholes 59 minutes
Paul Scholes jinked his way through a crowded penalty area to put United into a substantial lead with a goal which turned out to be the winner.

struck a deal at £505,000. Don't ask me what the £5,000 was for, because I don't know!

His first league game for us was against Wimbledon, so he certainly went in at the deep end. I think he was genuinely shocked at the level of commitment from opposing forwards – and that's putting it politely because this was in the days of the Wimbledon Crazy Gang! But because he is the man he is, he took it in his stride and blossomed into the best goalkeeper Manchester United have ever had and the best I have worked with. He ranks up there with Gordon Banks, Peter Shilton, Lev Yashin and all the other outstanding keepers. He is brave, quick and has a massive presence. He has been a model professional who has inspired us all on his way to becoming one of the most influential players in arguably the most successful period in the club's history.

Peter has made his mistakes, of course, mostly stemming from those moments when he is living out his dream of becoming a centre-forward. But the thing about him is that he has never made a mistake in a big game that was costly. When the chips are down his focus is intense.

I think the daily grind has got to him, and certainly it is hard work to maintain the level of fitness and commitment demanded at a club like Manchester United. When you weigh 16 stone throwing yourself around every day must take a lot out of you! I think he has found that he has to train even harder to maintain his standards and that he needs more time between games for recovery than he gets in an English League programme.

So he intends leaving in the summer for quieter waters, and he is determined to mark his departure by winning the championship again and, who knows, finally making it all the way in Europe. ❜

Paul Scholes struck twice to see United through to a 3–2 win.

22 November 1998	P	W	D	L	F	A	Pts
1 Aston Villa	13	8	4	1	20	10	28
2 Manchester Utd	13	7	4	2	27	14	25
3 Arsenal	14	6	6	2	14	6	24
4 Chelsea	12	6	5	1	21	12	23
5 Leeds Utd	14	5	8	1	20	11	23
6 West Ham Utd	14	6	5	3	18	15	23
7 Middlesbrough	14	5	7	2	23	16	22
8 Wimbledon	14	5	5	4	18	22	20
9 Liverpool	14	5	4	5	24	19	19
10 Tottenham Hotspur	14	5	4	5	18	21	19
11 Derby County	14	4	6	4	14	14	18
12 Leicester City	14	4	5	5	15	17	17
13 Charlton Athletic	14	3	7	4	21	21	16
14 Newcastle Utd	13	4	4	5	16	17	16
15 Sheffield Wednesday	14	4	3	7	13	14	15
16 Coventry City	14	4	2	8	12	20	14
17 Everton	13	2	6	5	7	14	12
18 Nottingham Forest	14	2	4	8	10	22	10
19 Southampton	14	2	4	8	12	30	10
20 Blackburn Rovers	14	2	3	9	14	22	9

Match Report

United opened confidently enough with a nice touch from Jesper Blomqvist that sailed just over the bar, and Sheffield Wednesday looked like a team that had just gone six games without a win! But then Wednesday perhaps recalled that Hillsborough is something of a bogey ground for United and they began to play with an assurance which seemed to have Peter Schmeichel worried.

After only 15 minutes, United's usually immaculate goalkeeper allowed a fierce, but nevertheless long-range, shot from Niclas Alexandersson to jump out of his arms and over the line. It was a rare mistake which Andy Cole soon wiped out after a brilliant exchange of passes with Dwight Yorke for an interval score of 1–1.

But with Benito Carbone in good flow and United stuttering again, the home team took an ascendancy which United could do little about. The visitors had a penalty appeal waved away after Alexandersson brought down Denis Irwin, but overall Wednesday were on top and in the 55th minute Wim Jonk latched on to Schmeichel's parried save from Andy Booth to put the home side ahead.

Alexandersson pounced again, this time on some defensive dithering, to complete a 3–1 victory for the Yorkshire club in the 73rd minute.

Manager's Report

'I can never quite make up my mind on the effect of European games on our league form before and after. It does seem we are vulnerable and with a big one against Barcelona next week, I wonder whether it accounts for the poor showing we made in this match against Sheffield Wednesday.

Certainly the results suggest we are not handling the two competitions of Champions League and Premiership at all well. A pattern has emerged indicating that we don't take in our stride the demands of switching from one to the other. There have been some notable exceptions, but overall, our hiccups in the League have nearly all come either immediately after or before a European tie.

GOAL NO. 1
Andy Cole 29 minutes
Gary Neville pushed upfield unchallenged to feed Andy Cole who quickly moved the ball square to Dwight Yorke on his right. Cole raced for goal to take a return pass from his partner and beat the goalkeeper from close range.

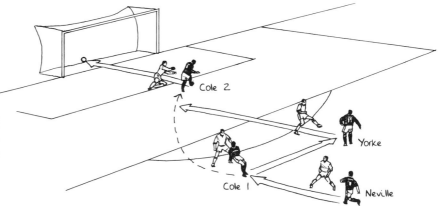

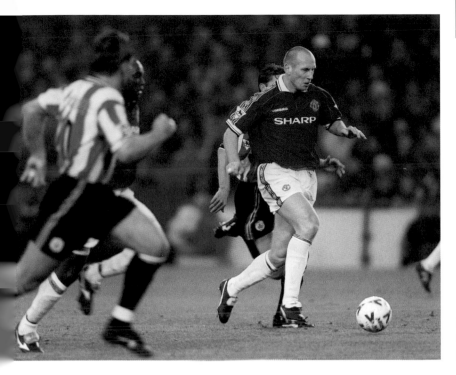

Left: Jaap Stam and his defence struggled to cope as United suffered a European backlash.

Below: Even Roy Keane could not prevent a 3–1 defeat.

This is simply unacceptable at our club and it is something that the players must take on board. Our squad is big and has quality. It has been built to cope with the demands of competing at the top level, which of course is what being a Manchester United player entails.

Perhaps some of our new players have not quite adjusted to this basic fact of football life, maybe some of our younger players are struggling to come to terms with the pressure, but what is crystal clear, in my mind at any rate, is that the players have got to get to grips with these expectations. We simply cannot afford – or tolerate – the under-performing displays at places like Derby County and in this game at Sheffield Wednesday which have cost us valuable points and let us all down.

We have a challenge on our hands if we are going to win the Premiership this season and I want to see a big improvement with the problem. I shall be examining in every detail, the attitude and standards of the players in our next league fixture at home to Leeds following next Wednesday's match in Barcelona.

I know Europe looms large in all our minds, and it is no secret that we would dearly like to go all the way this year after the near-misses, injuries and other setbacks of recent seasons. But it must not be at the expense of our challenge for the home championship, especially after missing out last season. We must never allow our standards to fall and I am determined that it must not happen again. **"**

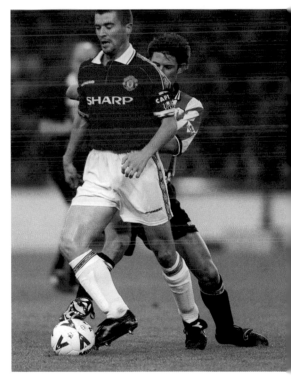

Sheffield Wednesday: Srnicek, Atherton, Hinchcliffe, Jonk, Thome, Walker, Alexandersson, Carbone, Rudi, Booth, Sonner

Manchester United: Schmeichel, G. Neville, Irwin (Brown 65), Keane (Solskjaer 83), P. Neville, Stam, Beckham, Scholes, Cole, Yorke, Blomqvist (Butt 57)

Group D	
Barcelona 3	Manchester Utd 3
Bayern Munich 2	Brondby 0

Match Report

Barcelona had to win to stay in the competition and they set about their task with the kind of resolve which was to test United all the way on a night of high drama and quality football.

United were dealt a blow so early in the game that they could have been forgiven for surrendering there and then. For in the very first minute Giovanni skewered United's defence with a centre which was cleanly hit home by Anderson to revive nightmare memories of the time Barcelona had destroyed United 4–0 in the Nou Camp Stadium in 1994.

But United are made of sterner stuff these days and in the 25th minute Dwight Yorke equalised after persistent work by Jesper Blomqvist. The score still stood at 1–1 at half-time with both teams in determined attacking mood and with hair-raising attempts at both ends.

Early in the second half Andy Cole combined brilliantly with Yorke to put United ahead, but the celebration was short-lived. Rivaldo took just four minutes to level with a free kick. The game continued to see-saw as Yorke struck again in the 68th minute, raising hopes of an incredible victory.

Rivaldo, more than living up to his reputation as a world-class performer, claimed another equaliser five minutes later with an over-head kick. The Spanish club continued to fight like tigers to stay in the competition. The Brazilian was within a whisker of a hat-trick when he hit the bar. Chances were created by both teams right until the final whistle. A draw was a fitting result for a superb match.

Jesper Blomqvist was the man behind United's opening goal, which wiped out Barcelona's early stunner.

Dwight Yorke scored twice in one of the most thrilling European matches of the season. Here he runs on to Jesper Blomqvist's pass to blast home his first in a sensational performance.

Manager's Report

❝ The reputation of a manager or coach is determined over many years and there is no doubting the high standing and respect in the game enjoyed by Louis van Gaal. I also recalled our 4–0 defeat against Barcelona in the Nou Camp in 1994, and set against this background I think it would have been understandable if we had gone to Spain to make sure we didn't lose.

But I always had this wonderful dream of having a team ready to attack and beat them. My job satisfaction is built around being involved in a game like that, putting my football beliefs up against van Gaal in the spirit of saying simply may the best team win! That's what this great night was about and if you re-run the video you will see that we had nine clear chances and Barcelona had 11 or 12.

What a fantastic game it was. I'll never forget it. Van Gaal is a disciple of English football and he was unstinting in his praise of United that night and our approach to the game. In turn, I cannot help but admire the ethic of Barcelona and their coach.

The game seesawed and I remember, when Rivaldo had just equalised to make the score 2–2, I went down to the side of the pitch to yell at my team: "Please defend properly." I was shouting into the wind and my words just came straight back at me. It was a night of complete abandon played exactly in the spirit of let the best team win.

Barcelona: Hesp, Reiziger, Sergi, Zenden, Okunowo, Xavi, Figo, Celades, Anderson, Giovanni, Rivaldo

Manchester United: Schmeichel, G. Neville, Irwin, Keane, Brown, Stam, Beckham (Butt 82), Scholes, Cole, Yorke, Blomqvist

GOAL NO.1
Dwight Yorke 25 minutes

Jesper Blomqvist won a tackle on the touchline deep in his own half and made rapid progress down the left before finding Dwight Yorke in the middle in space on the edge of the box. Yorke turned to score with a low right-foot shot just inside the post.

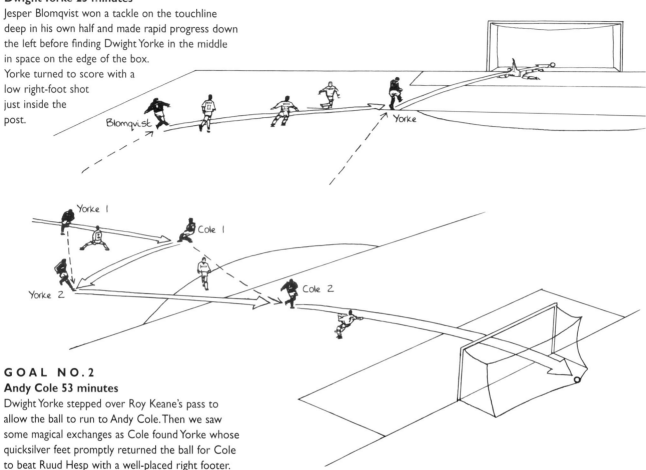

GOAL NO.2
Andy Cole 53 minutes

Dwight Yorke stepped over Roy Keane's pass to allow the ball to run to Andy Cole. Then we saw some magical exchanges as Cole found Yorke whose quicksilver feet promptly returned the ball for Cole to beat Ruud Hesp with a well-placed right footer.

GOAL NO.3
Dwight Yorke 68 minutes

Dwight Yorke had a headed goal ruled offside but he was quickly back to whip in front of the goal-keeper and score with a diving header from David Beckham's right-wing cross. And this one counted!

It's all very well a coach deciding on a strategy of attack, but he is not the one who has to go out there and actually do it! So I was very proud indeed as I watched my players go so boldly on the offensive and not only score three goals but stunning efforts, too.

I knew they were capable of playing to that level because I have watched their progress in Europe and seen them absorb all the qualities you need to cope with the demands of playing on a stage like the Nou Camp. Their belief now is tremendous.

I talk often about stepping up a level and this is what we achieved with this performance in an arena which is both impressive and frightening. They set about the task with flair and exuberance and the mental pictures of the goals they scored will remain with me for a long time.

I was especially pleased with the way the team shrugged off the goal scored against them in the opening seconds to come back and take the lead. Then Rivaldo produced his special moments, which rank alongside the goals scored by our dynamic duo up front, Dwight Yorke and Andy Cole.

I always felt that qualifying from this exacting group would probably go to the very last game, and that is what has happened with our fate now to be decided in what promises to be a gripping encounter against Bayern Munich at Old Trafford in a fortnight's time.

The winner takes all, or at least a place in the quarter-finals when the competition opens up again in March following the winter break. Meanwhile we must quickly put European thoughts to one side with our next Premiership game taking us to Leeds for a match in the cauldron of Elland Road, which in its own way will be every bit as demanding. ❥

Andy Cole was United's other scorer in magic parnership with Dwight Yorke.

		P	W	D	L	F	A	Pts
1	Aston Villa	14	8	5	1	22	12	29
2	Manchester Utd	14	8	4	2	30	16	28
3	West Ham Utd	15	7	5	3	20	16	26
4	Arsenal	13	6	7	2	15	7	25
5	Chelsea	13	6	6	1	22	13	24
6	Leeds Utd	15	5	8	2	22	14	23
7	Middlesbrough	15	5	8	2	24	17	23
8	Liverpool	15	6	4	5	26	19	22
9	Derby County	15	5	6	4	15	14	21
10	Wimbledon	15	5	5	5	19	25	20
11	Newcastle Utd	15	5	4	6	19	19	19
12	Tottenham Hotspur	15	5	4	6	19	23	19
13	Leicester City	15	4	6	5	16	18	18
14	Everton	15	4	6	5	10	15	18
15	Charlton Athletic	15	3	7	5	22	23	16
16	Sheffield Wednesday	15	4	4	7	14	15	16
17	Coventry City	15	4	3	8	13	21	15
18	Nottingham Forest	15	2	5	8	12	24	11
19	Southampton	15	2	4	9	12	31	10
20	Blackburn Rovers	15	2	3	10	14	24	9

Roy Keane after scoring his first goal of the season.

Match Report

The Manchester United players answered their manager's doubts about handling league games before and after major European fixtures by delivering a vibrant winning display against Leeds.

Alex Ferguson freshened up the team by including Ole Gunnar Solskjaer and Nicky Butt after omitting them both from the starting line-up against Barcelona. But he might have thought the message still hadn't sunk home when Jimmy Floyd Hasselbaink took advantage of some lax defending to put the visitors ahead with a shot that went in off the post on the half-hour.

United had made their presence felt, though, and Nicky Butt had headed fiercely for goal to produce a splendid save from Nigel Martyn. It was a marvellous effort by the Leeds goalkeeper, but not without cost. His acrobatic leap strained his back and he was replaced at the interval. Martyn might well have been feeling the effects of his injury when Solskjaer closed in from the left to beat him from a narrow angle and send the teams in for half-time with the score level.

It proved a timely strike for the Reds. They came out for the second half with a sharpened appetite and took the lead after just a few seconds play. Roy Keane moved into the box to thump home a cross with his left foot, a rare occasion which had Dwight Yorke pointing excitedly to his captain's left boot as they celebrated the goal. There was ample cause for celebration. Not only was it Keane's first goal of the season, but it was an emotional occasion for him. He was playing against Alf-Inge Haaland, the opponent involved when he suffered the knee injury that kept him out for the best part of last season.

The way Keane scored his goal summed up the Irishman's resilience, though it far from settled the match. The spirited Leeds side equalised when the talented Australian, Harry Kewell, bore down on Wes Brown and took the ball past him to beat Peter Schmeichel. Butt proved the saviour in the 78th minute when he turned like a born striker to take a ball from Phil Neville and blast it home for the winner and claim his first goal of the season.

For once, the twinkling partnership of Yorke and Cole had been outshone in front of goal by the boys from the engine room, Roy Keane and Nicky Butt.

Manager's Report

❝ Two things of significance came out of this game. Firstly we were up against a manager in David O'Leary who is clearly prepared to give young players a chance, and secondly we saw a talented bunch of youngsters who are a force to be reckoned with.

We did enough to win but they gave us a good insight into their potential and in the process gave us a fright. It looked as though we were OK leading 2–1 after going a goal behind, but Harry Kewell scored an equaliser. We got back in front with a winner from Nicky Butt, mainly I suspect because of our experience. A lot of Leeds' young players were playing at Old Trafford for the first time, quite a test, and it probably edged it for us.

Clearly they are going places. They are young players enjoying themselves, which always helps, and they take a positive approach, which is also an asset. Leeds normally defend like hell when they come to Old Trafford but today they really attacked us and, as I say, they gave us a big scare. It turned out to be the most entertaining encounter I have had against Leeds in my time at Old Trafford.

David O'Leary is the man who has changed things of course as he tackles his first job as a manager. It's already clear he is intent on bringing his own ideals into play and that he is encouraging his team to play creative football. It's refreshing to see. He is doing the game a service and I hope his beliefs work out. I have seen young coaches trying to change the way the game is played before, only to find the realities of football changing them, which is always a shame. I have seen managers change almost overnight and there is no doubt that the game can change the most inspired character. Let's hope it doesn't work out like that for David O'Leary. ✎

Manchester United: Schmeichel, G. Neville, P. Neville, Keane, Brown, Stam (Berg 77), Scholes (Sheringham 72), Butt, Cole (Giggs 65), Yorke, Solskjaer

Leeds United: Martyn (Robinson 45), Halle, Harte, Haaland, Hiden (Wetherall 26), Woodgate, Hopkin, McPhail, Hasselbaink, Ribeiro (Smith 85), Kewell

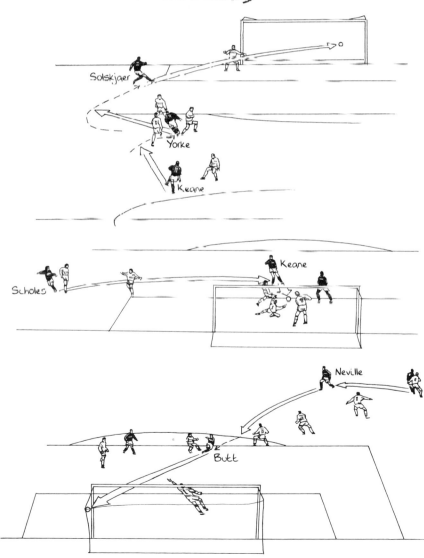

GOAL NO.1
Ole Gunnar Solskjaer 44 minutes
Roy Keane fed the ball up to Dwight Yorke who went past two defenders before slipping a pass to Ole Gunnar Solskjaer on his left. The Norwegian closed in and beat the struggling Nigel Martyn with a shot across the face of his goal.

GOAL NO.2
Roy Keane 46 minutes
Roy Keane smashed the ball into the roof of the net with a first-time strike as he ran on to a right-wing cross from Paul Scholes for his first Premiership goal in over a year.

GOAL NO.3
Nicky Butt 78 minutes
Phil Neville came down the left flank to find Nicky Butt in an advanced position on the edge of the penalty area. With all the nimble grace of an experienced striker, the midfielder stroked the ball in front of him, turned and scored with a cracking shot.

Fifth round	
Sunderland 3	Luton Town 0
Wimbledon 2	Chelsea 1
Leicester City 1	Blackburn Rovers 0
Tottenham Hotspur 3	Manchester Utd 1

Match Report

It was the end of the Worthington Cup road for United and there could be few complaints as Spurs emerged deserving winners.

The stature of the quarter-final and the quality of the opposition encouraged the manager to moderate the youth policy he had pursued in the earlier rounds of the competition. He used the full range of his senior squad, with Ryan Giggs back after injury, and only three juniors – Jonathan Greening, Michael Clegg and John Curtis, though Alex Notman came on as a late substitute, making his senior debut.

Spurs were still too strong for United, and though the first half was evenly contested, if uninspiring, the Londoners took the lead three minutes into the second half. A cross from Allan Nielsen was headed on by substitute Ruel Fox for Chris Armstrong to head beyond the reach of Raimond Van der Gouw.

Taking the lead moved Tottenham into a higher gear and was the signal for David Ginola to start revealing the full range of his talents. The Frenchman's display in this game was undoubtedly one that came to mind later in the season when his fellow professionals voted him Player of the Year as did the sports writers.

Ginola jinked his way down the left wing in the 55th minute before looping over a centre from which Armstrong scored at the near post.

The tempo rose as United tried desperately to get back into the game. Nicky Butt missed a good chance, though Steffen Iversen was equally guilty at the other end when he was wide from yet another of Ginola's pin-point crosses. United's response brought them the reward of a goal in the 70th minute when Teddy Sheringham, a former Spurs player and a target for jeers right from the start, silenced the home crowd with an accomplished goal headed in from Phil Neville's centre.

Sheringham led the United fight-back as the visitors threw caution to the winds in an attempt to grab an equaliser. They were caught pushing forward too enthusiastically five minutes from the end by the genius of Ginola who ran through them to score with a 25 yard rocket of a shot.

Young players Jonathan Greening (above) and Alex Notman (below) get their chance in the Worthington Cup.

Manager's Report

❛ Our visit to Tottenham was a day of frustration both on and off the field. On the morning of the match, Brian Kidd met with chairman Martin Edwards and director Peter Kenyon in London to discuss whether he would take up the opportunity to join Blackburn Rovers as their manager. He phoned me a couple of times and the message coming across was that he wanted to go to Blackburn. Deep down he wanted to try management and, in fact, I think at one point he actually approached Blackburn.

I have done my best to warn him. My fears are not about his capability as a manager but Jack Walker. Taking a line from the previous manager, it seems to me that one minute he regarded Roy Hodgson as a king and the next as some kind of fool. Such volatile, roller-coaster behaviour from the man who owns the club does not, in my view, make Blackburn the place for one's first job as a full manager.

Martin Edwards has offered Brian a lucrative deal to stay but Brian's mind is made up and there is nothing I can do about it. On reflection, if the ambition to become a manager has really taken hold, it is for the best that he leaves because if he stays, his frustration might fester and that would be no good for Brian, me or Manchester United. The only puzzle is that he has never previously indicated that he fancied becoming the man in charge.

From my point of view, Brian's departure could not be coming at a worse time with a key top-two battle in the Premiership against Aston Villa on Saturday and then the Champions League decider against Bayern Munich next week. I am worried about the disruption.

Brian has been an important figure in the success of this club, not just as my coach for the last eight years but going back to his days as a player and then the key work he did helping me to reorganise the structure of our youth system.

When I arrived at Old Trafford from Scotland, the club were not doing very well in the scouting department in the Manchester area. I brought Brian, who had been working for United's Community Football scheme, on to the scouting side. His local knowledge was invaluable in setting up closer contact with schools and junior football. The result was the arrival at United of players like Paul Scholes, Nicky Butt, Philip and Gary Neville, to name but a few, and I don't have to spell out the impact those particular players have made for both club and country.

Brian played a key role in that scouting revolution before I made him my assistant and coach working with the first team, but at my stage of management, nothing startles me any more. It's not the first time I have lost an assistant. Pat Stanton quit at Aberdeen to join Dunfermline while Archie Knox left as my Aberdeen assistant for Dundee. I brought Archie back and, of course, he came to Old Trafford with me. Then he did it a second time by moving to Glasgow Rangers.

When we finally got round to the Tottenham match, it was a frustrating experience as well, and naturally I was disappointed to lose. I thought we deserved at least a draw. People will no doubt say once again I fielded a weakened team but I always pick a side I consider capable of winning, and there wasn't much between the two teams.

I must say I was quite amused watching established international players celebrating at the end as if they had won the final. I suppose it must tell you something about how big we are. It was a compliment. It certainly didn't stop me having a drink with George Graham afterwards. He is a straight shooter, no greys, everything black and white, and I like that. ❞

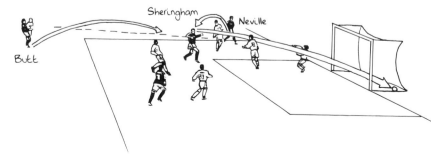

Butt Sheringham Neville

Tottenham Hotspur 3
Manchester United 1

Tottenham Hotspur: Walker, Carr, Sinton, Campbell, Calderwood (Fox 45), Nielsen, Young, Iversen, Anderton, Ginola, Armstrong

Manchester United: Van der Gouw, Clegg, Curtis (Beckham 86), P. Neville, Johnsen, Berg, Greening (Blomqvist 86), Butt (Notman 72), Solskjaer, Sheringham, Giggs

Ole Gunnar Solskjaer

GOAL NO.1
Teddy Sheringham 70 minutes
Nicky Butt sent Phil Neville away down the left side. The full-back, playing in midfield, centred for Teddy Sheringham to glance in a header against his old club.

		P	W	D	L	F	A	Pts
	6 December 1998							
1	Aston Villa	15	8	6	1	23	13	30
2	Manchester Utd	15	8	5	2	31	17	29
3	Leeds Utd	16	6	8	2	26	14	26
4	Arsenal	16	6	8	2	15	7	26
5	West Ham Utd	16	7	5	4	20	20	26
6	Chelsea	14	6	7	1	22	13	25
7	Middlesbrough	16	5	9	2	26	19	24
8	Wimbledon	16	6	5	5	21	26	23
9	Liverpool	16	6	4	6	27	21	22
10	Derby County	16	5	7	4	15	14	22
11	Tottenham Hotspur	16	6	4	6	21	24	22
12	Leicester City	16	5	6	5	18	18	21
13	Newcastle Utd	16	5	5	6	21	21	20
14	Everton	16	4	7	5	10	15	19
15	Sheffield Wednesday	15	4	4	7	14	15	16
16	Charlton Athletic	16	3	7	6	22	24	16
17	Coventry City	16	4	3	9	14	23	15
18	Blackburn Rovers	16	3	3	10	15	24	12
19	Nottingham Forest	15	2	5	8	12	24	11
20	Southampton	16	2	4	10	12	33	10

Paul Scholes gave United the lead.

Match Report

Aston Villa, though finishing seventh in the Premiership last season, have nevertheless surprised most people by dashing to the top of the table to face Manchester United as leaders one point ahead of the second-placed Reds.

John Gregory has steered his team to the top despite the blow of losing Dwight Yorke to Old Trafford, a transfer which quite naturally resulted in a torrid time for him from the home fans, and it was perhaps equally unsurprising that he had a quiet game.

The stage was set for a top-two tussle with an obvious bearing on the outcome of the championship, though as so often happens in this kind of drama the points were shared and nothing changed!

The game hardly lived up to its billing, especially in the first half when the tension seemed to affect both sets of players. The resulting patchy exhibition was conspicuous for its unforced errors. Andy Cole had a header cleared off the line but Villa probably shaded the first half. Dion Dublin, the former United forward, always looked capable of upsetting Jaap Stam and Wes Brown. But though Ugo Ehiogu and Lee Hendrie missed chances for Villa, they didn't create many real openings and the interval came with no score.

The second half brought an early bombshell for Villa as United dashed into the attack. Andy Cole's cross was palmed away by Michael Oakes only as far as Paul Scholes who buried it without giving the goalkeeper the chance to recover. The game was two minutes into the second half but, far from being crushed, Villa rose to the challenge and took just eight minutes to find an equaliser. Julian Joachim claimed the goal after taking a pot-shot from well outside the box, but it is doubtful if the ball would have gone in had it not struck Denis Irwin, taking a deflection wide of Peter Schmeichel.

Alan Thompson hit the United post but the visitors hung on for a draw to keep their mid-season rivals in their sights.

Manager's Report

❝ In the aftermath of Brian Kidd's departure, I made up my mind that I wouldn't rush to appoint a successor. So I've told my chief scout, Les Kershaw, and my experienced youth coach and scout, Eric Harrison, to go out and use their contacts in football to establish who are the best young coaches around in the country.

I am in no hurry because I am happy with Jimmy Ryan whom I have moved up from the reserves to the first-team squad. He played for the club, of course, and has been a marvellous servant. I trust him, too, which is important to me. I shall also make more use of Tony Coton, our goalkeeper coach, and perhaps give him a wider brief. He is a good observer and can spot details. Perhaps I shall take a bit more of the training myself, which I know I shall enjoy.

So the trip to Villa Park was really a matter of business as usual. Villa are top of the League and playing very well under John Gregory, a manager with forthright views and opinions. Some people describe

Left: Paul Scholes celebrates his goal.

Below: Dwight Yorke was given a hot reception by his old fans and by Ugo Ehiogu.

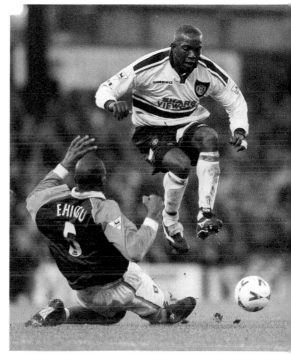

him as abrasive but I like his frankness. It's his character. He has never made any comment to concern me and I don't have a problem. His attitude is fine. He has certainly started well as a manager but, like all of us, he will have his ups and downs.

I remember when I was a young manager at St Mirren and we had put together a winning run of six or seven matches. I stuck my neck out and said I thought we would win the League and I couldn't, in fact, see us losing another game. We promptly went into freefall and finished fourth. I remember my assistant, Davie Provan, rather forcibly suggesting that in future it might be a good idea if I kept my big mouth shut. My only excuse is that I was 34 at the time. I have learned a lot since then!

We did well in the game. Both teams had their moments but when we got in front just after the interval through Paul Scholes I thought we won't lose now. There I go again I thought as Villa equalised, though it took a slice of luck for them to do it with a shot that took a wicked deflection off Denis Irwin to beat Peter Schmeichel.

In the circumstances of the week, a draw away from home against the leaders was not a bad result. I reminded myself it was December, not May, and that it wasn't necessary to get uptight. Plenty of time for that later! **⟩**

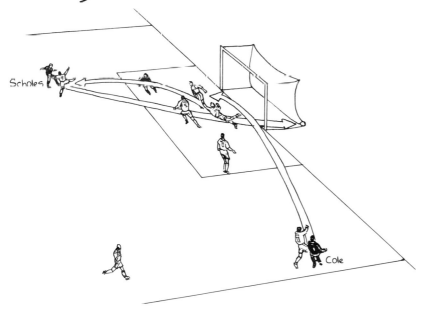

GOAL NO. 1
Paul Scholes 47 minutes
Andy Cole did the damage with a run down the right and a teasing cross which Michael Oakes reached but could not hold. The goalkeeper parried the ball away, Paul Scholes pounced and crashed in an unstoppable shot through a crowded goalmouth.

Aston Villa: Oakes, Barry, Wright, Southgate, Ehiogu, Watson, Taylor, Hendrie, Dublin, Joachim, Thompson

Manchester United: Schmeichel, G. Neville, Irwin, Keane, Brown, Stam, Beckham, Scholes, Cole (Butt 70), Yorke, Blomqvist (Giggs 45)

Group D	
Brondby 0	Barcelona 2
Manchester Utd 1	Bayern Munich 1

Andy Cole

Manchester United: Schmeichel, G. Neville, Irwin (Johnsen), Keane, Brown, Stam, Beckham, Scholes, Cole, Yorke (Butt 64), Giggs

Bayern Munich: Kahn, Babbel, Lizarazu, Kuffour, Salihamidzic, Jeremies, Zickler (Basler 81), Strunz, Elber (Jancker 81), Matthaus (Linke 61), Effenberg

Match Report

After a tense battle and 1–1 draw with Bayern Munich, Manchester United moved into the last eight of the Champions League and will go into the quarter-final draw with Bayern Munich, Olympiakos, Juventus, Inter Milan, Real Madrid, Dynamo Kiev and Kaiserslautern.

The game pulsed with passion when the stakes were high and winning through to the knock-out phase was at issue, but in the closing stages when it became apparent from the other venues that at 1–1 both teams would qualify, the match finished tamely with neither side doing much in attack and clearly prepared to settle for a draw.

Bayern were naturally content, with their position as group winners confirmed, while as soon as United heard the news from other games and knew they were on course to qualify as one of the two best runners-up, they lost their ambition.

Early on it was rousing stuff and it was fitting that the scorer of the all-important goal should be Roy Keane, an inspiring figure from the very start of a tough programme. Playing a captain's role, Keane strode on to a ball from Ryan Giggs, which kept low and true, to beat Oliver Kahn at a vital time just two minutes before the break. It was a deserved lead after near-misses from David Beckham and Andy Cole.

Ronny Johnsen, taking over from Denis Irwin at the interval, had a couple of chances to make the German team suffer but they came too soon in the second half before he had properly got his eye in. For the first chance, he took a fresh-air swing at the ball and for the next produced a wild blaze over the bar.

Bayern also pressed forward to attack and it took good goalkeeping by Peter Schmeichel to keep out a drive from Elber. Schmeichel was helpless in the 56th minute, though, when Thomas Strunz closed in from a fluffed corner kick and slid the ball across the face of the goal for Hasan Salihamidzic to force it over the line.

Bayern were back as group leaders and with United ready to settle for a runners-up ticket all the last ten minutes produced was a safety-first exercise with relief all round.

Manager's Report

❛ I have two abiding memories of this game. The first was at half-time when Markus Horwick, the secretary of Bayern Munich, showed me the scores of the other European games on the screen of his mobile phone. Why is it the Germans always seem further down the line in new technology than us?

The second was towards the end of the match when the score was level at 1–1, which meant Bayern were through as group winners while we were on line to qualify as one of the two best runners-up, a situation indicated as news from other venues came through. But Peter Schmeichel was rushing about his goal trying to hurry things up and I vividly recall Lothar Matthaus, who was now on the bench after being substituted, shaking his head at the mad English team!

I tried to tell Peter to settle down and eventually everyone realised the position. It meant a flat final few minutes, but the real significance was that we had scored 20 goals in a high-quality group and on the way shown great imagination and ability. I believe we are as good as anyone.

A lot of things will come into the equation when the competition reopens with the quarter-finals in March, especially injuries, but we have good ability and the right temperament to be successful. I just hope that the next stage will see us fresh and that I will have a reasonable squad to pick from.

We have been there before and the injury situation is always a worry. It is going to be a great test because there are some big, big names left in the competition. All eight are good enough to win it. They all have the history and tradition you associate with success in Europe.

I include ourselves in that. I just hope we can knock through the quarter-finals because once you have reached the semis anything can happen. I would certainly be pleased for the players because they are honest and they want to learn.

I was particularly pleased with their discipline in this match. They deserved to go through because it has been a difficult group. I thought we were in a good position after we had scored and we had the chances to have gone further ahead, but we were taxed when Bayern got what was a rather messy equaliser and we lost our composure for a spell. We got it back to ride the storm and in the end coped very well. The game petered out and fell away towards the end but you have to be sensible and I think we played it the right way.

The group has given us a roller-coaster ride. Some of the fixtures have gone as expected, but other games have produced shocks. Overall it has been unpredictable and competitive. Set against our high-scoring double over Brondby for instance, who would have thought the Danes would have opened up the group by beating Bayern Munich? I certainly expected the Germans to bounce back, which they did with a vengeance, beating Barcelona twice and effectively knocking them out of the competition.

Our strengths have been twofold – we have been difficult to beat and we have scored a lot of goals. We are the only team in our group without a loss, while at the same time we lead the entire competition with a total of 20 goals. Only Real Madrid, the present European champions, have come anywhere near that tally. You might ask questions of our defending at times, but nobody can accuse us of being negative or dull. Now we all look forward to the draw. ❞

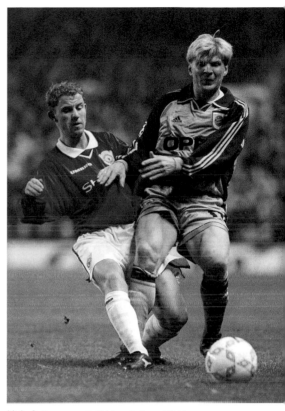

Nicky Butt came on to tighten up the midfield

GOAL NO.1
Roy Keane 43 minutes
Ryan Giggs seemed to make a mess of it when a cross from David Beckham flew over his head, but the Welshman turned and chased the ball to the touchline. He came back in on goal after beating Thomas Strunz and slid the ball into the path of the oncoming Roy Keane who kept his head down and scored with a blinding drive.

13 December 1998							
	P	W	D	L	F	A	Pts
1 Aston Villa	17	9	6	2	27	17	33
2 Manchester Utd	16	8	6	2	33	19	30
3 Chelsea	16	7	8	1	26	16	29
4 Middlesbrough	17	6	9	2	27	19	27
5 Leeds Utd	16	6	8	2	26	14	26
6 Arsenal	17	6	8	3	17	10	26
7 West Ham Utd	17	7	5	5	22	21	26
8 Wimbledon	17	7	5	5	22	26	26
9 Leicester City	17	6	6	5	21	19	24
10 Derby County	17	5	8	4	17	16	23
11 Tottenham Hotspur	17	6	5	6	23	26	23
12 Liverpool	17	6	4	7	27	22	22
13 Sheffield Wednesday	17	6	4	7	20	17	22
14 Everton	17	5	7	5	11	15	22
15 Newcastle Utd	17	5	6	6	21	21	21
16 Charlton Athletic	17	3	7	7	22	27	16
17 Coventry City	16	4	3	9	14	25	15
18 Blackburn Rovers	17	3	4	10	15	24	13
19 Nottingham Forest	17	2	5	10	15	30	11
20 Southampton	17	2	4	11	12	34	10

Match Report

At one time, this match looked like being a victory and sweet revenge for United's Worthington Cup defeat on the same ground ten days earlier, for the Reds were two goals up after 18 minutes and seemed set to cruise home. Then, towards the end of the first half, Gary Neville was sent off for two bookable offences. Down to ten men, United found it difficult to stem the Spurs tide and once again David Ginola was causing all the trouble. In fact, it was a tackle by Neville on the French winger that brought about the United defender's dismissal.

United fielded a more experienced team than the side they put out in the Worthington Cup, though it was one of the players who did play at White Hart Lane in the previous encounter who proved the main threat. Ole Gunnar Solskjaer and Teddy Sheringham were brought in to freshen up the team following the demanding European tie and it was Solskjaer who showed his appreciation of the squad rotation system by scoring both goals.

Ole Gunnar Solskjaer is congratulated by David Beckham and Teddy Sheringham for a fine display in which he scored both goals. The 2–2 draw made United the league leaders.

Ryan Giggs proved to be a handful for the Spurs defenders.

He grabbed his first after 11 minutes on a breakaway raid after Ian Walker had pushed a header from Ryan Giggs into his path. Seven minutes later he struck again, this time rounding off a tip-top cross from the always dangerous David Beckham.

Uriah Rennie, who flourished a total of seven yellow cards at United players during the course of a hotly competitive game, changed its course five minutes before the interval. He gave Neville his second caution for tussling with Ginola in a shirt-tugging incident that brought them both crashing down. On top of his booking for a foul on Allan Nielsen it meant he had to go and from then on Spurs were the dominant team.

The manager tried to hold the lead by putting on Henning Berg for Solskjaer at half-time and for a long time they battled superbly to keep the home team at bay. It wasn't until the 71st minute that United's defence cracked as Sol Campbell headed in a free kick taken by Darren Anderton.

United immediately regrouped and victory was in sight with just injury time remaining when Campbell, pushing forward from the centre-half position, equalised with a header, again from an Anderton pass.

The Reds left London feeling disappointed they had let it slip so late, but in the circumstances they had played stoutly for their point.

Manager's Report

We should have won comfortably. We played some of our best football and took a deserved two-goal lead.

But then enter Uriah Rennie, a man who represents a new breed of referee. He features on billboard advertising and is believed to have

Tottenham Hotspur: Walker, Carr, Sinton, Campbell, Young, Nielsen, Fox (Allen 83), Ginola, Anderton, Ferdinand, Armstrong

Manchester United: Schmeichel, G. Neville, P. Neville, Keane, Johnsen, Stam, Beckham, Butt, Solskjaer (Berg 45), Sheringham (Cole 75), Giggs (Blomqvist 87)

GOAL NO.1
Ole Gunnar Solskjaer 11 minutes

David Beckham launched one of many raids down his wing to curl a centre in for Ryan Giggs to make a diving header which Ian Walker did well to palm out. The Spurs goalkeeper was still in trouble, though, because the ball ran out to Ole Gunnar Solskjaer who rifled a shot into the back of the net on the half-volley from point-blank range.

GOAL NO.2
Ole Gunnar Solskjaer 18 minutes

David Beckham was also the supplier for Solskjaer's second goal with another great swinging centre which saw the nimble Norwegian nip in ahead of Sol Campbell to score with a first-time shot.

his own agent. He is a high-profile guy and there was no way he was going to let the stars of Manchester United and Tottenham upstage him.

He must have seen the way David Ginola was playing. There is no question, the French star dives, and although I have noticed he has made an effort to join in the spirit of the English game, he was going down all too easily in this match. It's disappointing to see him doing it so repeatedly. He has a rare talent and you say to yourself, why does he do it?

Anyway, Uriah Rennie bought the ticket and he sent Gary Neville off for a tackle on Ginola. It was his second yellow card and so he had to go. It was ludicrous. It not only left us with ten men, but nobody felt they were able to get near Ginola after that. I changed the people marking him. In turn I had Roy Keane, Ronny Johnsen, Henning Berg and Phil Neville on him in the hope that the referee would realise that they couldn't all be bad tacklers and that David Ginola was playing for free kicks and bookings. It didn't make any difference. The referee awarded free kick after free kick, and in the last 20 minutes Tottenham scored twice, the equaliser in injury time. They owed a lot to the referee.

I was so angry that when George Graham came to shake my hand I only half took his handshake and half threw it away. That was unfortunate, because really it was the referee and Ginola I was angry with. I don't know how George deals with it. It's perhaps difficult for him because the player is a great favourite with the crowd and maybe having such a rare talent is some compensation for the fans for not having the best of times in terms of results.

Ole Gunnar Solskjaer scored both our goals, ironic really because in the close season Spurs had come in for him. I put the situation to Ole and he wasn't sure whether he wanted to take up the offer and go. He asked my opinion. I said it was entirely up to him and that I wasn't forcing him out of the door. I told him he had been a model professional with United and that while I couldn't guarantee him a regular first-team place I could assure him that he would get plenty of football. He said he didn't want to leave Manchester United.

"Well, that's the matter over with," I replied. You could see the uncertainty in the boy and when he asked for my advice I said I honestly didn't think he should go. My words possibly took on more meaning for him as he banged his goals in today for a point which took us to the top of the table.

A few years ago, I never liked to go in front in case it started to make the players nervous but now they have the experience to handle it and my view is the quicker you take the lead the better. That way people have to catch you and it's not easy! ❥

Above: *Jaap Stam came under pressure but United hung on.*

Left: *Nicky Butt worked hard after the dismissal of Gary Neville.*

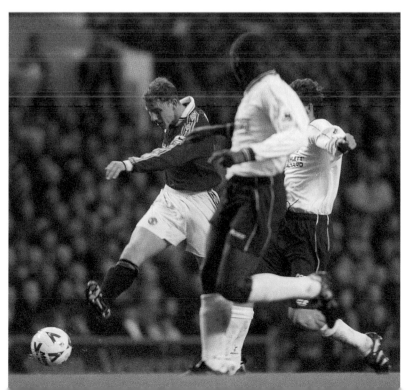

16 December 1998

		P	W	D	L	F	A	Pts
1	Aston Villa	17	9	6	2	27	17	33
2	Manchester Utd	17	8	7	2	34	20	31
3	Chelsea	17	7	9	1	27	17	30
4	Leeds Utd	17	7	8	2	28	14	29
5	Middlesbrough	17	6	9	2	27	19	27
6	Arsenal	17	6	8	3	17	10	26
7	West Ham Utd	17	7	5	5	20	21	26
8	Wimbledon	17	7	5	5	22	26	26
9	Leicester City	17	6	6	5	21	19	24
10	Derby County	17	5	8	4	17	16	23
11	Tottenham Hotspur	17	6	5	6	21	26	23
12	Liverpool	17	6	4	7	18	22	22
13	Sheffield Wednesday	17	6	4	7	21	17	22
14	Everton	17	5	7	5	10	15	22
15	Newcastle Utd	17	5	6	6	14	21	21
16	Charlton Athletic	17	3	7	7	22	27	16
17	Coventry City	17	4	3	10	14	23	15
18	Blackburn Rovers	17	3	4	10	15	24	13
19	Nottingham Forest	17	2	5	10	12	30	11
20	Southampton	17	2	4	11	12	34	10

Match Report

Chelsea are revealing a determined championship challenge and they certainly exploited United's inability to hold on to a lead in this match. In the three previous games, United have been in front only to concede late goals and finish with a draw, and this was no different. Andy Cole gave the Reds the lead just before the interval and a win looked on the cards until little Zola produced a delicious piece of magic for an equaliser just seven minutes from the end. Although the draw against Bayern Munich on the European scene was sound enough, valuable points have been dropped at Tottenham, Aston Villa and now Chelsea, a worrying run for the manager.

Perhaps in this match United were surprised by the ferocity of Chelsea's early challenge. Their foreign legion, ably encouraged by Dennis Wise, received five first-half bookings from referee Graham Barber. United established the bulk of command and though Cole missed an early chance he made no mistake seconds before the break, pouncing to score from inside the box after he had accidentally got in the way of a shot from Nicky Butt.

Dwight Yorke menaced Chelsea after an hour's play but was brought down and, sensing his team's inability to get the second goal that was needed to make the game safe, Alex Ferguson put on first David Beckham for Yorke and then Ryan Giggs for Blomqvist. They were substitutes as part of his rotation policy.

Chelsea had built up a good head of steam and in the 83rd minute substitute Gustave Poyet put Gianfranco Zola through with just Peter Schmeichel to beat. The Italian held off Wes Brown and as the goalkeeper came out, Zola scored with a neat chip curled high and wide of Schmeichel.

Celestine Babayaro almost added to United's defensive worries with a thundering shot near the end which flew narrowly wide to leave most supporters feeling a draw wasn't bad after all.

Chelsea's Dennis Wise closes in on Roy Keane.

Manager's Report

❝Sometimes you just have to hold up your hands! It's not that the other team are better than you, it's simply a matter of it being their day and Chelsea in this match struck all the right notes. I know it added to a run of draws but by the end I was quite pleased with this one because we could easily have lost.

We had one or two chances to kill them off in the second half after Andy Cole had given us the lead but generally I think the players found it difficult to get the ball down on a very lively pitch.

Chelsea, in comparison, played excellent football and persevered with it, showing the kind of consistency that has made them a potent force in the Premiership this season.

Gianfranco Zola's goal for the equaliser was tremendous. I must say he is one of those players you have got to admire, not just for his skill, but for his infectious enthusiasm for the game. He is a lovely mannered man, he doesn't get involved in kicking opponents, disputing decisions with referees or anything like that. His very demeanour puts him in the top drawer of footballers.

We have been fortunate to have great players of that kind at Old Trafford and I see the comparisons. I consider Zola one of the best of the foreign players to come to this country. The Italians don't usually let their very best players leave and Gianfranco Zola has been an exception.

As I say, all things considered, I was pleased with a point. I have always felt that getting something out of a game in which you don't play particularly well is the stuff of champions. I certainly hope so. What I do know is that overall we will play more good games than bad ones.❞

Manchester United: Schmeichel, G. Neville, Irwin, Keane, Brown, Stam, Scholes (Sheringham 85), Butt, Cole, Yorke (Beckham 61), Blomqvist (Giggs 77)

Chelsea: de Goey, Petrescu, Babayaro, Duberry, Lambourde, Le Saux (Poyet 45), Ferrer, di Matteo, Flo, Zola, Wise

Andy Cole is closely marked by Michael Duberry.

GOAL NO.1
Andy Cole 45 minutes
Jesper Blomqvist provided the cross which opened up the way towards Chelsea's goal. Nicky Butt collared the ball and drove it low at Ed de Goey only to find his shot hitting team-mate Andy Cole. Once he had recovered, Cole was quickly on to the rebound to score with a well-controlled drive.

		P	W	D	L	F	A	Pts
	20 December 1998							
1	Chelsea	18	8	9	1	29	17	33
2	Aston Villa	17	9	6	2	27	17	33
3	Manchester Utd	18	8	7	3	36	23	31
4	Middlesbrough	18	7	9	2	30	21	30
5	Leeds Utd	18	7	8	3	29	17	29
6	Arsenal	18	7	8	3	20	11	29
7	West Ham Utd	18	8	5	5	22	22	29
8	Wimbledon	18	7	5	6	23	29	26
9	Liverpool	18	7	4	7	29	22	25
10	Newcastle Utd	18	6	6	6	22	21	24
11	Leicester City	18	6	6	6	21	20	24
12	Derby County	18	5	9	4	18	17	24
13	Tottenham Hotspur	18	6	5	7	23	28	23
14	Sheffield Wednesday	18	6	4	8	20	19	22
15	Everton	18	5	7	6	12	17	22
16	Charlton Athletic	17	3	7	7	22	27	16
17	Coventry City	18	4	4	10	15	26	16
18	Blackburn Rovers	18	3	5	10	17	26	14
19	Southampton	18	3	4	11	15	35	13
20	Nottingham Forest	18	2	6	10	17	32	12

Andy Cole

Match Report

Everybody was pleased to see Bryan Robson back on his old stamping ground as manager of Middlesbrough, but allowing his team to sail into a three-goal lead in an hour was perhaps overdoing the warmth of the welcome!

The visit also brought Gary Pallister back to his old club but any temptation to compare the two opposing centre-halves vanished when Jaap Stam pulled out with an ankle injury. He would, though, have found it difficult to match the peerless performance of Pallister who did more than most to blunt United's lively opening. In marked contrast, United's latest of the season's six different defensive pairings, Ronny Johnsen and Gary Neville, slid slowly into trouble.

Their problems started after 24 minutes when Hamilton Ricard scored from Brian Deane's centre and just seven minutes later, with the defence under pressure following a free kick that wasn't properly cleared, Dean Gordon blasted in a shot to give Middlesbrough a two-goal interval lead.

Even in the second half United found it difficult to come to terms with Bryan Robson's highly motivated side and a mix-up at the heart of United's defence led to a third goal for the visitors just before the hour, this time from Brian Deane.

Contrary to the pattern of recent matches, United had a better ending than start. Maybe appalled at the beating they were taking on their own ground, they pulled themselves together with Nicky Butt heading in a cross from David Beckham in the 62nd minute.

A couple of minutes later Paul Scholes came off the bench to take over from David Beckham and made the score more respectable with a 70th minute goal from a penalty-area scramble.

United flung themselves forward in search of an equaliser but although Steve Vickers had to clear off the line at one point, it was not to be. At least the fans were satisfied that their team had made a valiant revival.

Manager's Report

'I missed this match because of the death of my brother Martin's wife. I wanted to be with him and the family. Ken Ramsden kept me up to date with the progress of the match by mobile phone and it was soon obvious we were not playing well. In fact, when we went 3–0 down I had a rush of guilt, but it was only fleeting. My place that day was in Scotland.

Now, a few days later, I've called all the players together at the training ground and I've told them enough is enough. I went over the goals on the video and told them how shocking they were for a club of our reputation and standing. I stressed it is not going to continue and will not be tolerated, even if it means playing four young lads at the back.

Sometimes the blunt truth is better than sympathising, telling them they were a bit unlucky or asking them what they think. Players will invariably come up with excuses, like a worm jumping up to deflect the ball! When they know you are not messing about, it can have a greater impact and I think that was what was needed.

At the same time, it is important to keep a balanced perspective on the season as a whole. We have just come through a particularly exhausting spell, yet we are still in contention in the League while at the same time qualifying for the next phase of the European Champions League. We have done a lot of travelling and played a lot of big games lately but it should get easier. We are starting a home run, and the fixtures are spread out a bit more. Playing twice a week including European games demands a lot, both mentally and physically.

With this defeat we have slipped down a place in the table. Chelsea, coming on strongly now, have jumped ahead of us and Aston Villa and are the new leaders. There are areas for improvement but now that we are able to put Europe on the back-burner until March and a quarter-final against Inter Milan, I think we will see an improvement in our Premiership results.

Europe remains the great challenge of course, but we have been down this road a few times now and we are knocking on the door with increased authority. We have players who want desperately to go all the way in the Champions League, and when you have people of that calibre, then you are in with a real chance of success.

We have had our defensive lapses but I also have to concede that playing with great attacking momentum sometimes leaves you vulnerable at the back. We have work to do as a unit to defend better against corner kicks and free kicks but at least we are still in touch in the Premiership and have moved forward in Europe. 🦅

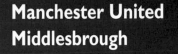

Manchester United 2
Middlesbrough 3

Manchester United: Schmeichel, G. Neville, Irwin, Keane, Johnsen, P. Neville (Solskjaer 79), Beckham (Scholes 64), Butt, Cole, Sheringham, Giggs

Middlesbrough: Schwarzer, Cooper, Gordon, Vickers, Festa, Pallister, Mustoe (Moore 72), Townsend, Ricard, Deane, Maddison (Beck 83)

David Beckham tries to get past Andy Townsend.

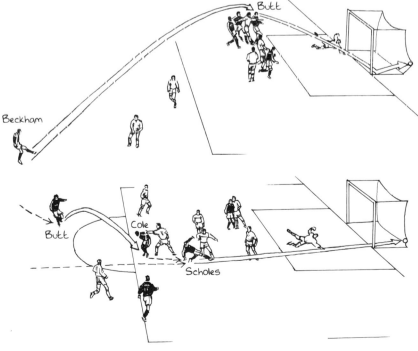

GOAL NO.1
Nicky Butt 62 minutes
David Beckham got a centre over from which Nicky Butt scored with a header to signal a United revival.

GOAL NO.2
Paul Scholes 70 minutes
It took Paul Scholes just six minutes to find the net after coming on as a substitute for David Beckham as the manager rang the changes to boost the fight-back. Scholes was on hand to stab the ball home after a goalmouth mêlée with Boro under intense pressure.

		P	W	D	L	F	A	Pts
1	Chelsea	19	9	9	1	31	17	36
2	Aston Villa	19	10	6	3	29	19	36
3	Manchester Utd	19	9	7	3	39	23	34
4	Leeds Utd	19	8	8	3	32	17	32
5	Arsenal	19	8	8	3	21	11	32
6	Middlesbrough	19	7	9	3	31	24	30
7	West Ham Utd	19	8	5	6	22	23	29
8	Wimbledon	19	8	5	6	25	30	29
9	Liverpool	19	8	4	7	32	23	28
10	Leicester City	19	7	6	6	22	20	27
11	Derby County	19	5	10	4	18	17	25
12	Newcastle Utd	19	6	6	7	22	24	24
13	Tottenham Hotspur	19	6	6	7	24	29	24
14	Everton	19	5	8	6	12	17	23
15	Sheffield Wednesday	19	6	4	9	20	20	22
16	Blackburn Rovers	19	4	5	10	19	27	17
17	Coventry City	19	4	5	10	16	27	17
18	Charlton Athletic	19	3	7	9	23	30	16
19	Southampton	19	3	4	12	15	37	13
20	Nottingham Forest	19	2	6	11	17	35	12

27 December 1998

Manchester United: Schmeichel, P. Neville, Irwin, Keane (Greening 66), Johnsen, Berg, Beckham, Butt, Scholes (Solskjaer 63), Sheringham, Giggs (Blomqvist 75)

Nottingham Forest: Beasant, Louis-Jean, Rogers, Quashie, Chettle (Doig 68), Armstrong, Stone (Hodges 77), Freedman, Shipperley, Johnson, Bart-Williams (Bonalair 54)

Nicky Butt closes in.

Match Report

At the halfway point of the league season, United are in third place with Chelsea in front on the same number of points as Aston Villa.

It's tight at the top but at least United's run of four games without a win has not proved too costly. Nevertheless, an emphatic 3–0 success against Nottingham Forest at Old Trafford was a welcome return to winning ways. Defeat would have seen the Reds slip down another two places, so beating Forest was timely indeed, especially as people were starting to talk about a crisis of confidence.

Their scoring hero was hardly one of their regular marksmen. United had both Dwight Yorke and Andy Cole missing through injury and Ronny Johnsen claimed the first two goals as United's flowing football came slowly but surely flooding back against a team admittedly struggling in bottom place. Johnsen also played a key role at the back, this time partnering Henning Berg in an all-Norwegian central defence. They did well together, too, keeping the team's first clean sheet since early November.

The early football was hardly inspiring. Both Johnsen's goals came from set pieces, the first after 28 minutes when he headed in David Beckham's corner kick. Beckham was also behind the second after 60 minutes with a free kick headed down by Berg and finished off by Johnsen.

Forest, without a Premiership win for 16 games, were clearly up against it. They were caught cold just a couple of minutes later by a sweeping move. The ball flowed through Teddy Sheringham and Beckham for Ryan Giggs to chip the advancing Dave Beasant.

As a spectacle, it was an ordinary game rescued by a piece of magic, but above all else for United, it had stopped the rot and given the team a big boost.

Manager's Report

❝ I was waiting today to study the reaction after my harsh words in midweek. I felt the situation called for a tough line, but a player like Jaap Stam had never heard anything so forceful from me before, and you can never be sure how people will respond.

In fairness, they looked like the old United against Forest, and the goal Ryan Giggs scored was the kind you could set to music. The rhythm of it was so sweet, it had a harmony all of its own, which is why I say it reminded me of a song. A nice piece of play from Denis Irwin, a touch from David Beckham and Ryan scored without breaking stride, just as a melody flows along. It's wonderful when you get football like that.

The other thing that struck me from this game was how things have changed at Nottingham Forest. In the days of Brian Clough it was always so difficult to score against them, they worked their tripe off and over the years had some clever players. No disrespect to the present people, but Dave Bassett has a mammoth job on his hands and you can't help thinking how the mighty have fallen.

I am just grateful that we have been able to keep the momentum going over the years at Old Trafford. We have had our unsuccessful moments but these falls from grace served to remind you that you must never take anything for granted. It's certainly what drives me on personally. I never want the struggle of 1989 and all that again!

So we will keep working and my aim now is to make sure that the players realise that every game is vital. It's nice to have people with nerves of steel who can rise to the biggest occasions without flinching, but in terms of winning a League, you need a team that can find inspiration come wet or shine from the dullest of fixtures.

I am urging the players to find total commitment and concentration for every match now, because out of this will come that vital ingredient of consistency. We face a lot more cut and thrust before anything is decided, but we must be in the thick of it.

It won't be easy because I believe the standard and competition among the leading clubs is greater than it has been for a long time. The arrival of quality players from abroad and the improved techniques of our home-produced youngsters, for those of us striving to produce our own players, has meant a bigger spread of ability.

It was a stronger challenge which, along with injuries, accounted for us losing out on the championship last season and has set up what is an intensely competitive battle again this winter. There isn't even a gap between the leading group and the chasing pack!

So I was pleased to see us take Forest in our stride. A few more clean sheets and the confidence will soon return to our defence. They were sensible in this match with nothing silly. A few more performances like that will soon see us back on track. 🍂

| Manchester United | 3 |
| Nottingham Forest | 0 |

Ronny Johnsen was a surprise scorer with two goals.

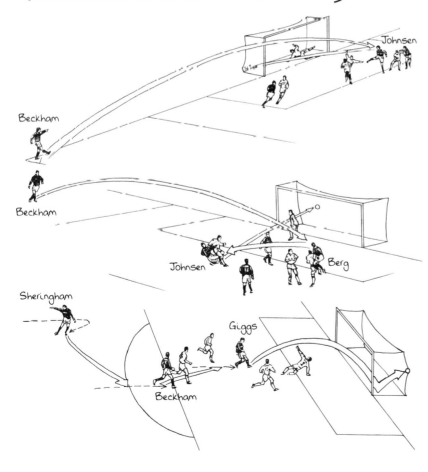

GOAL NO.1
Ronny Johnsen 28 minutes
A header from Ryan Giggs was saved at the expense of a corner which was taken by David Beckham. Ronny Johnsen scored from it with a crisp downward header.

GOAL NO.2
Ronny Johnsen 60 minutes
Hardly a prolific scorer, Ronny Johnsen probably surprised even himself by netting a second time to take his season's total to three. He and Henning Berg came forward from defence for David Beckham's free kick which Berg headed down for his partner to smash in powerfully.

GOAL NO.3
Ryan Giggs 62 minutes
A long clearance from Denis Irwin was moved on with a first-time touch to David Beckham who just as quickly sent Ryan Giggs in on goal. Giggs lifted a shot over Dave Beasant for a classic score.

		P	W	D	L	F	A	Pts
1	Aston Villa	20	11	6	3	31	20	39
2	Chelsea	20	9	10	1	31	17	37
3	Manchester Utd	20	9	8	3	39	23	35
4	Arsenal	20	9	8	3	22	11	35
5	Leeds Utd	20	8	9	3	34	19	33
6	West Ham Utd	20	9	5	6	24	23	32
7	Liverpool	20	9	4	7	36	25	31
8	Middlesbrough	20	7	9	4	32	26	30
9	Wimbledon	20	8	6	6	27	32	30
10	Leicester City	20	7	7	6	23	21	28
11	Derby County	20	6	10	4	20	18	28
12	Tottenham Hotspur	20	7	6	7	28	30	27
13	Newcastle Utd	20	6	6	8	24	28	24
14	Everton	20	5	8	7	13	21	23
15	Sheffield Wednesday	20	6	4	10	21	22	22
16	Blackburn Rovers	20	4	6	10	20	28	18
17	Coventry City	20	4	5	11	16	29	17
18	Charlton Athletic	20	3	7	10	23	31	16
19	Southampton	20	3	5	12	16	38	14
20	Nottingham Forest	20	2	7	11	18	36	13

Match Report

United are finding Chelsea a tough nut to crack. Honours were even with a 1–1 result at Old Trafford, and Stamford Bridge proved to be another ding-dong battle with a second draw and little to choose between the two teams.

A second clean sheet following the Forest fixture was satisfying, and if there had been any doubts about Peter Schmeichel following his announcement that he intends to quit Old Trafford at the end of the season, the great Dane answered them in this match in convincing fashion with a great display.

He had every opportunity to reveal his full armoury of talents in the first half which was dominated by Chelsea. They flung in wave after wave of attack, providing a string of chances for the little and large of their forward line, the diminutive Gianfranco Zola and the towering Tore Andre Flo. Schmeichel repeatedly saved from them both and his duel with Zola in one-on-one situations was a highlight of the match.

United were able to do little attacking in the first half and were confined mainly to a thrust from Andy Cole. He got round the goalkeeper but his finishing effort was cleared off the line by Michael Duberry. The second half was a different story with United much more in the game. Teddy Sheringham was brought on for the last half hour and he prompted an impressive attacking spell. Indeed ten minutes from the end, Chelsea were under such great pressure that Frank Leboeuf brought down David Beckham and was fortunate to escape a second yellow card from referee Mike Riley after an earlier booking for a foul on Cole. Even Leboeuf confessed at the end: 'I think I deserved to be sent off. I didn't do it on purpose but I touched his foot and grabbed him with my hands, so I think I maybe did deserve a red card.'

Nicky Butt shields the ball from Michael Duberry. United's resolute performance pleased the manager.

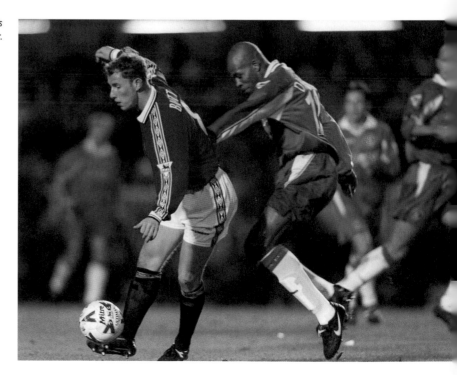

Left: Ryan Giggs was a key figure in United's late surge but Chelsea hung on to keep the game goalless.

Below: Roy Keane tussles with Roberto di Matteo.

So the honest if wayward Frenchman stayed on to see his team thwart United, while at the other end, the partnership of fit-again Jaap Stam and Ronny Johnsen went from strength to strength, perhaps inspired by the heroics of Schmeichel behind them.

Manager's Report

❝I am still in the mode of making sure we don't lose a goal. I have been stressing to the players that we must get back to basics and make sure we defend properly before throwing caution to the winds in attack. The way we had been playing was encouraging the opposition to think they were capable of beating us, and that's the last thing we want!

In the first half of this match against Chelsea we certainly had a lot of defending to do which we did with determination backed up by a lot of hard work. This gave us a solid platform for the second half when I think Chelsea tired. The result was that in the last half hour we overran them.

We should have got a win, but my main thought was that we started to look strong again. This is pleasing because now that we are on one game a week, we have started to use the midweek break for endurance training. Jimmy Ryan and our physiotherapist, Robert Swire, have prepared a fitness programme aimed at the run-in for the last lap of the season. Peter Schmeichel has already started the countdown, announcing after each fixture how many games we have left in an effort to keep our momentum and drive going.

I think we are already beginning to see the hard work pay off, and certainly in defensive terms I was pleased with this 0–0 result. Normally I would always prefer a 3–3 game for the entertainment value, but for the purpose of rebuilding our defensive confidence another clean sheet was a good result for us. Very often you get a goalless game and you think that was horrible but I wasn't ashamed of this by any means. ❞

Chelsea: de Goey, Petrescu, Babayaro, Duberry, Leboeuf, Le Saux (Goldbaek 88), Ferrer, Morris (Desailly 73), Flo, Zola, di Matteo

Manchester United: Schmeichel, G. Neville, Irwin, Keane, Johnsen, Stam, Beckham, Butt, Cole, Scholes (Sheringham 60), Giggs

Match Report

The big question was whether lightning could strike twice following Middlesbrough's shock league victory at Old Trafford a fortnight earlier. In the 53rd minute the answer looked like being yes as a free kick from Colin Cooper was headed on by Brian Deane for Andy Townsend to blast Boro into the lead.

United's powers of recovery came to the rescue with a goal from Andy Cole in the 68th minute, but even then it looked for quite a while as if Bryan Robson would at least get his old club back to the north east for a replay. It took a controversial penalty to swing the game back United's way with only eight minutes remaining. Referee Graham Barber ruled that Neil Maddison had brought down Nicky Butt. The Boro defender insisted, 'It wasn't a penalty. I made no contact.' Even Alex Ferguson conceded it had been a 'softish' award.

Gary Pallister seemed to be giving his goalkeeper advice on Denis Irwin's penalty methods, but Irwin put the dispute firmly out of his mind to beat Mark Schwarzer with a rasping spot-kick.

Once in front, United stepped up the pace and Middlesbrough accepted that there was going to be no repeat of their league upset. Helped by Ole Gunnar Solskjaer, Ryan Giggs confirmed victory by scoring for a 3–1 result which didn't really reflect the touch-and-go anxiety of the pivotal penalty moment.

Andy Cole led a charge and scored the first goal.

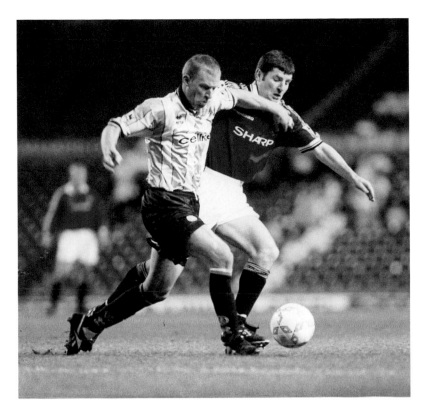

Denis Irwin

Manager's Report

❝The speedy return of Middlesbrough for this FA Cup third-round tie was an instant reminder of our league defeat a fortnight earlier, when I had told the players enough was enough, so it was clearly going to test our powers of recovery.

They have a system of playing three centre-backs which makes it difficult, and they have a lot of experience in the side with players such as Andy Townsend, Colin Cooper, Paul Gascoigne and Gary Pallister. It means that coming to Old Trafford holds no terrors for them.

Also scoring three goals on their last visit here suggested they would be feeling pretty confident and that is how it started. Despite battering their goal, they didn't panic and there was good control in their play. When they scored first, we knew we had another fight on our hands.

But as we have seen so often in the past, a goal against us often seems to wake us up, and there was an immediate increase in the tempo of our play and desire to turn things around. The crowd refused to give in and the supporters played a big part in helping to rouse us. Then we got the break every team needs for success in a Cup tie – we won the Nicky Butt penalty despite the controversy that followed it. I have watched the video several times and the Boro boy definitely caught him. I have seen similar penalties refused and it was a soft one but I cannot feel too embarrassed when you think of the number of appeals we have had turned down over the years on our ground. There

Manchester United: Schmeichel, Brown (P. Neville 75), Irwin, Keane, Berg, Stam, Blomqvist (Solskjaer 73), Butt, Cole (Sheringham 84), Yorke, Giggs

Middlesbrough: Schwarzer, Fleming, Gordon, Cooper, Maddison, Pallister, Mustoe (Stamp 62), Gascoigne (Beck 75), Ricard, Deane, Townsend

GOAL NO.1
Andy Cole 68 minutes

Ryan Giggs made all the running, cutting in to release a defence-splitting pass through the middle which Andy Cole was on to in a flash. The striker was just too quick for Gary Pallister as he collected the ball and turned to lift a rising drive into the roof of the net so quickly it seemed to blur into one movement.

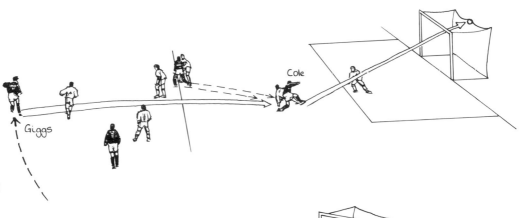

GOAL NO.2
Denis Irwin 82 minutes penalty

Gary Pallister was perhaps playing mind games when he drew on his time as a Manchester United player and went into conference with Mark Schwarzer as his goalkeeper prepared to face Denis Irwin's penalty. The chat didn't seem to have been of much help – the Australian keeper dived to his left but Irwin placed the spot-kick the other way.

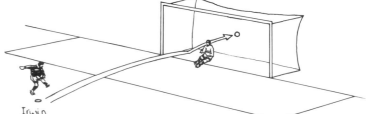

GOAL NO.3
Ryan Giggs 90 minutes

Ryan Giggs started a run from a deep position and as he scythed through the middle of a rooted Middlesbrough defence he played a one-two exchange with Ole Gunnar Solskjaer. It was pin-point passing and he didn't have to break stride before closing in to score with a shot which the goalkeeper touched but could not stop.

was a survey done not so long ago that showed we had the least percentage of penalty kicks of anyone considering the amount of possession and attacking we do at Old Trafford. I know Bryan Robson was aggrieved but I don't think he could deny at the end of the game that we deserved to win.

Just as important for me as winning through to the next round of the FA Cup was the fact that this time we had got the better of Middlesbrough. There are different ways of reacting to defeat. You can talk, you can drop players, you can sympathise, you can rant, but the one thing you must do is to get some purpose and desire into the team.

That's the start. Even great teams are not infallible and even the best players can suffer a loss of confidence. There are the rare ones, of course, who think the sun is always shining and that they can never have a bad game. I had a player at Aberdeen like that who couldn't get into the first team and he was always coming to say he couldn't believe

I wasn't picking him. He was a very limited player but his belief was unshakeable and it got him a career. I sold him and one year he became top scorer in Scotland.

Not everyone has that kind of self-belief and the issue for me after any bad spell is how quickly we can recover. We don't have to lose many games at Manchester United before the media reckon there is a crisis. I remember the season when we lost 5–0 at Newcastle and 6–3 at Southampton. Radio 5 Live ran a two-hour programme on the demise of Manchester United, virtually ignoring the fact that we were still second in the League and it was only October.

Happily, on this occasion we seem to have bounced back very quickly from the league crash against Middlesbrough, a game which might well prove to be the watershed of our season. It feels good to have the show back on the road.

The pressure of fixtures is also easing and we are getting one or two midweek breaks. I think we can see the benefits already with a fresher look about the team. ❥

Ryan Giggs says well done to Denis Irwin on the Irishman's penalty before going on to score a magnificent goal himself.

		P	W	D	L	F	A	Pts
1	Chelsea	21	10	10	1	32	17	40
2	Aston Villa	21	11	7	3	31	20	40
3	Manchester Utd	21	10	8	3	43	24	38
4	Arsenal	21	9	9	3	22	11	36
5	Leeds Utd	21	8	9	4	34	20	33
6	Wimbledon	21	9	6	6	29	33	33
7	Liverpool	21	9	5	7	36	25	32
8	West Ham Utd	21	9	5	7	25	27	32
9	Middlesbrough	21	7	10	4	32	26	31
10	Leicester City	21	7	8	6	23	21	29
11	Derby County	21	6	10	5	21	20	28
12	Tottenham Hotspur	21	7	7	7	28	30	28
13	Newcastle Utd	21	6	6	9	24	29	24
14	Everton	21	5	9	7	13	21	24
15	Sheffield Wednesday	21	6	5	10	21	22	23
16	Blackburn Rovers	21	5	6	10	21	28	21
17	Coventry City	21	5	5	11	20	29	20
18	Southampton	21	4	5	12	19	39	17
19	Charlton Athletic	21	3	7	11	24	34	16
20	Nottingham Forest	21	2	7	12	18	40	13

Match Report

Alex Ferguson's feeling about his team looking fresh and fired up was borne out in this runaway romp over West Ham. The kick-off was delayed 45 minutes because of a generator breakdown but there was certainly no power failure from United who lit up the day with a sustained performance, their goals coming steadily throughout the match.

The significance of the game was the partnership of Dwight Yorke and Andy Cole who between them claimed three of the four goals. It took just ten minutes for a shimmering move to light up the match with Yorke the scorer. Cole made it 2–0 for the interval after Nicky Butt had hit the post. Shaka Hislop, the West Ham goalkeeper, had strikes coming at him from all directions throughout the whole 90 minutes.

United had Raimond Van der Gouw in goal. Peter Schmeichel is away on holiday in Barbados in an effort to ease his massive frame through a hectic season. The manager has judged the break perfectly. There was little for Van der Gouw to do, and it wasn't long before the second half became a repeat of the first.

Cole scored again in the 68th minute, this time taking an astute pass from Yorke in a reversal of the build-up for Yorke's goal. The partnership is blooming. Solskjaer, on for Butt in the 78th minute, wasted no time joining the other strikers on the scoresheet. It took him just three minutes to latch on to a rebound and head in the fourth goal.

United perhaps eased up and some pretty football by the Hammers gave Frank Lampard the chance to burst through and score a couple of minutes from the end. It must have been scant comfort against a team who had steadily taken them apart.

Manager's Report

❛ The kick-off was delayed for 45 minutes because of a power failure which plunged the corridors near the dressing-rooms into semi-darkness and prompted Harry Redknapp, the West Ham manager, to say to me, "This could be the best chance we have ever had of winning at Old Trafford!"

Sadly for Harry, the lights came back on and we were electric as well! It was a good show. You only really feel confident when you start getting a run of good results and this is what is happening. Three wins in a row is no big deal for this club but the bonus is that we are

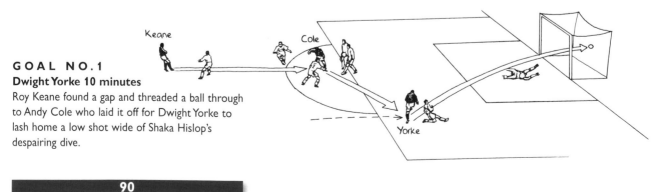

GOAL NO.1
Dwight Yorke 10 minutes
Roy Keane found a gap and threaded a ball through to Andy Cole who laid it off for Dwight Yorke to lash home a low shot wide of Shaka Hislop's despairing dive.

United quickly made up for a late start when Dwight Yorke scored after ten minutes to trigger a runaway win.

beginning to score freely with it, three against Forest, the same against Middlesbrough and today four.

West Ham are a team with good principles on the way the game should be played. Their players all want to take the ball and pass well. Our fans look forward to an entertaining game when the Hammers are the visitors, perhaps helped by the fact that in my time I think we have always beaten them at Old Trafford. I hope that continues for my final two years as well.

Our record at Upton Park is not bad either, though we still regard it as a bogey ground because we have lost two league championships there.

Dwight Yorke got us off to a good start with a great touch from Andy Cole who had an outstanding game and scored the next two. Ole Gunnar Solskjaer came on for the last quarter of an hour and he quickly grabbed a goal, too, which meant all our strikers had scored.

Our punters had a frustrating time waiting for the game to start, but I think most of them would agree it was worth waiting for.

I played Wes Brown at right-back and he did well. I played him in that position in the Champions League and he had a particularly good game against Barcelona, but I am coming round to the view that he is a centre-half. He has a presence about him and I'm encouraged by that. **"**

Manchester United: Van der Gouw, Brown (Johnsen 78), Irwin, Keane (Cruyff 84), Berg, Stam, Blomqvist, Butt (Solskjaer 78), Cole, Yorke, Giggs

West Ham: Hislop, Pearce, Lazaridis, Potts, Ferdinand, Ruddock, Lampard, Sinclair (Cole 45), Berkovic, Hartson, Lomas

GOAL NO. 2
Andy Cole 40 minutes

Jesper Blomqvist, prompted by Roy Keane, jinked his way square from the left wing to slide the ball into the path of the oncoming Nicky Butt. The midfield man's shot came back off the post but only as far as Andy Cole who punished the rebound.

GOAL NO. 3
Andy Cole 68 minutes

Denis Irwin did most of the hard work, fighting for the ball after coming up on an overlap. Once he had it under control he fed the ball to Dwight Yorke who found a gap in the defence for Andy Cole to run through and score with a measured shot.

GOAL NO. 4
Ole Gunnar Solskjaer 81 minutes

Dwight Yorke cleverly slipped the ball to Ryan Giggs but the winger's drive hit the goalkeeper and looped up into the air. The ever-ready substitute, Ole Gunnar Solskjaer, coolly headed over Shaka Hislop to complete a devastating forward display.

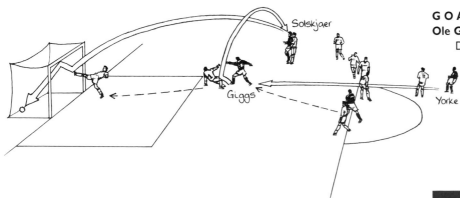

		P	W	D	L	F	A	Pts
	17 January 1999							
1	Chelsea	22	11	10	1	34	18	43
2	Manchester Utd	22	11	8	3	49	26	41
3	Aston Villa	21	11	7	3	31	20	40
4	Arsenal	22	10	9	3	23	11	39
5	Leeds Utd	22	9	9	4	36	20	36
6	Liverpool	22	10	5	7	43	26	35
7	Wimbledon	22	9	7	6	29	33	34
8	West Ham Utd	22	9	5	8	25	31	32
9	Middlesbrough	22	7	10	5	32	28	31
10	Derby County	22	7	10	5	22	20	31
11	Tottenham Hotspur	22	7	8	7	28	30	29
12	Leicester City	22	7	8	7	25	27	29
13	Sheffield Wednesday	22	7	5	10	25	22	26
14	Newcastle Utd	22	6	7	9	26	31	25
15	Everton	21	5	9	7	13	21	24
16	Blackburn Rovers	22	5	6	11	21	29	21
17	Coventry City	22	5	5	12	21	31	20
18	Charlton Athletic	22	3	8	11	26	36	17
19	Southampton	22	4	5	13	20	46	17
20	Nottingham Forest	22	2	7	13	18	41	13

Leicester City: Keller, Kaamark (Campbell 74), Ullathorne, Taggart, Walsh, Izzet, Lennon, Wilson (Parker 74), Cottee (Fenton 89), Zagorakis, Guppy

Manchester United: Schmeichel, Brown (P. Neville 45), Irwin, Keane, Berg, Stam, Beckham, Blomqvist, Cole, Yorke, Giggs

GOAL NO.1
Dwight Yorke 10 minutes
United made the first goal look easy as Andy Cole took the Leicester defence with him on a dummy run. He stepped over the ball to leave Dwight Yorke with a simple finish from Denis Irwin's probing cross.

Match Report

The rampant Reds simply carried on at Filbert Street where they had left off against the Hammers. This was a six-goal romp with the tornado twosome of Dwight Yorke and Andy Cole once again in the thick of the scoring action and revealing an almost uncanny understanding as they claimed five of the goals with a hat-trick for Yorke.

Leicester were missing several senior players, but even so, it was an awesome display of scoring power from United's two front players and once again the goals were orchestrated throughout the match.

Yorke started the scoring spree with a goal after ten minutes which was answered 25 minutes later by a stunning equaliser from Theo Zagorakis, a sizzling shot from outside the box as Leicester showed the fighting qualities they normally summon up for a match against United.

The score was level at a goal apiece at the interval but Cole quickly stepped into the firing line with a couple of goals. Leicester were still not quite buried and just about stayed in the game with a goal from Steve Walsh, but United were in scoring mood now and they finished off with two more goals from Yorke and a final effort from Jaap Stam to underline their free-flowing form.

Walsh, the former Wigan centre-half, described the problems involved in facing the United strikers.

'Andy Cole and Dwight Yorke link up well. They know where each other is going. They've got these little link-ups and flicks. It's through your legs and see you later,' he explained. 'You have to try to work out where they are going to go. You have to second guess them, but we guessed wrong most of the time. They are quick, sharp and very clever players. They are a class act together, right up there with the best. Having Yorke alongside him has certainly made Andy Cole a better player.'

Manager's Report

When I first bought Dwight Yorke I had no fixed idea of the eventual partnership. My mind simply revolved round what Yorke could add to the team.

We have had various pairings up front over the years. Brian McClair and Mark Hughes was my first and with Brian's ability to drop off and his stamina it worked well.

The arrival of Eric Cantona changed the whole picture of course.

He was undoubtedly the catalyst for our first championship in the Premier League and we moved on for a fantastic double in 1994. With the pace of Andrei Kanchelskis and Ryan Giggs on the wings we were a threat to anybody playing around the halfway line. The result was that the opposition started to drop back to the edge of their box so they wouldn't get caught by the speed of our wingers and that was when I decided to buy Andy Cole. We needed razor sharpness in the box as well as his goals of course.

Teddy Sheringham was a great signing to replace Eric Cantona when he decided to retire but at that point I also felt there was a need to bring someone in who could manufacture things on his own. The outstanding player in world terms was Ronaldo but our wage structure ruled out the possibility of signing him. So I looked around in this country and Dwight Yorke was the man. The matter of developing a partnership I knew would emerge in the course of time, and it certainly has.

We are in an incredibly rich scoring seam with a hat-trick for Dwight in this match and two goals for Cole. It could easily have been the other way round, because the lovely feature of their play has been the way they work for each other with an instinctive and unselfish understanding. Between them they have scored 31 goals already this season. You can almost see their telepathy working out on the training pitch.

The whole team performance was incredibly good against Leicester and with that kind of backing our strikers were like lightning.

We play Liverpool next weekend. Gerard Houllier has been quoted as saying that he considers his duo of Robbie Fowler and Michael Owen can become the most lethal pair in the Premiership. I would be inclined to agree with him if it wasn't for Cole and Yorke!

It was nice to see Jaap Stam joining the strikers with a goal, his first for the club. He gets a bit of stick in the dressing-room for his failure in front of goal when he comes up for corner kicks. He blames the crosses and says when he is at the front post the cross goes to the back and when he is at the far post it falls short. He says it is an English plot against the Dutch. My view is I don't much mind, provided he keeps them out at the other end! 〞

Beckham

Stam

Leicester City 2
Manchester United 6

GOAL NO.2
Andy Cole 50 minutes
United went up a gear in the second half. Ryan Giggs lobbed a high ball down the middle for Andy Cole to chase. The striker quickly mastered the bounce and held off two defenders to score with a low shot across the face of goal.

GOAL NO.3
Andy Cole 62 minutes
Roy Keane prodded a pass through the middle to Dwight Yorke who made the third goal with a lightning turn and a short ball forward for Andy Cole to run on to and shoot under the oncoming goalkeeper.

GOAL NO.4
Dwight Yorke 64 minutes
A lob down the field from Denis Irwin had Andy Cole chasing hard towards the by-line. Kasey Keller dashed out of goal but slipped and watched despairingly as Cole rounded him to thread home a goal from the narrowest of angles.

GOAL NO.5
Dwight Yorke 86 minutes
Gerry Taggart made a mess of his header as he tried to steer Denis Irwin's long clearance to one of his full-backs. Andy Cole picked up the loose ball and sped away to rattle the bar with a rising drive. Dwight Yorke easily put away the rebound.

GOAL NO.6
Jaap Stam 90 minutes
David Beckham took a short corner on the left and the ball was played back to him as he came deep to cross to the far post. Jaap Stam, up for the corner kick, found himself virtually unmarked and he cleanly sidefooted the ball wide of the hapless Kasey Keller to score his first goal for Manchester United.

Fourth round	
Aston Villa 0	Fulham 2
Barnsley 3	Bournemouth 1
Blackburn Rovers 1	Sunderland 0
Bristol Rovers 3	Leyton Orient 0
Everton 1	Ipswich Town 0
Leicester City 0	Coventry City 3
Newcastle Utd 3	Bradford City 0
Portsmouth 1	Leeds Utd 5
Sheffield Wednesday 2	Stockport County 0
Swansea City 0	Derby County 1
Wimbledon 1 REPLAY	Tottenham Hotspur 1
Tottenham Hotspur 3	Wimbledon 0
Wrexham 1 REPLAY	Huddersfield Town 1
Huddersfield Town 2	Wrexham 1
Manchester Utd 2	Liverpool 1
Wolverhampton W. 1	Arsenal 2
Oxford Utd 1 REPLAY	Chelsea 1
Chelsea 4	Oxford Utd 2
Sheffield Utd 4	Cardiff City 1

Match Report

Liverpool made a dream start with a goal in the third minute, but United have become famous for their powers of recovery and this was one of the games which established their right to say we are never beaten until the final whistle.

United were still trying to come to terms with Liverpool's whirlwind opening when Jamie Redknapp sent full-back Vegard Heggem moving down their right flank. Heggem's high centre found the home defence pulled out of position and Michael Owen enjoyed an unchallenged header at goal. He didn't miss and from then on United had a tough nut to crack.

United fans were slowly losing hope as they watched their team battering away at a stubborn defence without making much impression. It seemed they were destined not to score.

Roy Keane seemed to have found an opening with a shot that hit the post and careered along the line until Paul Ince scrambled it clear. Players of both sides looked to see what the linesman was doing, but there was no flag. Keane hit the woodwork again and time was running out.

Alex Ferguson had one last ploy to try; he took off two defenders, replacing them with Ronny Johnsen as an attacker in midfield and Ole Gunnar Solskjaer up front in support of Dwight Yorke and Andy Cole. Liverpool wobbled in the face of the suddenly souped-up attack and two minutes from the end of normal time they cracked. From David Beckham's free kick, the class combination of Cole and Yorke sprang to the rescue with Yorke bagging the equaliser.

The competition between the recognised strike forces of the two clubs was now even, but the winner was United's fringe striker, the super sub making a name for himself with his knack of coming off the bench to score. He left it on the late side, in fact into time added on, with the tie seemingly heading for an Anfield replay. Solskjaer, having been on the park for ten minutes, snatched possession from Paul Scholes and rifled in the winner.

Manager's Report

❝It's difficult to know what to say about this match because it had everything. Without question it raised the old spectre of us making a careless start. I have lost count of the number of times I have said to the players, let's start the game right and make sure we defend properly. I don't know why I waste my breath. Someone said recently we should start all our games a goal down, then we would know where we stood and could start playing properly right from the kick-off!

You prepare for the game properly, analyse the opposition, go through the tactical thing, make your plans, prepare the set-pieces and talk about the various functions of the team and then you watch in horror the kind of opening we made in this match, and against Liverpool of all teams.

I can still see their goal. It started from a throw-in on the halfway line and they scored from it. They got Heggem away and Michael

Ole Gunnar Solskjaer swings his boot for a late winner.

Owen scored from his cross which fell between three of our markers. I can tell you, there were a few words about it at half-time.

I also took advantage of the break to reorganise. Our problem was that Liverpool had massed in midfield, and when their centre-backs allowed Dwight Yorke to drop off into midfield, we were getting choked. I explained that Yorke must not be the source of our attack and that we must spread our play wider to make it more difficult for them to defend and then Yorke could come back into it in the last third of the field.

We did well in the second half. Our attacking was relentless and our pursuit of victory was quite incredible. That's not something that comes from a manager's instructions or the drawing board; it comes from within the players. That's what we saw in this match.

It was always going to be hard to score goals against Liverpool of course. I didn't realise how hard until I watched Roy Keane twice hit a post, and I must confess that five minutes from the end I had decided that it wasn't going to be our year in the FA Cup again.

Liverpool thought they had it won. When Jamie Redknapp was substituted he came off applauding the Liverpool fans as if to say we're through, but fortunately our strikers did not lose hope and we had an equaliser from Ole Gunnar Solskjaer.

When we got the equaliser I had a gut feeling that it wasn't finished. I was checking my watch – as usual – and shouting to Jaap Stam to get the ball forward because at that point they were passing it across the back four. I could see Liverpool were in disarray with signs of panic and, sure enough, when we did get the ball into their box, Paul Scholes was there to fight it clear for Ole Gunnar. What a finish, and against such great rivals! It was the kind of victory supporters will never forget. I certainly won't.

The commitment and willingness to persevere in the face of stubborn resistance on a day when luck also seems to have deserted you is a sure sign of quality in a team. ❯

Manchester United: Schmeichel, G. Neville, Irwin (Solskjaer 81), Keane, Berg (Johnsen 81), Stam, Beckham, Butt (Scholes 68), Cole, Yorke, Giggs

Liverpool: James, Heggem, Harkness, Carragher, Matteo, Bjornebye, Ince, Berger, Fowler, Owen, Redknapp (McAteer 71)

Jaap Stam goes tight on Michael Owen.

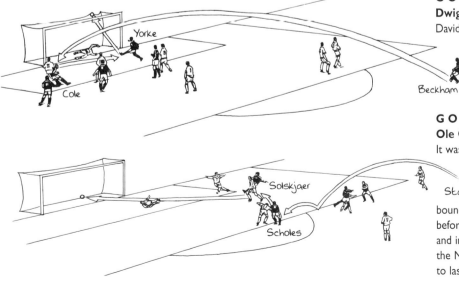

GOAL NO.1
Dwight Yorke 88 minutes
David Beckham floated in one of his free-kick specials towards the far post where Andy Cole neatly laid it back across goal to give Dwight Yorke a simple chance which he sidefooted home from close range.

GOAL NO.2
Ole Gunnar Solskjaer 90 minutes
It was well into stoppage time when Jaap Stam belted the ball forward and into the Liverpool penalty area. Just inside the box, Paul Scholes cleverly brought the bouncing ball under control and surged forward before finding Ole Gunnar Solskjaer better placed and in the right position for a shot. He stopped and the Norwegian promptly took the ball off his toes to lash in a left-foot shot too hot for David James.

FA Carling Premiership
31 January 1999

		P	W	D	L	F	A	Pts
1	Manchester Utd	23	12	8	3	50	26	44
2	Chelsea	23	11	10	2	34	19	43
3	Aston Villa	23	12	7	4	35	22	43
4	Arsenal	23	11	9	3	24	11	42
5	Leeds Utd	23	9	9	5	36	23	36
6	Liverpool	23	10	5	8	44	28	35
7	Wimbledon	23	9	8	6	29	33	35
8	Derby County	23	8	10	5	23	20	34
9	West Ham Utd	23	9	6	8	25	31	33
10	Middlesbrough	23	7	11	5	32	28	32
11	Tottenham Hotspur	23	7	9	7	29	31	30
12	Leicester City	23	7	9	7	25	27	30
13	Newcastle Utd	23	7	7	9	28	32	28
14	Sheffield Wednesday	23	7	5	11	25	23	26
15	Everton	23	5	9	9	13	25	24
16	Coventry City	23	6	5	12	23	32	23
17	Blackburn Rovers	23	5	7	11	22	30	22
18	Southampton	23	5	5	13	23	46	20
19	Charlton Athletic	23	3	8	12	26	37	17
20	Nottingham Forest	23	3	7	13	19	41	16

Dwight Yorke goes close.

Match Report

This was a valuable win with the points taking United to the top of the table by a point from Chelsea and Aston Villa. It was another late show, however, with the winning goal not arriving until the game had gone into stoppage time. Indeed, the hard-working Charlton gave United more worries than you might expect from a team near the foot of the table and clearly struggling to come to terms with their new life in the Premiership.

Alan Curbishley's defensive strategy with three centre-backs frustrated United for long spells. Alex Ferguson said he thought they had coped with his front men, Dwight Yorke and Andy Cole, as well as anyone this season.

Nicky Butt went close with a shot which flew wide. Ryan Giggs at least got his effort on target but he was thwarted by an excellent save from Simon Royce. Another wide drive, this time from Henning Berg, made the fans wonder how so many goals had gone in so easily against Leicester and West Ham.

United survived a couple of penalty appeals but the second half was mainly constant pressure from United coming up against a packed and hard-working defence. Roy Keane had a fierce drive blocked following a corner and Butt was off target again.

But once again, a canny substitution seemed to break down the opposition's resistance. This time after bringing on Ole Gunnar Solskjaer for David Beckham, the manager introduced Paul Scholes to replace Butt with just eight minutes remaining. As the game moved into injury time, Scholes flung over a centre for Yorke to snatch all the points and move his team into the top spot.

Manager's Report

❝I have been to the Valley with our youth team and I said to the players for whom it would be a new experience, be ready for a terrific atmosphere. Looking at old pictures, it was obviously an impressive place when this giant bowl held 80,000, and the new stand has helped retain a tremendous aura.

Although struggling near the bottom of the table, they have an appetite to play which always gives a team a chance and that is how it was in this game. It took us a long time to win, in fact to the very last minute, but when you are going for championships, I don't really care when we score. My players have shown time and time again that they seem to relish taking us all to the brink. We have been there so often you can become immune to the knife-edge journey. It can leave you with fraught nerves but it's part of our club and everything worked out well in the end. Dwight Yorke's late effort takes us to the top of the table. Overall, I think that's a fair reward for the football we have been playing lately – running free in front of goal and then grinding out this kind of result with a late goal.

At the same time it has got to be said that both Villa and Chelsea have given us a leg up by losing this weekend. Staying at the top may also be slightly easier than getting there.

Chelsea have been the surprise packet because with Gianluca Vialli signing so many new players you could never be sure when they would all start to knit together. He has certainly succeeded in getting together a group of players from the top drawer with the likes of Zola. I am a bit concerned about their challenge, though I still feel Arsenal are the team to beat if we are going to win the League. They have the experience and the confidence of having been there. Aston Villa have led the Premiership for most of the season but there are signs of them starting to drop off a bit and Arsenal remain the danger as far as I am concerned. ❜

Charlton Athletic: Royce, Brown, Powell, Redfearn, Rufus, Tiler, Jones, Kinsella, Hunt (Bright 78), Pringle (Parker 83), Robinson

Manchester United: Schmeichel, G. Neville, Irwin, Keane, Berg, Stam, Beckham (Solskjaer 71), Butt (Scholes 82), Cole, Yorke, Giggs

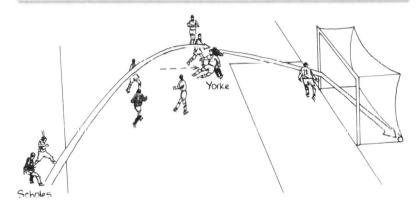

GOAL NO.1
Dwight Yorke 90 minutes
Gary Neville sent Paul Scholes off on a run, the substitute ploughing past his marker to whip over a centre which at long last caught the Charlton defence off balance. Dwight Yorke flung himself at the ball and, though under challenge from Keith Jones, he was first there to score with a powerful header just inside the post.

Below left: *Ryan Giggs in elusive mood.*

Below: *Gary Neville initiated the late winner.*

		P	W	D	L	F	A	Pts
1	Manchester Utd	24	13	8	3	51	26	47
2	Chelsea	23	11	10	2	34	19	43
3	Aston Villa	23	12	7	4	35	22	43
4	Arsenal	23	11	9	3	24	11	42
5	Leeds Utd	23	9	9	5	36	23	36
6	Liverpool	23	10	5	8	44	28	35
7	Wimbledon	23	9	8	6	29	33	35
8	Derby County	24	8	10	6	23	21	34
9	West Ham Utd	23	9	6	8	25	31	33
10	Middlesbrough	23	7	11	5	32	28	32
11	Tottenham Hotspur	23	7	9	7	29	31	30
12	Leicester City	23	7	9	7	25	27	30
13	Newcastle Utd	23	7	7	9	28	32	28
14	Sheffield Wednesday	23	7	5	11	25	23	26
15	Everton	23	5	9	9	13	25	24
16	Coventry City	23	6	5	12	23	32	23
17	Blackburn Rovers	23	5	7	11	22	30	22
18	Southampton	23	5	5	13	23	46	20
19	Charlton Athletic	23	3	8	12	26	37	17
20	Nottingham Forest	23	3	7	13	19	41	16

Manchester United: Schmeichel, G. Neville, Irwin, Keane, Johnsen, Stam, Scholes, Butt, Solskjaer, Yorke, Giggs (Blomqvist 11)

Derby County: Hoult, Carbonari, Prior, Powell (Hunt 80), Dorigo, Stimac, Laursen, Bohinen, Wanchope, Carsley, Harper (Burton 71)

Match Report

Dwight Yorke admits he wears his shirt collar turned up like Eric Cantona because when he was at Aston Villa he admired Cantona and liked his style. Now the comparison is even closer as Yorke follows in the Frenchman's famous footsteps with his habit of scoring vital winning goals. A Yorke goal turned the Cup tie against Liverpool and his late strike beat Charlton at the weekend. In this match, a Yorke goal secured another three points. He has scored seven goals in the last five outings. Vintage Eric Cantona indeed!

His all-important strike against Derby came in the 65th minute and was nicely taken with the help of Nicky Butt. Up until then, United had again struggled to turn command into goals.

Yorke said, 'It does seem I'm making a habit of scoring winners but the main thing is that we got three points. I will probably get all the headlines again but I must thank my team-mates. They have been fantastic and I couldn't ask for a better bunch of lads around me.

'It doesn't matter who scores and I don't really know exactly how many I have scored. It's not the be all and end all for me. I just hope we can carry on from here. There's a long way to go and we're not getting carried away, but I would be very disappointed if we didn't win one trophy this season.'

Manager's Report

❝ My heart fell when I watched Ryan Giggs walk out of the match after only 11 minutes with a recurrence of his hamstring problem. It rekindled bad memories for me, and is a timely reminder of how things can change, because it was a similar injury that seemed to trigger most of our difficulties last season.

It's a particular worry when we come to the European matches, and I have to decide whether to keep him out of games in order to have him fit for the Champions League.

Players of pace are always susceptible to hamstring strains, especially one of Ryan's physique. There's not a lot of fat on his muscle and it's one of those characteristics that you have to accept.

I am glad I signed Jesper Blomqvist. He took over well and allowed us to keep our shape. We won the game with yet another goal from Dwight Yorke, midway in the second half.

It was always going to be a difficult game for me personally because I knew I had to approach Jim Smith after deciding that Steve McClaren is going to be our man to replace Brian Kidd. We have taken our time but all the reports point to Steve. So I had the task of approaching Derby. I waited in the corridor which leads from our press conference room back to the dressing-rooms while Jim did his bit with the media. My office was full of people and it was the only quiet place to catch him. I said I needed to speak to him and I can see him now leaning against the wall with his hands behind his back. I think he knew right away what it was going to be about because he realised we hadn't filled our coaching vacancy.

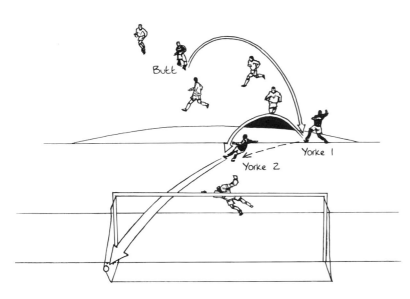

Butt

Yorke 1

Yorke 2

GOAL NO.1
Dwight Yorke 65 minutes
Nicky Butt chipped a pin-point pass through to Dwight Yorke who moved so quickly it looked as if he might have been offside. There was no flag and Yorke finished with the deadly accuracy that has brought him seven goals in the last five games.

"No," he said, as I explained I was sorry but I had to do the best for Manchester United and I needed his permission to approach Steve McClaren. He said he couldn't stop me and that in his opinion we will be getting a great man who will do a terrific job for us. I phoned Steve and have arranged to meet him in Derbyshire tomorrow.

In the meantime, I just hope Ryan's injury is not too serious and that we got him off in time. Before he was injured last season we had been going well and getting some great results such as the 5–3 win over Chelsea in the FA Cup. Then when Ryan dropped out we suddenly ran into a spate of other injuries which knocked us right out of our stride. We faltered in the championship race and failed to get past Monaco in the Champions League.

You learn from experiences like that of course, and I think we are now much better equipped to stave off the same kind of collapse. We are far stronger in depth now with Jaap Stam, Dwight Yorke and Jesper Blomqvist with us, and I also have some great youngsters coming along who will hold us up in an emergency. Mark Wilson, Jonathan Greening, John Curtis and Michael Clegg give me a back-up which I think should enable us to cope with set-backs like those that troubled us this time last year. ❧

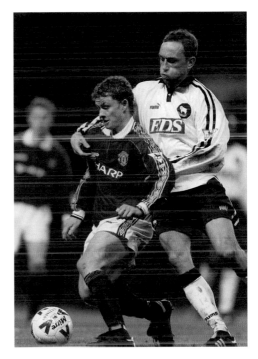

Derby kept Ole Gunnar Solskjaer (above) quiet but couldn't do much about the pin-point chip from Nicky Butt (left) that opened up the way for Dwight Yorke's vital goal.

		P	W	D	L	F	A	Pts
1	Manchester Utd	25	14	8	3	59	27	50
2	Chelsea	24	12	10	2	35	19	46
3	Arsenal	24	12	9	3	28	11	45
4	Aston Villa	24	12	7	5	36	25	43
5	Liverpool	24	11	5	8	47	29	38
6	Derby County	25	9	10	6	25	22	37
7	Leeds Utd	24	9	9	6	36	24	36
8	Wimbledon	23	9	8	6	29	33	35
9	West Ham Utd	24	9	6	9	25	35	33
10	Middlesbrough	24	7	11	6	33	31	32
11	Tottenham Hotspur	24	7	10	7	29	31	31
12	Newcastle Utd	24	8	7	9	29	32	31
13	Leicester City	24	7	9	8	25	29	30
14	Sheffield Wednesday	24	8	5	11	27	23	29
15	Blackburn Rovers	24	6	7	11	25	31	25
16	Coventry City	24	6	6	12	23	32	24
17	Everton	24	5	9	10	14	27	24
18	Southampton	24	5	5	14	23	47	20
19	Charlton Athletic	23	3	8	12	26	37	17
20	Nottingham Forest	24	3	7	14	20	49	16

GOAL NO.1
Dwight Yorke 2 minutes
Roy Keane pulled the ball back from the by-line for Paul Scholes to chip forward and Dwight Yorke to score a simple opener.

Match Report

The manager used to claim that his team lacked the ruthless streak to kill off opponents. Not any more, following this extraordinary demonstration of power, precision, pace and pulverising goals.

Dwight Yorke launched the scoring spree in the second minute, and though Alan Rogers got one back, Forest paid for their temerity as Andy Cole quickly restored the visitors' lead.

The score was still 2–1 at the interval, but then the roof fell in for Forest. Cole and Yorke each scored again before Ole Gunnar Solskjaer added to his super-sub reputation by coming on for the last 18 minutes and scoring four goals.

It was United's biggest away win in the League since their Newton Heath days and left the experienced Dave Beasant stranded somewhere between anger with his defence and admiration for United.

'It was the lowest of the low. It has taken me twenty years to concede that many goals in a match,' said the Forest goalkeeper. 'The Andy Cole and Dwight Yorke partnership is unbelievable. I've faced great strikers in the past but you don't normally see two at a time like that. And even more frightening is that they can bring on Ole Solskjaer who would be in anyone else's first team from the start.'

Manager's Report

❝It was Steve McClaren's first trip as United's new coach but I kept Jimmy Ryan with us. I have been aware for some time of a weakness in our set-up. If I have to tell a player he is not playing, invariably I don't have much time to spend discussing it with him. I always try to be sensitive, stress his value to us and his importance in the squad, but prior to a game there's a lot of other things to do. Also, in the context of being dropped, the player may be too disappointed to take everything in.

I can see a role here for Jim, talking things through with the player and explaining in detail. He does it well. In any case, Jim has done such a great job between Brian Kidd leaving and Steve McClaren arriving that I thought we would miss him.

The sheer size of the senior squad has increased enormously since the old days. You are talking virtually two teams now and I think I need more support. My job has grown so big with so many demands on my

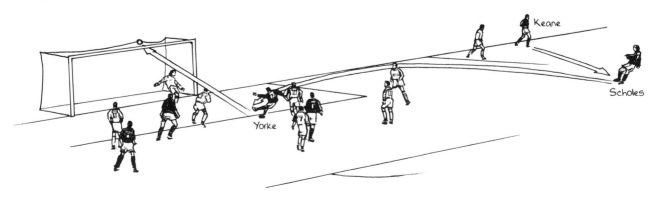

Nottingham Forest: Beasant, Harkes, Rogers, Armstrong, Palmer, Hjelde, Stone, Gemmill (Mattsson 57), Van Hooijdonk, Johnson (Porfirio 74), Darchville (Freedman 26)

Manchester United: Schmeichel, G. Neville, P. Neville, Keane (Curtis 72), Johnsen, Stam, Beckham, Scholes, Cole, Yorke (Solskjaer 72), Blomqvist (Butt 76)

Andy Cole struck after seven minutes to open the floodgates.

time that despite starting meetings by eight in the morning I scramble to get through in time for training.

We are chasing three trophies at the moment and I have told Jim that although Steve has come on board I want him to stay with us. He is such a loyal person I knew there wouldn't be a problem.

But what a start for Steve – his first game and an 8–1 win. As Jim Ryan said to him, "It's got to be all downhill now."

Forest could have scored three or four in the first half, though I have got to say that we could as well! It was a very exciting game and we led 2–1 at half-time when I made the point that we must make sure we took the chances in the second half that would inevitably come our way. And that's what happened with Cole and Yorke each scoring again to make sure of victory.

With just under 20 minutes to go, I brought on Ole Gunnar Solskjaer for Yorke and Ole scored four in ten minutes, an incredible feat. The only one in the dug-out who may not have been celebrating was Dwight. He was on a hat-trick again when I brought him off. His usual smile looked a little fixed as he no doubt thought those four goals might have been his!

Ole is a fantastic finisher. If I ever feel guilty about the teams I pick and the players I leave out, it invariably centres round him. He really deserves better than the number of games I give him, but the other factor that influences me is that he is better than anyone else at the club as a substitute. He can come on and not be disturbed by it. He finds the flow easily and has scored an amazing number of goals as a sub. I am sure he hates being called a super sub, and it's unfair, but the fact is . . . he is! **❜**

GOAL NO.2
Andy Cole 7 minutes
A long ball from defence was chased by Andy Cole. The keeper came out but Cole skipped past him to chip the ball into the empty net.

GOAL NO.3
Andy Cole 50 minutes
Dave Beasant saved from Dwight Yorke but the rebound came straight to Andy Cole who hit it home from point-blank range.

GOAL NO.4
Dwight Yorke 67 minutes
Jesper Blomqvist cut in from the left, beat his man and then shaved the post as he tried to squeeze a shot past Beasant. The ball came out nicely to Dwight Yorke who successfully finished off the move.

GOAL NO.5
Ole Gunnar Solskjaer 80 minutes
David Beckham neatly fed the overlapping Gary Neville on his right and the full-back's low cross was tapped in at the far post by Ole Gunnar Solskjaer.

GOAL NO.6
Ole Gunnar Solskjaer 88 minutes
Beckham found Solskjaer with a long diagonal ball down the middle. Beasant beat out the Norwegian's first attempt but Solskjaer pounced on the rebound and took the ball round the keeper to blast into the roof of the net.

GOAL NO.7
Ole Gunnar Solskjaer 90 minutes
Paul Scholes advanced through the middle and cleverly fed Solskjaer on his left to set up an inviting hat-trick which the striker duly collected with an explosive shot on the volley.

GOAL NO.8
Ole Gunnar Solskjaer 90 minutes
Nicky Butt centred from the right. Paul Scholes mishit his shot but the ball spun to his left for Solskjaer to make no mistake for his fourth goal.

Fifth round	
Arsenal 2	Sheffield Utd 1
Barnsley 4	Bristol Rovers 1
Everton 2	Coventry City 1
Huddersfield Town 2 REPLAY	Derby County 2
Derby County 3	Huddersfield Town 1
Leeds Utd 1 REPLAY	Tottenham Hotspur 1
Tottenham Hotspur 2	Leeds Utd 0
Sheffield Wednesday 0	Chelsea 1
Manchester Utd 1	Fulham 0
Newcastle Utd 0 REPLAY	Blackburn Rovers 0
Blackburn Rovers 0	Newcastle 1
Arsenal 2	Sheffield Utd 1

Match Report

United had to fight hard to get through this fifth round of the FA Cup. The tie was quite different from the scoring extravaganza of the previous match against Nottingham Forest.

Fulham, though missing their two main strikers through injury, played with the confidence of a team heading their division, albeit the Second, and with a top-class display from Maik Taylor in their goal, they made United fight every inch of the way.

Having already knocked out Premier clubs Southampton and Aston Villa, Fulham squared up to the Reds with solid football, but they could do little when Andy Cole struck in the 26th minute. As a 19 year old, Cole had played at Fulham on loan from Arsenal and had a thin time. He made no mistake with this chance from Ole Gunnar Solskjaer, even though a deflection off Chris Coleman helped to deceive the goalkeeper.

Fulham, far from crushed, were close to equalising a few moments later when Dirk Lehmann broke through and it took a timely tackle by Gary Neville to stop him.

There was also a tricky moment for United fans in the second half as John Salako closed in but Peter Schmeichel denied him. Taylor was equally good at the other end, especially against Dwight Yorke when he tipped the United striker's close-range shot over the bar.

United won through in the end but they made hard work of it.

Dwight Yorke chests the ball down.

Manager's Report

The press seized on Kevin Keegan's first visit to Old Trafford since his days as manager of Newcastle and regurgitated our spat all over again.

Managers have their arguments, like couples do in marriage, but it's not the end of the world. Kevin was upset at the time at the way we were gaining ground on him for the championship and I have always understood his reaction. I am sure he would have preferred to say what he did face to face but there wasn't the opportunity.

Kevin is an emotional man and at the time he was angry. I understand that because I am inclined that way a bit myself and from time to time there are disputes off the field as well as on it. You couldn't go through a managerial career without arguments, and I have had plenty of those! I had a raging row with George Graham soon after coming down from Scotland but now we are the best of friends. I count myself a pal of Howard Wilkinson's, too, but I have had upsets with him.

Once I have made my point – and no doubt the other guy will have had his say too – we will get on with things, just as Kevin and I have done. The moment has gone and that's how it should be.

I have nothing but respect for what Kevin achieved at Newcastle and what he has done getting Fulham to the top of the table, and a few words spoken in the heat of the moment take nothing away from the respect I have for him, and which I hope he has for me. But certainly I could have done without the matter being dragged up again by the press. It made a disappointing build-up to what at the end of the day was a peaceful Cup tie!

Manchester United: Schmeichel, G. Neville, Irwin (Greening 45), P. Neville, Berg, Stam, Beckham, Butt, Cole (Johnsen 88), Yorke, Solskjaer (Blomqvist 68)

Fulham: Taylor, Finnan, Brevett, Smith, Coleman, Symons, Collins (Uhlenbeek 87), Salako (Trollope 74), Lehmann (Betsy 59), Hayward, Hayles

Jesper Blomqvist, a late substitute, tries to dribble his way through against a spirited Fulham team.

Fulham have been on a good Cup run, and I'm glad we got them at Old Trafford. I would not have relished a trip to Craven Cottage against a team fired up by Kevin. I rested one or two and played Phil Neville in the middle of the park, as well as using three up front in the absence of Ryan Giggs, still nursing his hamstring along. I felt it was a chance to exercise the full squad and I was able to give young Jonathan Greening a go in the second half.

I had Jesper Blomqvist on the bench but didn't feel I was taking chances because putting three strikers out meant there was every chance of one of them scoring! Andy Cole obliged, and though we didn't score again, I never felt that there was even the hint of a Cup shock. ❥

GOAL NO. 1
Andy Cole 26 minutes
Nicky Butt found Ole Gunnar Solskjaer lurking at the far post with a high ball from the right. The Norwegian nimbly brought the cross under control before cutting it back for Andy Cole to strike first time and, with the help of a deflection, claim the only goal of the game.

18 February 1999	P	W	D	L	F	A	Pts
1 Manchester Utd	26	14	9	3	60	28	51
2 Chelsea	25	12	11	2	36	20	47
3 Arsenal	25	12	10	3	29	12	46
4 Aston Villa	25	12	7	6	37	27	43
5 Leeds Utd	25	10	9	6	38	25	39
6 Liverpool	25	11	5	9	47	30	38
7 Derby County	25	9	10	6	25	22	37
8 West Ham Utd	25	10	6	9	27	36	36
9 Wimbledon	24	9	8	7	29	35	35
10 Newcastle Utd	25	9	7	9	33	33	34
11 Middlesbrough	25	7	11	7	33	36	32
12 Tottenham Hotspur	24	7	10	7	29	31	31
13 Leicester City	24	7	9	8	25	29	30
14 Sheffield Wednesday	24	8	5	11	27	23	29
15 Everton	25	6	9	10	19	27	27
16 Blackburn Rovers	25	6	8	11	26	32	26
17 Coventry City	25	6	6	13	24	36	24
18 Charlton Athletic	25	5	8	12	29	37	23
19 Southampton	24	5	5	14	23	47	20
20 Nottingham Forest	25	3	7	15	21	51	16

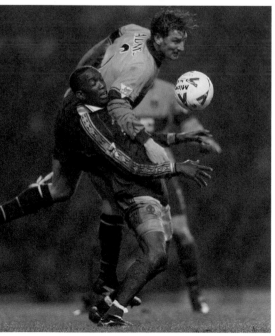

Tony Adams jumps all over Dwight Yorke.

Match Report

This was the big shoot-out, the clash of the two teams expected to be battling it out for the title in May. Victory for either would have been of enormous psychological as well as points value, but as so often happens in this kind of situation honours ended even.

Both teams were up for it with United creating the early chances, most of them saved by the excellent David Seaman. Dwight Yorke could do little right. Perhaps unnerved by missing with a header, he was wide of the target when, in the absence of Denis Irwin, he took a 30th minute penalty awarded against Ray Parlour for bringing down Ronny Johnsen. He also picked up a rare booking and failed to beat Seaman after being set up by Ryan Giggs and Andy Cole. Even Roy Keane seemed caught up by the nervous tension and missed a couple of fair opportunities.

Arsenal were little better until, riding their luck early in the second half, they took the lead. The goal was superbly made by Kanu's neat sidestep and shot which was blocked by Phil Neville for Anelka to net the rebound.

Cole was the most confident of United's attacking players and it was fitting that he should emerge the scorer against one of his old clubs with a smartly taken and valuable equaliser in the 61st minute. Phil Neville swung over a curling centre from the left which was headed in by Cole to inspire a late flurry of attacks which forced Arsenal to defend grimly for their point.

In that sense, United were unlucky not to snatch a winner. However, there was a great deal of relief among the home troops that the reigning champions, rated by most people as posing United's greatest threat for the league title, had been kept at bay.

Manager's Report

❛The players knew they should have won this one. The pitch had a lot to do with it, cutting up badly after an awful lot of rain which continued to lash down during the game. I think we will have to have at least part of it returfed because it is deteriorating all the time now.

Our frustrations also stemmed from missing a penalty and seeing Arsenal take the lead early in the second half with the flukiest of goals. Kanu's shot was blocked and the ball rolled with great good fortune into the path of Anelka who couldn't miss from such close range.

There is nothing you can do about that kind of goal, save keep your nerve, and I'm delighted to say that that was exactly what we did, and without too long a wait for the equaliser. Phil Neville got in a good cross for Andy Cole to score. Cole and Yorke gave Tony Adams and Steve Bould a hard time. In fact, I have to say it is the shakiest I have ever seen Adams.

A draw was a good result for Arsenal and I know they are not going to go away in terms of the championship. That's fine by me, but I also know that if someone wants to go the distance with us, they will have to be strong and special to overtake us. Naturally, I had hoped we

Manchester United: Schmeichel, G. Neville, P. Neville, Keane, Johnsen, Stam, Beckham, Butt (Giggs 77), Cole, Yorke, Blomqvist (Scholes 61)

Arsenal: Seaman, Dixon, Winterburn (Vivas 77), Vieira, Bould, Adams, Parlour, Kanu (Garde 62), Anelka, Hughes, Overmars (Diawara 84)

Steve Bould gives Andy Cole little room to manoeuvre in this clash, but the United striker had the last word when he struck on the hour with a header that earned United a key point.

would beat them in this match. The share of the points means they are still on our coat tails.

There was so much at stake that we tended to cancel each other out. In terms of tension and both teams' desire to win, I found it an engrossing contest. From the performance point of view, we created more chances. On another night, they would have gone in. So in that respect I was pleased. The team dug in and once again showed themselves difficult to beat. On reflection, it was not a bad result for us either!

Certainly the idea of a draw wasn't on the agenda for either manager. It was the last thing on my mind, and I am sure Arsene Wenger had no thoughts of trying to play safe either. Both of us set out to try to win the match, and there you have the essence of both clubs, quality football played in a positive and attractive way.

But we do need a better stage and I shall be having words about what can be done to improve our playing surface. **"**

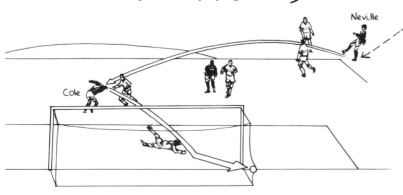

GOAL NO.1
Andy Cole 61 minutes

David Beckham, moving into the middle, passed out wide to his left to Phil Neville who immediately started to weave his way inside. The full-back rounded off his run with a dipping cross which was met by a firm header from Andy Cole, beating David Seaman and sailing inside the post.

21 February 1999							
	P	W	D	L	F	A	Pts
1 Manchester Utd	27	15	9	3	61	28	54
2 Chelsea	26	13	11	2	39	21	50
3 Arsenal	26	13	10	3	34	12	49
4 Aston Villa	26	12	8	6	37	27	44
5 Leeds Utd	26	11	9	6	39	25	42
6 Liverpool	26	11	6	9	49	32	39
7 Derby County	26	9	10	7	25	24	37
8 West Ham Utd	26	10	7	9	29	38	37
9 Wimbledon	25	9	9	7	29	35	36
10 Newcastle Utd	26	9	7	10	34	35	34
11 Middlesbrough	26	7	12	7	33	36	33
12 Sheffield Wednesday	25	9	5	11	31	24	32
13 Tottenham Hotspur	25	7	11	7	29	31	32
14 Leicester City	25	7	9	9	25	34	30
15 Everton	26	6	9	11	19	28	27
16 Charlton Athletic	26	6	8	12	31	37	26
17 Blackburn Rovers	26	6	8	12	27	36	26
18 Coventry City	26	6	6	14	24	37	24
19 Southampton	25	6	5	14	25	48	23
20 Nottingham Forest	26	3	7	16	22	54	16

Match Report

The warning bells are ringing early for Coventry, which is perhaps why they staged the kind of gritty display they usually produce to escape relegation by the skin of their teeth.

It was one of those results that had to be ground out, and the fact that United came home winners was due as much to Peter Schmeichel as the glorious goal scored by Ryan Giggs 11 minutes from the end.

The United goalkeeper did particularly well to palm away a crashing shot from George Boateng shortly before the break; and then late in the game, with the help of Henning Berg clearing his save from Darren Huckerby, he successfully protected United's slender but important lead. It was vintage Schmeichel from the days before announcing that he could no longer keep up with the demands of Old Trafford and that he wanted to swim in calmer waters.

Coventry certainly made the going this afternoon pretty choppy but the goalkeeper was in command. In fact, he launched the move that brought United the points. Schmeichel's long throw set the Reds off on a counterattack. Giggs, making his first start for three weeks after his hamstring problem, raced the full length of the field to finish.

United were far from their fluent best with the normally volatile Cole and Yorke for once subdued, and considering the hard work put in by Coventry, United did well to get back on the winning trail.

Manager's Report

❝ I was hoping to beat Arsenal to give us a safety cushion but they are still on our coat tails. So it is all the more vital that I give each game a priority rating and decide which is really important to us and where and when I can change things around to rest players.

The picture is quite clear now. I feel we can go all the way in Europe, we are in the quarter-final of the FA Cup and we are top of

Ryan Giggs scores.

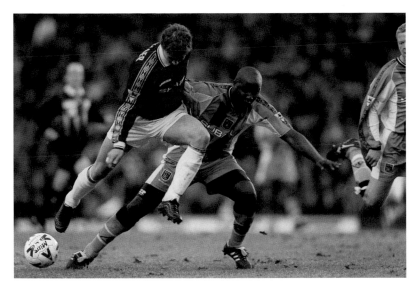

Ole Gunnar Solskjaer leaps into action.

the League. I picture about 60 games for us so we must pace ourselves and it's a matter of trying to keep all the players fit.

We are monitoring Ryan Giggs all the time. He is an important player for us, especially in the Champions League. He came on as a sub against Arsenal after injury and changed the game for us. At Coventry today, his performance emphasised his value. He finished off a marvellous move which started with a corner at our end. Schmeichel caught it and by the time Yorke and Beckham had moved the ball along, Ryan, who had been defending the front post, had arrived in their goalmouth to score. It was a brilliantly exciting goal and I knew straightaway that it had won the game for us. They tried hard to get back at us but we defended quite comfortably.

Peter Schmeichel was back to his very best. He had one exceptionally good save in the first half but it was his general dominance and presence in the box that was the big plus for us. ⟩

Coventry City: Hedman, Nilsson, Burrows (Soltvedt 86), Williams, Shaw, Telfer, Huckerby, Whelan (Aloisi 65), Froggatt, McAllister, Boateng

Manchester United: Schmeichel, G. Neville, Irwin, Keane, Johnsen, Stam (Berg 45), Beckham, Scholes, Cole (Solskjaer 74), Yorke (P. Neville 87), Giggs

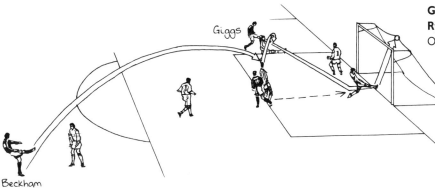

GOAL NO.1
Ryan Giggs 79 minutes
One of Peter Schmeichel's mighty throws launched the winning raid as time was beginning to run out. Dwight Yorke picked it up and the ball was moved smoothly through Ryan Giggs to David Beckham who crossed into the goalmouth. Richard Shaw got his head to the centre but it was too high for him and the ball went through to Giggs who scored with a half-hit shot across the face of goal. Shaw tried to retrieve but couldn't manage it.

	28 February 1999	P	W	D	L	F	A	Pts
1	Manchester Utd	28	16	9	3	63	29	57
2	Chelsea	27	14	11	2	41	22	53
3	Arsenal	27	13	11	3	35	13	50
4	Aston Villa	27	12	8	7	38	31	44
5	Leeds Utd	26	11	9	6	39	25	42
6	West Ham Utd	27	11	7	9	31	38	40
7	Liverpool	27	11	6	10	50	34	39
8	Derby County	27	9	11	7	26	25	38
9	Wimbledon	26	9	10	7	30	36	37
10	Sheffield Wednesday	26	10	5	11	34	25	35
11	Newcastle Utd	27	9	8	10	35	36	35
12	Tottenham Hotspur	26	7	12	7	30	32	33
13	Middlesbrough	27	7	12	8	34	39	33
14	Leicester City	25	7	9	9	25	34	30
15	Everton	27	6	10	11	20	29	28
16	Charlton Athletic	27	6	9	12	31	37	27
17	Coventry City	27	7	6	14	28	38	27
18	Blackburn Rovers	27	6	8	13	27	38	26
19	Southampton	26	6	5	15	26	50	23
20	Nottingham Forest	27	3	8	16	22	54	17

David Beckham jumps to it.

Match Report

As Roy Keane summed up afterwards, 'It wasn't pretty but we got the points.' Keane emerged the hero. On the bench with next week's European quarter-final against Inter Milan in mind, he was summoned for the second half as United got increasingly bogged down against a team they were expected to beat. Keane duly obliged and performed like a true captain, not only scoring but lifting those around him to a higher standard of play.

'Scoring was a relief,' he said, 'not only because of the situation in the match but also because I have been a bit unlucky in front of goal recently.

'The manager had told me he was thinking of resting me. I wanted to play but you have to look at the system and I realise it has worked well for us. I am not arrogant enough to think I'm exempt from the rotation system. I was just happy to get on and do something.'

Keane's 80th minute goal was followed four minutes later by one from Dwight Yorke, and although Matthew Le Tissier hit a spectacular consolation effort it was too late to influence the outcome of the game.

Manager's Report

'I rested Roy Keane for this match. I tend to take more of a risk at home and he had been feeling his hamstring a bit tight so I wanted to give him a break. I put him on the bench along with Andy Cole and Denis Irwin, who at 33 needs the occasional rest. Leaving Denis out also enabled me to keep Phil Neville going. He is loyal and patient, brought up at Old Trafford and red through and through. He deserves to be recognised for that and I can't wait to give this type of player the opportunity of playing in the team.

As it turned out, I think I waited too long before making changes because this was one of those stagnant performances that haunts us from time to time, especially before a big European match, and of course we meet Inter Milan on Wednesday.

That's obviously on my mind, but by half-time my patience had worn out. At the end of the day, we also want to win the League and dropping points against Southampton is hardly the right recipe.

So I brought Roy off the bench for the second half and the improvement in our play was instant. He gave us the purpose that we had been lacking and though we had to wait until the 80th minute it was Roy who scored our first goal. That's the value of the substitution system we have today. You can still have your top players in reserve on the bench if things are not working out as you planned, and with Roy's key help, we squeezed through 2–1.

It's a funny thing about Southampton. Of all the teams that come to Old Trafford, they are the ones with the best attitude. They always come to try to beat us. They have been like that ever since they played five at the back only to concede two early goals, scored I think by Ryan Giggs. Since then they always strive to make a proper game of it, and all credit to them.

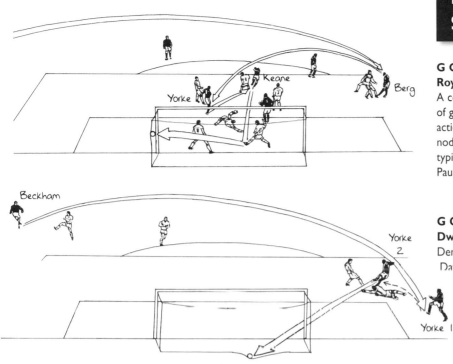

GOAL NO.1
Roy Keane 80 minutes

A corner kick from David Beckham to the far side of goal was headed back into the thick of the action by Henning Berg. Dwight Yorke neatly nodded the ball into the path of Roy Keane who typically kept his shot low and it screamed past Paul Jones with the help of a deflection.

GOAL NO.2
Dwight Yorke 84 minutes

Denis Irwin's booted clearance from defence sent David Beckham racing away down the right flank. His cross found Dwight Yorke in the clear, and with a rapid sidestep round the keeper he clipped the ball into the empty net.

Dwight got our second goal, but it was Matt Le Tissier who had the last word with a superbly hit shot. Le Tissier has a great talent, which is probably why, in my time, he has been continually linked with a transfer to Old Trafford. People are always speculating and there is no doubting his ability. Indeed, I have often wondered how he would have fared as a United player. We shall never know, of course, because it's too late now but there is no doubt he has been one of the most gifted, if not the hardest working, players to grace the game in the last decade.

Although it wasn't one of our best performances it nevertheless took our unbeaten run to 13 matches following the débâcle against Middlesbrough. All but two of the 13 have been won so it has been a good spell. We have made the most of the break from Europe.

When I think back to December and the rather difficult period we went through, I marvel at what the team has achieved since the turn of the year. The players have done everything I have asked of them and pulled off some notable success in both League and Cup.

They have taken games by the scruff of the neck and struck a level of form which has hardly wavered. We have ranged from scoring sprees to games where they have simply ground out a result. It's not always possible to deliver an extravaganza but then the Premiership is very competitive and hotly contested these days so it would be unreasonable to expect runaway scores all the time. ❯

Manchester United: Schmeichel, G. Neville, P. Neville (Irwin 79), Scholes, Johnsen, Berg, Beckham, Butt (Keane 45), Solskjaer (Cole 68), Yorke, Giggs

Southampton: Jones, Dodd, Colleter, Marsden, Lundekvam, Monkou (Benali 51), Hughes, Oakley, Beattie, Ostenstad (Le Tissier 68), Bridge

David Beckham produced one of his masterly crosses for the second goal.

Quarter-final, first leg	
Bayern Munich 2	Kaiserslautern 0
Juventus 2	Olympiakos 1
Manchester Utd 2	Internazionale 0
Real Madrid 1	Dynamo Kiev 1

Dwight Yorke leaps for the first of his two goals, rocking the Italians.

Match Report

The manager was banking on crosses to undo the Italians and that is just how it worked out after six minutes with David Beckham delivering the perfect centre for Dwight Yorke to beat Pagliuca with a firm header.

The move was repeated just before half-time to put United in the driving seat, and although it proved to be a tense and dramatic second half, United emerged with a healthy 2–0 lead from this hard-fought first leg. United missed opportunities to score and almost paid for it when Diego Simeone headed in from a corner, but the goal was disallowed for pushing in the crowded goalmouth.

Peter Schmeichel was heroic in goal with several spectacular saves. In the last minute, Henning Berg helped with a clearance off the line.

Manager's Report

'Now I just have a smell about Europe. I really think we have a terrific chance to go all the way. I just have to make sure we don't shoot ourselves in the foot.

The emphasis against Inter Milan was twofold. We had to defend the centre of midfield and at the same time get our crosses in. We had watched them several times and I felt sure we could score from centres.

They had been making changes and they seemed to be in some confusion about what was their best team. They didn't seem sure about their left-hand side. Silvestre was there sometimes, then Milanese and also Aron Winter. As it turned out, Winter played at Old Trafford, so they had a right-sided midfielder playing in the left wing-back position, which didn't seem ideal to me.

Their main thrust is playing one up, Zamorano, who can be a handful, with Baggio and Djorkaeff tucked in behind him. From the pace point of view, they are not going to kill you but the vital part is still in the centre of midfield where I wanted our midfield players to get nice and close to force them wide. They are not dangerous there and happily our full-backs played a key part closing down Baggio and Djorkaeff. This left Ronny Johnsen and Jaap Stam to look after Zamorano, which they did well. It was a good tactical performance.

Yes, in the second half we had to ride our luck with a couple of threatening moments. Henning Berg, who came on at half-time for the injured Johnsen, played fantastically well and his goalline clearance at the end was an important stop. Inter also had a goal disallowed for a push, which the video later showed was in fact a foul, but nevertheless it was a close call.

David Beckham hit two great crosses and Dwight Yorke scored with two terrific headers, but it was our tactical discipline that really won the game for us. The players earn ten out of ten for that. To go away for the second leg with a two-goal advantage is clearly wonderful.

I think we also did quite well in the planning department to ignore all the speculation about Ronaldo. Their star has been injured for some time and all kinds of stories have been coming out of Italy suggesting that he would be flying in late by private jet. I wouldn't have been surprised if someone had reported he would be landing by helicopter on the pitch.

| Manchester United | 2 |
| Internazionale Milan | 0 |

Manchester United: Schmeichel, G. Neville, Irwin, Keane, Johnsen (Berg 45), Stam, Beckham, Scholes (Butt 69), Cole, Yorke, Giggs

Inter Milan: Pagliuca, Bergomi, Colonnese, Zanetti, Galante, Djorkaeff, Cauet, Winter, Zamorano (Ventola 68), Baggio, Simeone

Jaap Stam and Roy Keane were outstanding as United kept the Inter attack at bay.

We decided that Ronaldo wouldn't play, at least in the first leg. If he had it would have been as big a problem for them as us. They would have had to change their whole way of playing and at that point it wouldn't have made sense.

So we didn't allow ourselves to get bogged down in the big Ronaldo debate. Maybe they do it to try to confuse you, but we simply concentrated on our own game plan and I stressed the need for discipline with our tactics. That way I felt confident we could handle them, and I wasn't far wrong.

Our concentration was first-class and I am sure we can score over there. That would leave Inter needing to score four goals to win – a tall order against us, or against anyone at this level in Europe. 〉

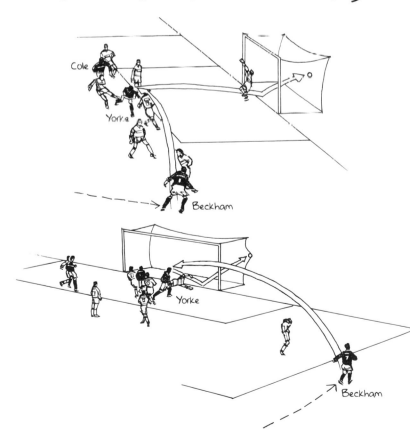

GOAL NO. 1
Dwight Yorke 6 minutes
Forewarned is not necessarily forearmed. David Beckham delivered a quality cross with too much pace for Pagliuca to reach and the Inter defence was rooted as Cole and Yorke charged into them. Yorke got a superb glance to steer in the first goal and deliver an early shock for the visitors.

GOAL NO. 2
Dwight Yorke 45 minutes
Beckham continued to test Inter with his raking centres and there was an inevitability about the second goal coming as virtually a carbon copy of the first – another unstoppable header from Yorke as he ran in to meet yet another Beckham centre.

Sixth round	
Arsenal 1	Derby County 0
Manchester Utd 0 REPLAY	Chelsea 0
Chelsea 0	Manchester Utd 2
Newcastle Utd 4	Everton 1
Barnsley 0	Tottenham Hotspur 1

Match Report

The television vote for Chelsea goalkeeper Ed de Goey as man of the match tells the story of this goalless sixth-round tie at Old Trafford. The 32-year-old Dutchman was in constant action while Peter Schmeichel was almost a spectator at the other end.

United, despite the manager's shake-up as he juggles his squad to keep everyone rested and on their toes, dominated the match and bombarded the visitors' goal only to find de Goey in fantastic form.

Paul Scholes led the shooting assault until he was sent off five minutes from the end, and might well have had a hat-trick, while Gary Neville hit a post and David Beckham missed a good chance.

Chelsea lost Roberto di Matteo just before the break, red-carded after being booked twice for rash tackles, but as so often happens against ten men, it didn't make it any easier for the full-strength side!

Nevertheless, it was a good result considering that Yorke and Cole had been left on the bench, and neither Giggs nor Stam had figured.

Manager's Report

‘ I made changes following last week's game with Inter Milan in an attempt to freshen up the side and avoid the dip that we sometimes suffer after major games in Europe.

I was also trying to bear in mind that Chelsea have a good record at Old Trafford. I think we have beaten them four times in my 13 years with United. Some teams enjoy coming to Old Trafford and Chelsea are one of them. They have a lot of experienced, well-travelled players and I think playing on our stage appeals to them.

But I knew I needed to work the system and make full use of my

Manchester United   **0**
Chelsea   **0**

Manchester United: Schmeichel, G. Neville, Irwin, Keane, Brown, Berg, Beckham, Scholes, Solskjaer (Cole 82), P. Neville (Yorke 73), Blomqvist (Sheringham 82)

Chelsea: de Goey, Petrescu (Newton 45), Le Saux, Ferrer, Lambourde, Desailly, Goldbaek, di Matteo, Flo (Forssell 61), Zola (Myers 80), Morris

United were on top but David Beckham (left) couldn't find a way through, and even the overhead acrobatics of Dwight Yorke (far left) failed to beat man of the match Ed de Gocy.

squad. So I put Dwight Yorke and Andy Cole on the bench and played just Ole Gunnar Solskjaer up front.

Knowing Chelsea's strengths, we also decided to man-mark Zola. In my view, the little guy is the best Italian player to come to this country – Italy don't normally let their top players go until they are on the way down – and in the past he has caused us some problems. We put Phil Neville on to him to keep him quiet, and Phil did a very good job. There wasn't much from Zola and ten minutes from the end they took him off.

In terms of possession, my changes were more than justified because we ran most of the game and we were unlucky not to win. Chelsea were down to ten men for the whole of the second half and it is difficult to say how the game would have gone had they not had di Matteo sent off.

The dismissal was for a second bookable offence and was down to the referee's interpretation. For me Paul Durkin is probably the best referee on the list. He and Graham Poll are ahead of the rest. When he puts his mind to it, Poll can be a very good referee indeed. I have got to say, though, that in this match Durkin was not his usual self. It was as if he was in a bad mood. He also sent Paul Scholes off in the closing minutes and he came in for a bit of criticism. When I saw him at the replay, I asked him if he had had a row with his wife before our last game. In fairness, he was first-class in the second tie.

Although Chelsea celebrated – and from their point of view a draw with ten men at Old Trafford is a fair achievement – I said to our players and staff that a replay was the best possible result for us. Without a second game on the Wednesday we would have been going to Liverpool for a league game. They have not played for a fortnight while we have been on the treadmill of playing Saturday, Wednesday and Sunday. The last thing I wanted was to go to Anfield with them waiting for us all fresh and fired up. As far as I am concerned, Liverpool can wait until later in the season! 〞

Match Report

Most punters considered United had blown it when they failed to beat Chelsea at the first attempt on their own ground, but Alex Ferguson had other ideas. He sent a full-strength side to London and the Reds racked up their game to produce a brilliant display.

Chelsea, believing they had done the hard part, also went up a gear and the result was a fascinating, quality Cup tie.

United emerged triumphant but they were tested every inch of the way. Crucial for United was being able to take the lead after only four minutes when Dwight Yorke punished some slack defending with a sharply taken goal. But Chelsea were not down for long and it took a great instinctive save from Peter Schmeichel to stop Zola scoring. The United goalkeeper went on to make several more crucial saves until Yorke struck again in the 59th minute to put the tie beyond Chelsea's reach.

The Londoners still came back for more but Schmeichel crushed the stirrings of a revival with a couple more super saves.

Andy Cole battles for the ball and then celebrates with scorer Dwight Yorke, rocking imaginary cradles to mark the arrival of David Beckham's baby.

Manager's Report

❛I felt we were really ready for the replay. I brought Yorke and Cole back and we went for it with all guns blazing. Stam and Giggs were back, too, and we were up for it, everyone feeling we could reach the semi-finals.

And we got a fantastic performance, not just from my team, but from Chelsea as well. Usually, it is very difficult to assess the opposition when you have beaten them because you are full of the positive things your own team have accomplished. Occasionally though, you are aware that there have been two great performances. It doesn't happen often, but this was one of those nights, and I am sure Vialli, despite being beaten, will have been saying well done to his players.

There was some terrific football from both teams. Zola was buzzing, a delight to watch, and in terms of exquisite skill I think Dwight Yorke's second goal stands comparison with anything. We were on a counterattack, Cole won the ball and gave it to Dwight. Chelsea hesitated. The keeper came ever so slightly off his line as Dwight moved towards him, and with the outside of his foot, Dwight chipped him. Absolutely magnificent!

I think it's the fourth time we have knocked Chelsea out of the FA Cup in the last six years, and this really was worthy of a clash between the top two teams in the Premiership.

So now we are through to the semi-finals of the FA Cup, and at this stage anything can happen. I don't like to build things up too much, but there is no escaping the fact that everyone is assessing our chances of doing the treble. Naturally we will go for everything, we always do, but I don't honestly think it is a realistic target. Deep down we know we aren't going to do it because it would take a football miracle for us to win the League, the FA Cup and the European Cup.

But when I look at each competition on its own, I cannot escape the feeling that we are going well. Our lead in the Premiership is now four points and, although it was in the Cup, we have just beaten Chelsea, our nearest rivals. In the FA Cup, we are one step away from Wembley and I know we are capable of going to the final. Europe obviously remains the most elusive, but we must be favourites to reach the semi-finals of the Champions League after taking a two-goal lead over Inter Milan in the first leg.

So, who knows, we'll just have to keep going and see what happens. We are, of course, entering that stage of the season when every game really counts but at least we have arrived at this point in good shape. People still occasionally criticise me for making changes and resting players – tinkering with the team as they put it – but now is the time when I think everyone will appreciate the value of that strategy.

David Beckham is a case in point. He had a three-week break around Christmas, as did Paul Scholes and Gary Neville. We sent them away on holiday. I haven't hammered the strikers, either. They have had their breaks and I think they are all coming to a peak at just the right time. We are in a very strong position and we are all eager to see what happens next. ❚

Chelsea: de Goey, Le Saux, Babayaro, Lambourde, Leboeuf (Myers 45), Desailly, Morris (Goldbaek 72), di Matteo, Flo (Forssell 72), Zola, Wise

Manchester United: Schmeichel, G. Neville, Irwin, Keane, Borg, Stam, Beckham, Scholes, Cole (P. Neville 71), Yorke (Solskjaer 85), Giggs (Blomqvist 76)

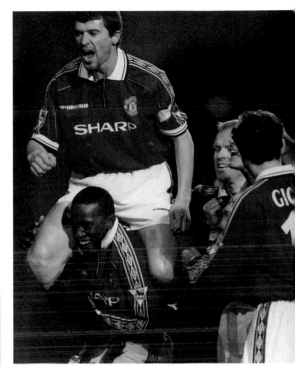

Dwight Yorke has to carry Roy Keane as well as score the goals!

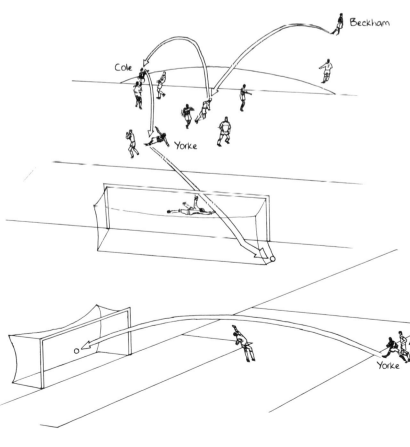

GOAL NO.1
Dwight Yorke 4 minutes
Frank Leboeuf failed to clear a free kick from David Beckham, a mistake pounced on by Andy Cole who quickly headed the ball towards his partner. The ever-ready Dwight Yorke turned sharply to volley home from eight yards and deliver a fourth-minute shock to the London club.

GOAL NO.2
Dwight Yorke 59 minutes
Cole again made the running by winning possession to give Yorke sight of goal. Measuring the advancing goalkeeper coming off his line, Yorke chipped him with a delicacy which sent his manager into raptures.

		P	W	D	L	F	A	Pts
	14 March 1999							
1	Manchester Utd	29	17	9	3	65	30	60
2	Arsenal	29	15	11	3	40	13	56
3	Chelsea	28	14	11	3	41	23	53
4	Leeds Utd	29	14	9	6	45	26	51
5	Aston Villa	29	12	8	9	39	34	44
6	Derby County	29	11	11	7	31	28	44
7	West Ham Utd	29	12	7	10	32	39	43
8	Wimbledon	29	10	10	9	33	41	40
9	Liverpool	28	11	6	11	52	37	39
10	Tottenham Hotspur	29	9	12	8	34	34	39
11	Newcastle Utd	29	10	8	11	38	39	38
12	Middlesbrough	28	8	12	8	37	39	36
13	Sheffield Wednesday	29	10	5	14	35	32	35
14	Leicester City	28	8	10	10	28	37	34
15	Coventry City	29	8	7	14	31	40	31
16	Everton	29	7	10	12	22	32	31
17	Charlton Athletic	29	6	10	13	33	40	28
18	Blackburn Rovers	29	6	9	14	29	41	27
19	Southampton	29	7	5	17	27	56	26
20	Nottingham Forest	29	4	8	17	26	57	20

Two goals for Andy Cole.

Match Report

United's win maintained their four-point lead at the top of the table, and Andy Cole outclassed Alan Shearer in the battle of the strikers.

Although Nolberto Solano gave Newcastle an early lead, it was Cole who grabbed the headlines with a goal in each half, which must boost his hopes of making the next England squad.

Once in front United cruised to a comfortable win against a team looking dangerously low in morale.

Manager's Report

❛One thing is crystal clear – Coley does like playing against Newcastle! He has a superb scoring record against his old club and his two goals in this match gave us the points.

I was a little apprehensive before the game because I am always wary of a team enjoying a good Cup run. Newcastle's history is based on the FA Cup and goes back to the fifties when they won it three times in five years. They have been in numerous finals and though they have never quite done it consistently in the League, I nevertheless wondered if their Cup success this season might give them a lift against us and we were going there at the wrong time.

I knew for sure they would be revved up, their fans as well. You talk about natural passion, and no matter how badly they are playing, their supporters are with them through thick and thin. The volume in their stadium is always full blast. I talked to our players about the need to handle the crowd. Over the years, we have done that quite well.

Newcastle certainly gave their supporters something to cheer in the 16th minute when they surprised us from a free kick. Peter Schmeichel expected Alan Shearer to hit one of his usual rockets but instead Nolberto Solano ran from the line-up to bend a brilliant ball into the top corner. Peter got a hand to it but it was a token gesture.

Now the battle was really on. I had been on the point of leaving my seat in the directors' box because I felt we needed to step up the tempo a bit. Once they scored we livened up anyway and within ten minutes Andy Cole had got the equaliser. The pitch was dry and bumpy and when Andy scored a second goal it was a matter of digging in.

It was a quiet performance from Newcastle, despite their fans' fervour, and they didn't produce much of a threat. On this occasion, there wasn't any real atmosphere around the club which makes me think about the grapevine gossip that Ruud is not a popular manager and that Alan Shearer is not getting on with him. Certainly Shearer was a shadow of his normal self and I was disappointed with his performance. I know he is capable of producing a lot more than he did. When you see that kind of thing, you have to worry for the manager's future.

There is nothing wrong with the spirit in our camp, though. Afterwards in the dressing-room, the players were high, hugging and clapping each other, shaking hands and having a fantastic time after returning to league football with a win.

I noticed that Dwight Yorke wasn't there and when he finally strolled in I asked him where he had been.

Newcastle United: Given, Barton (Maric 84), Charvet, Domi, Dabizas, Georgiadis (Lee 45), Hamann, Solano, Shearer, Ketsbaia (Saha 62), Speed

Manchester United: Schmeichel (Van der Gouw 45), G. Neville, Irwin, Keane, Berg, Stam, Beckham, Scholes (P. Neville 87), Cole, Yorke, Giggs (Johnsen 74)

Once in front, United shut up shop with Denis Irwin producing his usual efficient and consistent performance.

"Oh, I've just been talking to someone," he replied.

What a personality, a ray of sunshine and you'll never change his cool West Indian temperament. He misses a chance and smiles at the crowd. He doesn't smile at me, though. He's not that laid back!

I took Peter Schmeichel off at half-time and announced that he had a touch of flu and didn't feel well. The truth is he hurt his back in the warm up and it was troubling him. I gave out the flu line so as not to give Inter Milan any encouragement before our match on Wednesday. **"**

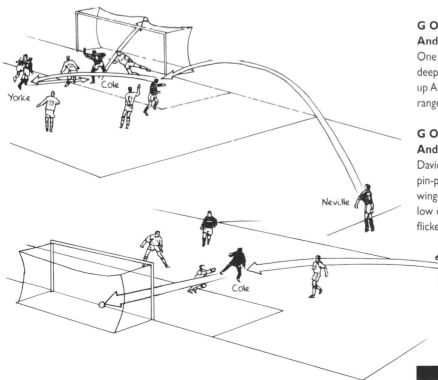

GOAL NO.1
Andy Cole 25 minutes
One of Gary Neville's mighty throws was headed deeper into the goalmouth for Dwight Yorke to set up Andy Cole with a chance he buried from close range.

GOAL NO.2
Andy Cole 51 minutes
David Beckham switched the play with one of his pin-point long crosses to Ryan Giggs. The left winger wasted no time finding Andy Cole with a low centre which the one-time Newcastle striker flicked past Shay Given.

European Champions League

Quarter-final, second leg
17 March 1999

Quarter-final, second leg	
Dynamo Kiev 2	Real Madrid 0
Internazionale 1	Manchester Utd 1
Kaiserslautern 0	Bayern Munich 4
Olympiakos 1	Juventus 1

Match Report

Inter Milan complained bitterly after Gilles Veissiere had turned down three penalty appeals, but in fact the Italians paid the price for trying to con the French referee with bogus claims.

United were worried when substitute Nicola Ventola gave the home team the lead and they didn't relax until Paul Scholes, coming on quarter of an hour from the end for Ronny Johnsen, had scored an equaliser on the night. A score draw was United's best result on Italian soil for 40 years following six defeats. Scholes now joins Norman Whiteside as the only other United player to score in a major competition in Italy. No wonder confidence was leaping skywards.

Manager's Report

'The bonus in the Newcastle game was being able to play Ronny Johnsen for all but the last quarter of an hour on his return from injury. I had it in mind to play him in the centre of midfield against Inter in case Ronaldo dropped in there; it's what he likes to do and he is the best in the world operating in that position.

My other concern for the match was the refereeing. You hear all manner of stories about corruption in the European competitions. UEFA are aware of the issue and one of the things they do now is to wait until a couple of days before the match before announcing the name of the official. But regardless of dishonesty, referees do get influenced by some of the major clubs and in the build-up I made the point that in the volatile atmosphere of the San Siro Stadium, the referee would have to be strong. I said the Italians would be ducking and diving and referee-baiting. Inter were not very happy with me but the French official, Gilles Veissiere, was superb. He refused to be intimidated and he didn't fall for any of the play-acting.

We still had to be strong ourselves and I knew going to Milan would show us what we are made of. The players answered all the questions with a fabulous display. There are always moments when you have to ride your luck. Some people try to identify what is important in a game of football and forget about the luck element. I don't and we had our share of good fortune in this match. Having said that, we showed tremendous resolve in terms of refusing to bow down to the atmosphere. We had the courage to play.

Above: *Ronny Johnsen held nothing back on his return to the starting line-up after injury.*

Right: *Dwight Yorke is chased by Giuseppe Bergomi.*

Dwight Yorke was up against Taribo West, the Inter player with the green hair.

The key tactically was to get the ball to our full-backs because I didn't think Ronaldo and Simeone would have the energy to hunt the ball down. That way Gary Neville and Denis Irwin could control the game, which they did for most of the time. In fact, Simeone was substituted after half an hour, and he had been the one in the tunnel beforehand winding his team up and shouting across at our players.

As the game went on, I had the feeling that it was going our way. We kept good possession of the ball and dictated the pattern of play. We made a few mistakes at the end but that can happen when you know you are nearly there and start to sit deeper with not as much thrust. This was when Ventola scored and I waited for the fireworks but instead we got the break – Ze Elias, another of the substitutes, missed a great chance. My response was to bring on Paul Scholes, fresh legs and good imagination with his adventurous passing. They started to feel it and he scored the equaliser for us.

I have had the good fortune to take United teams to Barcelona, Turin, Dortmund, Munich and the San Siro and it is just an incredibly proud feeling when you watch them expressing themselves with distinction.

We have had a bad record against Italian clubs, which is why this was such an important match for us and an even more significant result. The facts tell you that to succeed in Europe you have got to get past the Italian clubs, something that had eluded us. Now this splendid aggregate win of 3–1 takes us into the semi-finals. It was an unforgettable night.

I see the Italian big guns as a barometer of our progress and with Inter Milan now out of the way, I think we are entitled to feel we can go all the way. ❯

Inter Milan: Pagliuca, Bergomi (Moriero 69), Colonnese, Zanetti, West, Silvestre, Cauet, Zamorano, Ronaldo (Ventola 60), Baggio, Simeone (Ze Elias 32)

Manchester United: Schmeichel, G. Neville, Irwin, Keane, Johnsen (Scholes 77), Stam, Beckham, Berg, Cole, Yorke, Giggs (P. Neville 82)

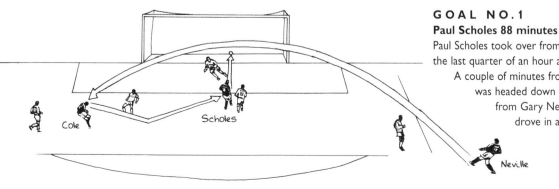

GOAL NO.1
Paul Scholes 88 minutes
Paul Scholes took over from Ronny Johnsen for the last quarter of an hour and changed the game. A couple of minutes from the end, the ball was headed down to him by Andy Cole from Gary Neville's centre, and he drove in a goal.

21 March 1999							
	P	W	D	L	F	A	Pts
1 Manchester Utd	30	18	9	3	68	31	63
2 Arsenal	30	16	11	3	42	13	59
3 Chelsea	29	15	11	3	44	23	56
4 Leeds Utd	30	15	9	6	49	27	54
5 West Ham Utd	30	13	7	10	34	39	46
6 Aston Villa	30	12	8	10	39	37	44
7 Derby County	30	11	11	8	32	32	44
8 Wimbledon	30	10	10	10	34	44	40
9 Liverpool	28	11	6	11	52	37	39
10 Tottenham Hotspur	29	9	12	8	34	34	39
11 Middlesbrough	29	9	12	8	39	40	39
12 Newcastle Utd	30	10	8	12	38	41	38
13 Sheffield Wednesday	30	10	5	15	35	33	35
14 Leicester City	28	8	10	10	28	37	34
15 Coventry City	30	8	7	15	31	42	31
16 Everton	30	7	10	13	23	35	31
17 Blackburn Rovers	30	7	9	14	32	42	30
18 Southampton	30	8	5	17	28	56	29
19 Charlton Athletic	29	6	10	13	33	40	28
20 Nottingham Forest	30	4	8	18	27	59	20

A rare goal for Gary Neville.

Match Report

Although Everton are struggling in the bottom half of the table, this emphatic win was both significant and encouraging for supporters beginning to weigh up the prospects of a treble success. The team's record on their return to domestic football after big glamour games in Europe has been poor. Half of their dropped points in the Premiership so far have been in the games immediately after a European fixture.

So this was an important victory, despite a poor first half by both teams when the Reds did indeed look as if they were suffering from a Champions League hangover. Fortunately, Peter Schmeichel was as alert as ever and he saved well from Marco Materazzi's free kick, one of the rare moments of goalmouth action in a flat first half.

United came to life after the interval and a sparkling burst of three goals in 12 minutes did for Everton and suggested that Alex Ferguson has found the answer to his post-Europe problems.

Also encouraging was the way that David Beckham found his scoring boots with his first goal for nearly five months and Gary Neville remembered the way to goal with his first for nearly two years!

Don Hutchison scored for Everton ten minutes from the end but the late talking point for United fans was the bright display from Jonathan Greening after coming on for the last 20 minutes.

Manager's Report

❛ You always know that coming into a league game on the back of a big European match is going to be hard, but the team are on a run and so I wasn't unduly worried about the visit of Everton.

It's easy to send the players out in this kind of situation. Everyone is up for it, confidence is growing and there is so much to aim for.

I try to play my part by bringing in a little freshness where I think it is important; on this occasion some of the decisions were made for me by the FA with both Roy Keane and Paul Scholes suspended. I rested Ryan Giggs and Denis Irwin bringing in Phil Neville along with Nicky Butt and I decided to play three up with Ole Gunnar Solskjaer joining Yorke and Cole.

I don't consider I weakened the team to any great extent, although it did mean having three youngsters, Brown, Greening and Curtis, on the bench. That's no big deal because they are all promising players and I'm glad of the opportunity to put them in at Premiership level.

I was particularly pleased to give Nicky Butt a game because he was terribly disappointed at being left out in Milan without even a place on the bench. I feel for guys like Nicky who have their heart and soul in the club. I could see how hard he took it and I said to him, "Look, Nicky, you'll play in a lot of other big games," and I know I'll be proved right. I don't like to see the boys I have brought up so disappointed.

It worked out a comfortable win and we were three up before they had scored. Ole Gunnar Solskjaer got the first, and no doubt he was glad to get this one after making the starting line-up. So often he has got his goals coming on as a sub because he arrives with his scoring trigger already cocked. If the tempo has gone or the team fire has died down, I know the golden boy is always ready.

The next goal came from Gary Neville, "one a year" as he is known in the club. I suspect his scoring is not as much as that!

Then we had one from David Beckham who has a curious scoring pattern. One season he got nearly all his usual dozen or so goals from inside the box, the following year he scored them nearly all from outside the penalty area. This season he is way down the scoring list from anywhere. I can't think of any particular reason unless he has been concentrating too much on staying wide for his crossing. He is a good header of the ball and is capable of great finishing. We must try to get him into the box more. He will be well pleased with this goal from about 25 yards. ❩

Dwight Yorke in juggling mood as United begin to think about the treble.

Manchester United: Schmeichel, G. Neville, P. Neville, Berg, Johnsen, Stam, Beckham (Greening 71), Butt, Cole (Sheringham 71), Yorke, Solskjaer (Curtis 89)

Everton: Myhre, Weir, Ball, Dacourt, Short, Unsworth, O'Kane (Jeffers 61), Materazzi, Bakayoko (Cadamarteri 5), Hutchison, Grant (Degn 68)

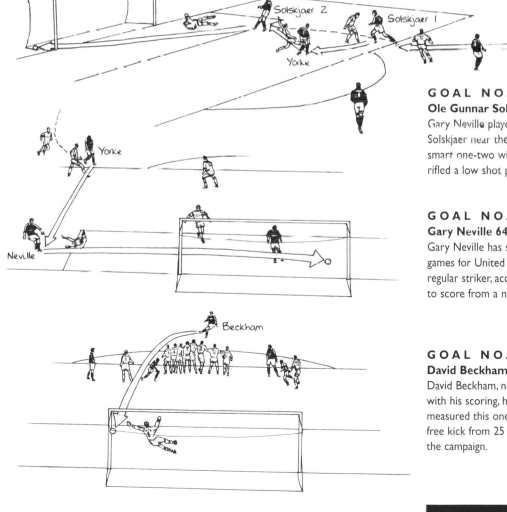

GOAL NO.1
Ole Gunnar Solskjaer 55 minutes
Gary Neville played the ball up to Ole Gunnar Solskjaer near the edge of the box and after a smart one-two with Dwight Yorke the Norwegian rifled a low shot past Thomas Myhre.

GOAL NO.2
Gary Neville 64 minutes
Gary Neville has scored twice in over 200 senior games for United but he took this one like a regular striker, accepting a pass from Dwight Yorke to score from a narrow angle.

GOAL NO.3
David Beckham 67 minutes
David Beckham, normally in double figures with his scoring, has lagged this season but he measured this one perfectly with a lovely curling free kick from 25 yards out for his fifth goal of the campaign.

		P	W	D	L	F	A	Pts
4 April 1999								
1	Manchester Utd	31	18	10	3	69	32	64
2	Arsenal	31	16	12	3	42	13	60
3	Chelsea	30	16	11	3	45	23	59
4	Leeds Utd	31	16	9	6	52	28	57
5	West Ham Utd	31	13	8	10	34	39	47
6	Aston Villa	31	12	9	10	39	37	45
7	Derby County	31	11	11	9	35	36	44
8	Liverpool	29	12	6	11	55	39	42
9	Newcastle Utd	31	11	8	12	42	44	41
10	Wimbledon	31	10	11	10	35	45	41
11	Middlesbrough	30	9	13	8	39	40	40
12	Tottenham Hotspur	30	9	12	9	34	36	39
13	Leicester City	29	9	10	10	30	37	37
14	Sheffield Wednesday	31	10	5	16	36	35	35
15	Coventry City	31	9	7	15	33	43	34
16	Blackburn Rovers	31	7	10	14	32	42	31
17	Everton	31	7	10	14	25	38	31
18	Southampton	31	8	6	17	28	56	30
19	Charlton Athletic	30	6	10	14	33	41	28
20	Nottingham Forest	31	4	8	19	28	62	20

Match Report

The Juventus coach stayed at home, which is just as well for United's chances in their semi-final first leg against the Italian giants next Wednesday! This was a poor display by United which, had they seen it first hand, could only have boosted the Juventus morale.

The Reds made a sloppy start with John Hartson looking for an anxious moment as if he was going to exploit a misunderstanding between Peter Schmeichel and Denis Irwin as the pair of them hesitated over a pass back. After five minutes, another fluffed pass back really did prove costly as Jason Euell raced past Gary Neville to score.

Euell was close to increasing the home team's lead and would have done so but for a fine save by Schmeichel. United got back into it and Neil Sullivan distinguished himself with a save of Schmeichel proportions, a full-length dive to deny Paul Scholes. But the Dons' keeper couldn't keep David Beckham out a minute before the interval. Denis Irwin returned one of Beckham's crosses into the goalmouth for him to rifle home.

United roused themselves even more in the second half without being able to score. They dictated play but found Sullivan in tip-top form, especially when he saved from Jesper Blomqvist with a flip of his trailing leg as he dived the wrong way.

Schmeichel saved from Marcus Gayle but Sullivan was the busier of the keepers and pegged United to a draw by frustrating Scholes again, along with Yorke, Cole and Roy Keane.

Manager's Report

❝ I had Roy Keane and Paul Scholes back in the fray, but with no Jaap Stam it allowed me to play Ronny Johnsen in the middle to get on with his recovery. He and Henning Berg have a good understanding which they also take into the Norwegian national team together. I regard Jaap as my main central defender but I am very confident if I have to go with Ronny and Henning.

Jesper Blomqvist building up for an attack on goal. He sent the goalkeeper diving the wrong way but Neil Sullivan saved with a trailing leg.

Wimbledon: Sullivan, Hughes, Kimble (Ardley 81), Perry, Blackwell, Thatcher, Hughes (Roberts 83), Earle, Hartson (Cort 68), Euell, Gayle

Manchester United: Schmeichel, G. Neville, Irwin, Keane, Johnsen, Berg, Beckham, Scholes, Cole, Yorke, Blomqvist (Solskjaer 73)

Paul Scholes returned to action (left) while David Beckham (below) marks his goal with a long hard look at the visiting supporters.

Wimbledon are not the easiest of teams to play against, especially on their own ground. Right from the start they ask questions of you by throwing the ball into your penalty box, and if you don't stick your head in, you are in big trouble.

In this match, they had the additional advantage of a very good start when Gary Neville got caught with a difficult long kick out and his attempted pass back fell short. Jason Euell seized it and the Dons were a goal up after only five minutes.

David Beckham levelled the score just before the interval, a good time for us to get a goal, and I was able to sort out a few things during the break. We had much more purpose about us in the second half. We were the dominant team without being able to score, something that was down to us, but also to Neil Sullivan, the Wimbledon goalkeeper, who played extremely well.

We should have won comfortably but had to settle for 1–1. The main thing when you are going for a league title is to get at least something from the game, which we did with a point.

Reflecting over the weekend and putting everything into perspective, I am not too unhappy. An away point against Wimbledon is not too bad and we have taken our unbeaten run to 20 matches, reinforcing our reputation as a team that is very difficult to beat.

Maybe one or two of the players had begun to think about the European Cup semi-final against Juventus next week, and who could blame them, for that is a big one! ❜

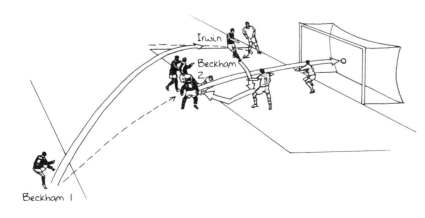

GOAL NO.1
David Beckham 44 minutes
David Beckham started and finished the scoring move. He crossed from the right to the far side where Denis Irwin collected and moved towards goal, on the way cheekily nutmegging Michael Hughes. Beckham was following up at full tilt and when Irwin's cross came off a defender into his path, he blasted the ball home from the edge of the six-yard box.

Semi-final, first leg	
Dynamo Kiev 3	Bayern Munich 3
Manchester Utd 1	Juventus 1

Match Report

As the old cliché would have it, this was a game of two halves. From being given a footballing lesson by Italian masters in the first half, United slowly but surely came to terms with the occasion and ended the match the dominant team, convinced that they deserved more than a 1–1 draw. The bookmakers still changed their minds, however, no longer making them favourites to win the Cup, perhaps influenced by the fact that United have never won in Italy against Juventus!

United kept their heads up, boosted by the lifeline goal from Ryan Giggs and cheered by the way Teddy Sheringham came on as a substitute for the last quarter of an hour and changed the face of the game.

England manager Kevin Keegan was watching and had no doubts about Sheringham's impact.

'The substitution was a masterstroke. It wasn't happening for Dwight Yorke on the night and when Sheringham came on he turned the game. Ryan Giggs got the goal but it was Sheringham who put United on top in that last phase,' he said.

Dwight Yorke demonstrates what he does so well – shielding the ball from an opponent.

Manager's Report

❝ When I get to a semi-final I always try to think back and draw on the experience of other big games, even back to when I was at Aberdeen. I go over in my mind the preparation, the tactics and even the little things. I recall the Dortmund semi-final and although we lost I know that with my present team if we get as many chances I will be happy.

Normally there are not a lot of goals in a semi-final and I thought if we could win 1–0 at home to Juventus I would be more than satisfied because they have fantastic experience in Europe and have been over the course time and time again.

I am also aware that although they have usually beaten us in the past they have found it difficult at Old Trafford. I knew that they would be coming in the knowledge that they would have to run all night and perform to be successful. So there was no great trepidation on my part. We have played them a number of times and my players have accumulated information. We spoke about Zidane because great teams invariably have an axis and for a few years now Zidane has been the main man for Juventus.

He has the cleverness to play right up front but he also has the ability to play in midfield. He is strong with good control and can play his one-twos. He can be hard to play against when he drops into the hole behind the strikers. It's becoming the way to play in Europe. Eric Cantona used to play like Zidane for us.

The way we hoped to handle it was to get at their right-back through Ryan Giggs who usually does well on the European stage. I wanted Ryan to get forward as the third attacker. David Beckham had the same role if play was on the other side. I wanted Juventus to have to defend against three all the time. Unfortunately, Ryan and David took the plan too literally with the result that they both stayed forward,

Manchester United: Schmeichel, G. Neville, Irwin, Keane, Berg (Johnsen 45), Stam, Beckham, Scholes, Cole, Yorke (Sheringham 79), Giggs

Juventus: Peruzzi, Pessotto, Mirkovic, Montero (Ferrara 68), Juliano, Deschamps, Di Livio (Tacchinardi 77), Conte, Inzaghi (Esnaider 88), Davids, Zidane

Teddy Sheringham (left) can't understand the decision, but it didn't stop him setting up Ryan Giggs (below) for an all-important goal.

which left Zidane, Deschamps and Davids over-running us in midfield against Roy Keane and Paul Scholes.

At the same time our full-backs were tied down by Di Livio and Conte without much help from our wide players. The result was complete domination by Juventus in the first half and we could well have been two or three goals down instead of the one scored by Conte. At the break I was angry that the players hadn't grasped what we should have been trying to do.

I changed things, asking David to play tight in midfield leaving Ryan to play from deep and run through the channels as the extra attacker – and the game completely changed.

People have quite rightly pointed out that we were outplayed in the first half but in the second it was us doing the over-running and we could have scored five.

Although Ryan equalised right at the end, we are at a disadvantage because they have scored an away goal. They only need a goalless draw in the second leg and they will go through.

Nevertheless, I'm pleased with our performance in the second half and that we were able to break their domination. They didn't give us any problems at all in the second half, which gives me something solid and encouraging to work on for the trip to Turin.

Hats off to the players for the way they recognised the problem and did something about it. Juventus will feel they are favourites and rightly so but they may live to regret our late goal. I have a gut feeling we can take our second-half form over there for the second leg. Something tells me that we are going to win. **,**

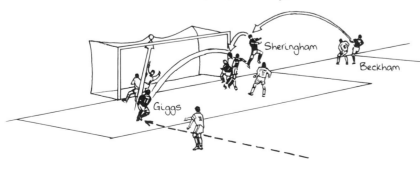

GOAL NO.1
Ryan Giggs 90 minutes

Teddy Sheringham put Juventus in trouble when he headed a cross from David Beckham into the six-yard box. Ferrara's attempted clearance was slammed into the net from point-blank range by Ryan Giggs.

Semi-final	
Newcastle Utd 2	Tottenham Hotspur 0
Manchester Utd 0 REPLAY	Arsenal 0
Arsenal 1	Manchester Utd 2

Arsenal: Seaman, Dixon, Winterburn, Vieira, Keown, Adams, Vivas, Parlour, Anelka (Kanu 100), Bergkamp, Overmars (Ljungberg 90)

Manchester United: Schmeichel, G. Neville, Irwin (P. Neville 85), Keane, Johnsen, Stam, Beckham, Butt, Cole (Scholes 113), Yorke, Giggs (Solskjaer 99)

It was a tough tie, as Andy Cole, here watched closely by Martin Keown, will testify.

Match Report

United considered they had won this tie in the 38th minute when Ryan Giggs raced away down the left wing to fling over a centre which Dwight Yorke headed down for Roy Keane to hit a piledriver past David Seaman. However, the linesman's flag was up and it later emerged that he was signalling offside against Yorke at the outset of the move. United argued that with play on the other flank, Yorke had not been interfering with play, but referee David Elleray was not convinced and the goal was disallowed.

United's indignation was such that the normally mild Denis Irwin was booked for dissent.

Both sides had their chances but missed and the Villa Park tie went into extra time. When Nelson Vivas was sent off early in the first period for elbowing Nicky Butt, it seemed as if United would force an advantage, but Yorke slipped up, while at the other end it took a super save from Peter Schmeichel to keep out Fredrik Ljungberg.

Manager's Report

❝ It's an exciting time. Here we are, coming out of a European semi-final with high hopes for the second leg because we didn't lose, we got a draw, and then we are meeting Arsenal in the semi-final of the FA Cup just one step from Wembley.

David Elleray's decision to disallow Roy Keane's goal so incensed Martin Edwards that it had him making really out-of-character comments about the referee; not that I blame him. It was absurd not letting the goal stand. The linesman who flagged Dwight Yorke offside was the one who got slaughtered, and certainly it was a horrendous mistake because play at the time was on the other side of the field.

I point the finger at the referee because he had at least a minute to get it right and bail out his assistant. A lot of things disturb me about

Mr Elleray, but chiefly his influence over other referees. I don't think we are seeing the best referees in the Premiership. What we are getting is a lot of David Elleray's friends instead of league officials such as Tony Heilbron for instance, and this is unhealthy for football.

What made the whole situation even more frustrating for us was the fact that we were the better side. We should have won, and would have done if Roy Keane's goal had been allowed. I thought when we got into extra time and they were down to ten men that we would easily do it, but it didn't seem to make any difference to Arsenal. Mind you, they get plenty of practice playing with ten men. What is it, 29 players sent off in Arsene Wenger's time? I suppose they are used to it.

I said to our players before the tie, the last thing we want now is a replay, whatever you do don't come back in with us involved in an extra match at this busy juncture. Fat lot of notice they take of me. Now we must go back to Villa Park for another demanding match in three days' time.

On the journey home, I discussed the situation with Steve McClaren and Jim Ryan, explaining that we must change the team. I am adamant that if we are going to win the things we want to win, we must have some fresh legs and give the ones who have been playing regularly a break. We are top of the League and we are in the semi-final of the Champions League. There is so much to lose and in a list of priorities I have to be blunt and say the FA Cup comes third. I am determined to bring in some different players.

It's a testing time for me as manager and for my coaches. I have got to show judgement in picking the sides but have the courage to make those changes. The tricky part is sticking to your purpose when a result goes against you.

I am sure there will be some raised eyebrows when I announce the team for the replay, but this is why I have constructed a squad of players equipped to handle the string of mighty matches now coming our way. ➜

Nicky Butt also found the Gunners in determined mood as he goes flying in a collision with Tony Adams.

Match Report

In a rip-roaring match United moved into the final of the FA Cup with a victory deservedly gained by ten men in extra time. It was one of the most memorable matches of the season and reached a sensational climax when Ryan Giggs conjured up one of the most magical runs in football to score the winner.

There was drama virtually from the start with the manager rotating his squad to send out an attack led by Teddy Sheringham and Ole Gunnar Solskjaer with Jesper Blomqvist on the wing. Sheringham, distraught at being left out of the first game following his outstanding contribution against Juventus, was taunted by the Arsenal fans but he quickly silenced them when he set up the opening for David Beckham to give United a 17th minute lead.

Peter Schmeichel successfully answered the first of several testing moments when he saved from Dennis Bergkamp and then stopped Emmanuel Petit.

United roared back in the second half with Solskjaer and Blomqvist going close but Arsenal gave as good as they got and, with the help of an unlucky deflection off Jaap Stam, Dennis Bergkamp scored a 69th minute equaliser.

The match really turned against United five minutes later when Roy Keane was sent off for two bookable offences, especially when Arsenal were awarded a penalty for Phil Neville's trip on Ray Parlour. Schmeichel pulled off a magnificent save to send the game into extra time.

Again the Reds seemed to be up against it only to find Giggs racing past man after man from his own half as if he had the ball tied to his bootlaces. He finished brilliantly to win the tie.

Arsenal: Seaman, Dixon, Winterburn, Vieira, Keown, Adams, Parlour (Kanu 104), Ljungberg (Overmars 62), Anelka, Bergkamp, Petit (Bould 119)

Manchester United: Schmeichel, G. Neville (Yorke 91), P. Neville, Keane, Johnsen, Stam, Beckham, Butt, Solskjaer, Sheringham (Scholes 76), Blomqvist (Giggs 61)

Ryan Giggs finishes explosively after a magical run through the Arsenal team to score the winner in an unrelenting Cup tie.

Manager's Report

❛I left out Andy Cole, Dwight Yorke, Ryan Giggs and Denis Irwin for the replay. It surprised a lot of people, including the directors. I think some of them have given up trying to understand some of my selections. You can sometimes hear the hush when they come into the dressing-room before a match and see the line-up. It's written on their faces – what on earth is he doing now? I used to banter with Mike Edelson about my choice of team but he says he has given up arguing because he is fed up with querying a selection and then we win.

We certainly won this one, and what a terrific, fantastic Cup tie. It had everything, a fine goal from Beckham, our captain sent off, Peter Schmeichel's penalty save, extra time and then the crowning glory of the Giggs goal.

The last thing we wanted was a replay and I have been worrying about the effects it might have on us, but it's turned out to be the best thing that could have happened. The players are so upbeat now. The FA Cup was never our top target, but getting through to Wembley is an incredible feeling and you can see the players lapping it up.

The champagne was spraying everywhere in the dressing-room afterwards. Sir Bobby Charlton always seems to wear a nice jacket to

GOAL NO.1
David Beckham 17 minutes

A sweeping move launched by Peter Schmeichel's long kick came off an Arsenal player to David Beckham who interchanged with Teddy Sheringham before scoring with one of his famous benders from a distance of about 25 yards.

GOAL NO.2
Ryan Giggs 109 minutes

Ryan Giggs, initially rested, was called back into action after an hour and became the scoring hero with a classic goal. After intercepting a pass from a tired Vieira in his own half, he simply flew past at least five opponents in a scything run before thundering a shot over the head of the helpless David Seaman.

Giggs whirls round after his superb goal, which took his team to Wembley.

matches and this one got a soaking. He didn't seem to mind. Clearly he is not as fussy as our goalkeeper. If Peter thinks champagne might become the order of the day, he covers up his clothes hanging on the peg with towels.

Everything and everyone was bubbling. We were all so high we could have flown back along the motorway to Manchester.

I know I have been very lucky to have managed such great players as Eric Cantona, Roy Keane, Mark Hughes, Bryan Robson and David Beckham, but when I see Ryan Giggs performing as he did in this game for his goal, there is not a player in the world to touch him. We found the real Ryan Giggs. He can't be matched for the excitement he can provide. We still teased him about the great pass he got from Patrick Vieira to set him off on his scoring run.

So that's us into the final and I must immediately lock the thought away. That's the right place for it with so many important games still to come at this crucial part of the season. It's important we keep our feet on the ground, but Steve McClaren is organising a celebration lunch at an Italian restaurant in a few days' time. It's the team spirit and camaraderie that are going to make it difficult for us to be beaten. ❜

		P	W	D	L	F	A	Pts
	18 April 1999							
1	Manchester Utd	32	19	10	3	72	32	67
2	Chelsea	33	17	13	3	49	26	64
3	Arsenal	32	17	12	3	43	13	63
4	Leeds Utd	33	16	11	6	53	29	59
5	Aston Villa	34	14	10	10	45	39	52
6	West Ham Utd	34	14	9	11	39	41	51
7	Middlesbrough	34	12	14	8	46	42	50
8	Derby County	33	12	11	10	37	41	47
9	Liverpool	32	12	8	12	57	42	44
10	Tottenham Hotspur	32	10	13	9	36	37	43
11	Newcastle Utd	33	11	9	13	44	48	42
12	Wimbledon	33	10	11	12	37	50	41
13	Leicester City	32	9	13	10	34	41	40
14	Sheffield Wednesday	33	11	5	17	38	39	38
15	Everton	34	9	10	15	31	41	37
16	Coventry City	34	10	7	17	35	47	37
17	Charlton Athletic	33	7	11	15	35	44	32
18	Blackburn Rovers	33	7	11	15	35	46	32
19	Southampton	34	8	7	19	31	63	31
20	Nottingham Forest	34	4	9	21	30	66	21

Match Report

Rival fans are singing a slightly different tune now. When Teddy Sheringham first joined Manchester United, opposition supporters, especially those from London, delighted in reminding him that he had said he was leaving Spurs in order to win medals but had finished his first season at Old Trafford without a trophy. The fact that this season has seen him making fewer first-team appearances than any of the strikers has not helped his standing in the eyes of the fans either.

But Sheringham is now coming into his own, and he was an influential figure in knocking Arsenal out of the FA Cup as well as becoming the key man in the destruction of Sheffield Wednesday in this match at Old Trafford.

Benito Carbone fired a couple of warning shots for the visitors but the United steamroller was soon rolling as Sheringham set up Ole Gunnar Solskjaer for a goal in the 34th minute. The second-string spearhead was working with great understanding as Solskjaer returned the compliment with a centre glanced in by Sheringham for a two-goal interval lead.

Jesper Blomqvist made a key contribution as the manager juggled his players to keep them all fit and fresh for the demanding climax to the season.

Alex Ferguson repeatedly rings the changes but rarely leaves out Roy Keane.

Then Sheringham was involved in setting up a goal for Paul Scholes just after the hour as United cruised home despite the absence of the injured Giggs. Cole, Yorke, Beckham and Schmeichel were all held back for next week's crucial clash with Juventus.

Manager's Report

❝ Given our tough programme of the last few weeks, even our staunchest supporter would have forgiven us if we had slipped a bit, but the players just seem to be taking everything thrown at them in their stride, and despite a demanding FA Cup replay in midweek, the boys ran up a convincing win over Sheffield Wednesday.

What I am finding is an increasing momentum in the team spirit. Jimmy Ryan and I worked hard on that after Brian Kidd left and it continued to be high on our agenda when Steve McClaren joined us. Steve's arrival helped considerably because it gave us an extra body on the senior coaching staff which enabled us to concentrate even more on the mood and attitude of the players.

There is no question in my mind, they are absolutely flying and it is a pleasure to recall the happiness of the dressing-room after knocking Arsenal out of the FA Cup. The atmosphere about the place tells me that these guys are not going to fail us in any game.

Beating Wednesday 3–0 at Old Trafford is not exactly a landmark occasion in the history of Manchester United; you might even say it was expected of us, but at the same time I am sure there are a few people who might have anticipated a slip-up. Happily, we were never in any danger.

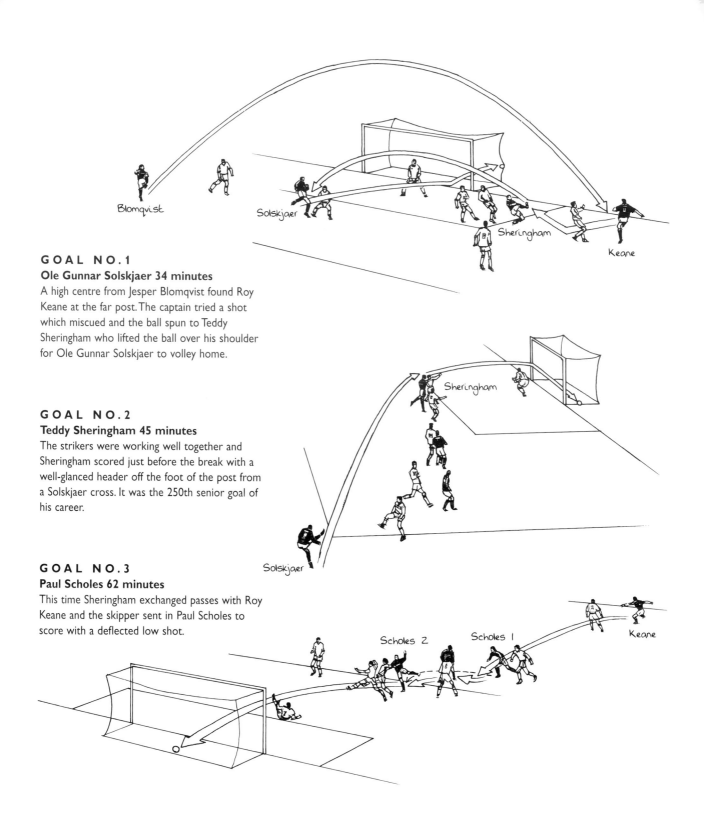

GOAL NO.1
Ole Gunnar Solskjaer 34 minutes

A high centre from Jesper Blomqvist found Roy Keane at the far post. The captain tried a shot which miscued and the ball spun to Teddy Sheringham who lifted the ball over his shoulder for Ole Gunnar Solskjaer to volley home.

GOAL NO.2
Teddy Sheringham 45 minutes

The strikers were working well together and Sheringham scored just before the break with a well-glanced header off the foot of the post from a Solskjaer cross. It was the 250th senior goal of his career.

GOAL NO.3
Paul Scholes 62 minutes

This time Sheringham exchanged passes with Roy Keane and the skipper sent in Paul Scholes to score with a deflected low shot.

I kept Ole Gunnar Solskjaer and Teddy Sheringham in the team after their efforts against Arsenal. This was their chance and they deserved it. It was a pleasure to watch them play and the scoreline was a fair reflection of their efforts together. There could easily have been more goals.

In management you become sensitive to the mood of the players and I just know things are right. There is little for me to do except watch for any sign of complacency. I might even look overmuch for tell-tale indications of the players taking too much for granted, but I can't help it because it is simply a natural thing in my style of management. I always have a queue of doubts in my mind. It's part of my armoury. Maybe that's what sets us in such relentless pursuit of the trophies, especially this season with three targets in our sights.

The win keeps us at the top of the table by a point with a game in hand. The bonus is that Andy Cole and Dwight Yorke are fit and fresh for the big one, the second leg of our European semi-final against Juventus.

Two of the goalscorers with every reason to feel pleased – Teddy Sheringham and Paul Scholes.

Manchester United: Van der Gouw, G. Neville, P. Neville, Keane (Greening 63), Brown, Stam (May 63), Scholes, Butt, Solskjaer, Sheringham, Blomqvist (Irwin 75)

Sheffield Wednesday: Srnicek, Atherton, Hinchcliffe, Jonk, Thome, Walker, Alexandersson (Scott 55), Carbone, Sonner, Booth (Cresswell 71), Rudi

Semi-final, second leg	
Bayern Munich 1	Dynamo Kiev 0
Juventus 2	Manchester Utd 3

Match Report

Juventus stunned United with two quick goals from Filippo Inzaghi and the Italians must have thought they were home and dry. They had not reckoned with United's powers of recovery and by half-time Roy Keane and Dwight Yorke had scored to put United back in front by virtue of two away goals.

Andy Cole, who hit a post, scored in the second half to clinch an emphatic 3–2 victory on the night. Unhappily, Roy Keane and Paul Scholes were booked and will be suspended for the final.

Manager's Report

❝ One of my tactics throughout our European campaign, and especially in the days building up to this big game, was to keep saying at press conferences and in interviews that despite being away from home we would score. I put great emphasis on this, partly because I believed it to be true, but also to put doubt and concern in the minds of our opponents.

I said in Turin, not that it would be nice if we scored, but that we would most definitely get a goal. I took this positive attitude with the players, too. I said in my pre-match talk that if Juventus scored it

Andy Cole sealed victory with the third goal in an amazing recovery.

mattered not, because after drawing 1–1 in the first leg, just one away goal from us would put the game back in our court.

Although I had tried to ease their worries about conceding a goal, little did I anticipate that we would go two down, and in the first 11 minutes!

The first goal annoyed me because it was poor defending following a corner. The second didn't bother me because it was a deflection off Jaap Stam's boot and it was just bad luck.

I recognised that Juventus then had a tactical problem. They had to decide whether to go for a third goal and kill us off or sit back on the aggregate 3–1 lead and say to themselves, that's it, we're through!

Goals change games might be a cliché but it's nevertheless true and we at last started to get some momentum into our game. We raised the tempo and it was simply too much for Juventus. It was the finest display I have ever had from United with an intensity and speed of passing that was absolutely brilliant.

Roy Keane's goal after 24 minutes got us back into it and Juventus started to look concerned. What a remarkable performance from our captain. He was booked soon after scoring, which with a previous yellow card meant he was out of the final should we get there. But far from inhibiting him, the caution seemed to inspire him to make sure the others got to Barcelona. It was a truly selfless contribution

Roy Keane scores the first goal on the way to a significant win in Italy.

GOAL NO.1
Roy Keane 24 minutes
Roy Keane led the fight-back from the front, like the super skipper he is, to score with a glancing header at the near post from a David Beckham corner.

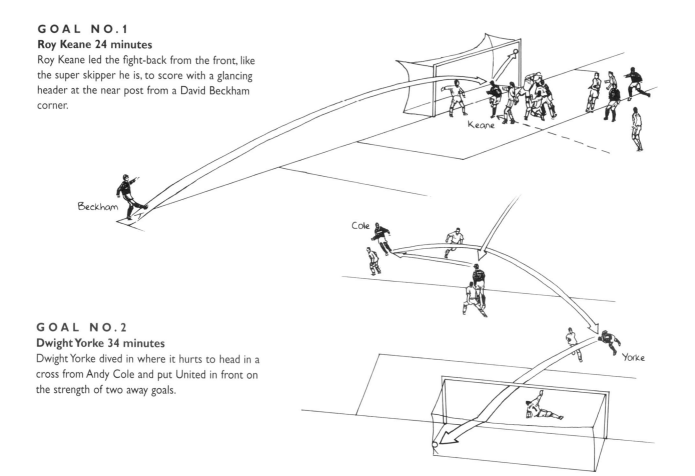

Beckham

Keane

Cole

Yorke

GOAL NO.2
Dwight Yorke 34 minutes
Dwight Yorke dived in where it hurts to head in a cross from Andy Cole and put United in front on the strength of two away goals.

and everyone responded. Dwight Yorke levelled the score on the night and that goal put us in front because we had now scored two away goals.

Juventus had to come at us. Tactically, they are very good and they made changes for the second half, bringing on Montero and Amoruso to replace Juliano and Birindelli. It was a gamble for them because Montero wasn't fully fit but full credit to him, he and Edgar Davids proved to be their two best players. They were superb. We changed our tactics, too, and went into a back four again, counterattacking well, particularly through David Beckham, and eventually we ground them down.

Their legs started to go in the last 20 minutes in the face of our ceaseless probing and I knew whoever scored next would come out on top. Fortunately it was us following Peter Schmeichel's long kick. Dwight Yorke beat the two central defenders. He was tripped by the goalkeeper but Andy Cole was there to hit the ball into the net.

Six minutes to go and we were in the final. Six minutes in which to relish the greatest football moment in my life, at least up to this point! I have always been happy with what I have achieved but the European Cup has eluded me. This is my eighth attempt and getting to

Barcelona is a fantastic experience. Juventus's manager, Carlo Ancelotti, was ever so gracious and their President wished us success in the final. Juventus are a big and great club. Class oozes out of them.

It is a great moment for Manchester United. We passed the test against Inter Milan and now we have knocked out another Italian giant. **,**

Juventus: Peruzzi, Ferrara, Birindelli (Amoruso 45), Pessotto, Juliano (Montero 45), Deschamps, Di Livio (Fonseca 80), Conte, Inzaghi, Davids, Zidane

Manchester United: Schmeichel, G. Neville, Irwin, Keane, Johnsen, Stam, Beckham, Butt, Cole, Yorke, Blomqvist (Scholes 68)

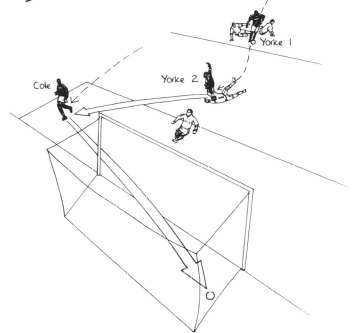

GOAL NO.3
Andy Cole 84 minutes
Juventus stopped a determined thrust by Dwight Yorke with a foul, but Andy Cole was on hand to smash the ball home and make the game safe.

Alex Ferguson relaxes in celebratory mood, as well he might – Manchester United are in the final.

	25 April 1999	P	W	D	L	F	A	Pts
1	Arsenal	34	19	12	3	54	15	69
2	Manchester Utd	33	19	11	3	73	33	68
3	Chelsea	34	17	14	3	49	26	65
4	Leeds Utd	34	16	12	6	54	30	60
5	Aston Villa	35	15	10	10	47	39	55
6	West Ham Utd	35	15	9	11	41	42	54
7	Middlesbrough	35	12	14	9	47	48	50
8	Derby County	34	12	12	10	37	41	48
9	Liverpool	34	13	8	13	60	44	47
10	Tottenham Hotspur	34	11	13	10	41	40	46
11	Leicester City	34	11	13	10	36	41	46
12	Newcastle Utd	35	11	11	13	46	50	44
13	Wimbledon	35	10	12	13	39	56	42
14	Sheffield Wednesday	35	11	7	17	39	40	40
15	Everton	35	10	10	15	35	42	40
16	Coventry City	35	10	7	18	35	48	37
17	Blackburn Rovers	34	7	11	16	36	49	32
18	Charlton Athletic	35	7	11	17	37	52	32
19	Southampton	35	8	8	19	31	63	32
20	Nottingham Forest	35	4	9	22	30	68	21

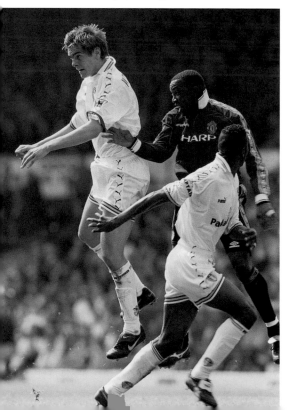

An aerial challenge from Dwight Yorke.

Match Report

Leeds started with the youthful enthusiasm that is the hallmark of their team these days under David O'Leary. Within a couple of minutes Lee Bowyer had whistled a header narrowly over the bar and it took a smothering block by Peter Schmeichel to stop Alan Smith in his tracks.

It was an unnerving start for United's new pairing in central defence. Wes Brown was in for the injured Ronny Johnsen and David May was pulled in late for Jaap Stam following a flare-up of Stam's Achilles injury during the pre-match warm-up.

It was no great surprise when the always threatening Harry Kewell pounced on slack defending to send in Jimmy Floyd Hasselbaink who scored with a shot that went in off the post.

United continued to live dangerously, but with Roy Keane beginning to exert more influence in midfield in the second half, the Leeds goal came under threat as well. Ten minutes after the break, Andy Cole equalised and right at the end Dwight Yorke could have snatched all the points. The striker cut in from the left and after an exchange of passes with substitute Teddy Sheringham had Nigel Martyn in his sights only to shoot high and wide.

Manager's Report

❝The game at Elland Road was what you would expect, starting with the usual hateful welcome from the Leeds fans as the coach rolled into the ground on a boiling hot day.

With Ronny Johnsen out with injury I had brought in Wes Brown to play alongside Jaap Stam. At least, that was the plan until Jaap felt his Achilles in the warm-up and had to drop out. This meant a rare appearance for David May who would have been one of the substitutes after a long absence through injury. For 45 minutes, David and Wes looked as though they were playing their first-ever game together, which at this level they probably were!

Leeds were the better side and went one up after half an hour through Jimmy Floyd Hasselbaink. They showed a freshness in the hot conditions which was lacking in our boys who were taking a long time to settle. It couldn't have been easy for them, of course, after the mental and physical demands of the midweek match against Juventus.

But they had come too far now for tiredness to beat them. Excuses about being weary just did not come into it, and at half-time there was a general revving up, as you might expect from a Manchester United team a goal down.

I didn't miss the point of asking them if they were the team we had talked about after Wednesday night. I asked them to consider whether this was the spirit everyone had been remarking on after the great recovery against Juventus. They replied in convincing fashion and were terrific as they clawed their way back to 1–1 with another Cole goal. We should have won the match but Dwight Yorke missed a sitter. As usual he turned round and smiled. It was just as well he was out of throttling range!

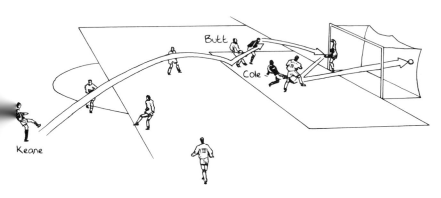

Butt
Cole
Keane

GOAL NO.1
Andy Cole 55 minutes

Nicky Butt made a penetrating run into the box and was picked out unerringly by Roy Keane. Butt's header was parried by Nigel Martyn but it only reached Andy Cole who snapped up the loose ball and prodded it over the line from just three to four yards out.

So it was a hard-won point and, away at Leeds perhaps, on reflection, not a bad result.

There is certainly a silver lining ahead with a week's break, a chance for the players to recover from the little injuries, aches and pains that come with playing twice a week and no recovery time. Rest also brings back energy, again important for the final push with crucial games to play.

Training is minimal now because it's simply not an issue. Mental fitness and freshness are the key. If the players feel strong in their minds, they will be strong on the pitch.

Overall, I am satisfied. I know some supporters will be thinking about the two points that have got away, but we have to be realistic. We are not going to win every game, and I am just grateful for the way they have come out of the match with something after draining semi-finals in two competitions.

Above all, they have once more demonstrated their phenomenal character coming from behind. They just don't know when they are beaten, and my feelings as we went home from Elland Road were of incredible pride and optimism. 〞

Leeds United: Martyn, Jones, Harte, Woodgate (Wetherall 59), Radebe, McPhail, Batty, Smith, Hasselbaink (Wijnhard 87), Kewell, Bowyer

Manchester United: Schmeichel, G. Neville, Irwin (P. Neville 71), May, Brown, Keane, Beckham (Scholes 84), Butt, Cole, Yorke, Blomqvist (Sheringham 76)

Roy Keane took a grip on the game in the second half and with a typical drive forward the captain started the scoring move for a hard-won point.

		P	W	D	L	F	A	Pts
	2 May 1999							
1	Arsenal	35	20	12	3	55	15	72
2	Manchester Utd	34	20	11	3	75	34	71
3	Chelsea	35	18	14	3	52	27	68
4	Leeds Utd	35	17	12	6	59	31	63
5	Aston Villa	36	15	10	11	48	41	55
6	West Ham Utd	36	15	9	12	42	47	54
7	Middlesbrough	36	12	15	9	48	49	51
8	Liverpool	35	14	8	13	63	46	50
9	Derby County	35	12	12	11	37	42	48
10	Tottenham Hotspur	35	11	13	11	43	43	46
11	Leicester City	35	11	13	11	37	43	46
12	Newcastle Utd	36	11	12	13	47	51	45
13	Wimbledon	36	10	12	14	40	58	42
14	Sheffield Wednesday	36	11	7	18	39	42	40
15	Everton	36	10	10	16	36	45	40
16	Coventry City	36	11	7	18	37	49	40
17	Southampton	36	9	8	19	33	64	35
18	Blackburn Rovers	35	7	12	16	36	49	33
19	Charlton Athletic	36	7	12	17	37	52	33
20	Nottingham Forest	36	5	9	22	32	68	24

David Beckham's free kick was a winner.

Match Report

It's tight at the top! United went into this match in second place, one point behind Arsenal, albeit with a game in hand. They came out of it in exactly the same position with four games to go.

United's two drawn league games in April have proved costly. The Gunners wiped out a four-point gap to leapfrog into the lead, but there is no stopping the Reds now. The pressure is on and United are certainly up for it.

In an all-action start, Paul Scholes bustled through to make a diving header, well saved by Michael Oakes. Oakes didn't know much about a free kick from David Beckham, though – it was headed off the line at the other end of his goal by Gareth Southgate – and the Villa goalkeeper was certainly stranded when Steve Watson put the ball past him for an own-goal under pressure from Scholes.

Villa were not finished yet, however, and Julian Joachim scored a first-half equaliser from Steve Stone's centre, which could have taken a slight deflection off David May.

United won the game immediately after the break with a free-kick special from David Beckham. Denis Irwin had a penalty saved after Phil Neville had been pushed over. Had he been able to beat Oakes, it would have spared the home supporters an anxious last few minutes.

Manager's Report

❝ Andy Cole had an injury so I left him out and brought Teddy Sheringham back. Ronny Johnsen returned for Wes Brown and David May continued with Jaap Stam still nursing along his Achilles problem.

It was a nervous game, maybe because we are now into May with everyone sensing that there is not long to go. We have to weather that, though, and for an hour or so we did well.

We enjoyed the bonus of an own-goal by Villa, but then we went slack and they drew level. Julian Joachim's goal knocked us back on our heels for a bit, and at half-time, I concentrated on reminding the players of the qualities which had first made them championship challengers. I urged them to get back to passing the ball properly. It was a matter of getting back on track and they didn't waste any time when they went out for the second half.

David Beckham gave us the perfect start by hitting one of his amazing free kicks. For some reason Villa had only two men in their defensive wall. I bet they don't do that again, at least against Beckham.

We should have won more comfortably but Denis Irwin missed a penalty, the first miss I can recall in my time, and it shocked us all. But we eased through 2–1 and I console myself with the thought that there comes a time when winning is more important than the actual performance. This was certainly one of those days with just four league games to go!

It's a tense period of course, but not exactly how one writer described it when he referred to "treble torture" and said we were "facing days of hell" in our quest for glory. Certainly my nerves are tingling and the expectations weigh heavily, but if I am honest, I am enjoying every minute of every day. We are on a rollercoaster, perhaps,

Manchester United: Schmeichel, G. Neville, Irwin, May (Brown 79), Johnsen, Scholes, Beckham, Butt, Yorke, Sheringham, Blomqvist (P. Neville 63)

Aston Villa: Oakes, Stone, Wright, Southgate, Calderwood, Watson, Taylor, Draper (Thompson 67), Dublin (Vassell 76), Merson, Joachim

Steve Watson runs the ball into his own net under the eye of Dwight Yorke, giving United an easy start.

but I am just elated to be challenging on three fronts at this late stage of the season. The players are loving it, too. It's not something that should be taken for granted – this is a very special season. The treble wouldn't be worth striving for if there wasn't pressure. It's what happens in football at this level.

Already I feel that no matter what happens in these last few games we are witnessing something that may be impossible to repeat. We have nosed in front at the top of the table again, and to be playing in the finals of both the FA Cup and the Champions League, along with setting the pace for the Premiership, is no mean achievement.

I am proud of the way we have done it. We have scored well over a hundred goals this season and I don't think there has been a more entertaining or exciting team to watch.

I hope our fans are enjoying the ride because this is the pinnacle of football, and as I say, it's not torture, it's more like sheer bliss! ⟩

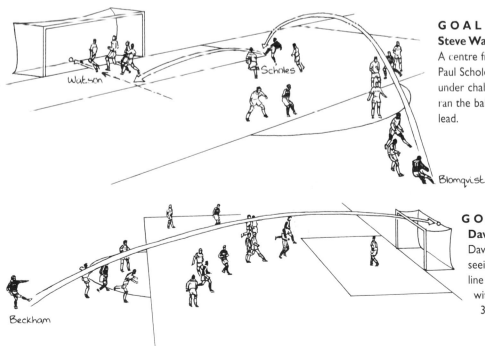

GOAL NO.1
Steve Watson 20 minutes (own-goal)
A centre from Jesper Blomqvist put Villa in trouble. Paul Scholes pulled the ball back across goal and under challenge from Dwight Yorke, Steve Watson ran the ball into his own net to give United the lead.

GOAL NO.2
David Beckham 47 minutes
David Beckham, perhaps still smarting from seeing an earlier free kick headed off the line by Gareth Southgate, made no mistake with this one, guiding it with precision from 30 yards into an unreachable top corner.

6 May 1999							
	P	W	D	L	F	A	Pts
1 Arsenal	36	21	12	3	58	16	75
2 Manchester Utd	35	20	12	3	77	36	72
3 Chelsea	36	19	14	3	53	27	71
4 Leeds Utd	36	17	12	7	59	32	63
5 Aston Villa	36	15	10	11	48	41	55
6 West Ham Utd	36	15	9	12	42	47	54
7 Liverpool	36	14	9	13	65	48	51
8 Middlesbrough	36	12	15	9	48	49	51
9 Derby County	36	13	12	11	39	43	51
10 Tottenham Hotspur	36	11	13	12	44	46	46
11 Leicester City	36	11	13	12	38	45	46
12 Newcastle Utd	36	11	12	13	47	51	45
13 Wimbledon	36	10	12	14	40	58	42
14 Sheffield Wednesday	36	11	7	18	39	42	40
15 Everton	36	10	10	16	36	45	40
16 Coventry City	36	11	7	18	37	49	40
17 Southampton	36	9	8	19	33	64	35
18 Blackburn Rovers	35	7	12	16	36	49	33
19 Charlton Athletic	36	7	12	17	37	52	33
20 Nottingham Forest	36	5	9	22	32	68	24

Match Report

United set off in fine style. Dwight Yorke's great goal from David Beckham's 22nd minute cross and a penalty scored just before the hour seemed to have locked up all the points. But matches with Liverpool are renowned for surprises and they scored two goals in the last 20 minutes, forcing a draw.

United hotly disputed the first of these goals – a Jamie Redknapp penalty, the result of a harsh decision against Jesper Blomqvist. What really aggravated United was referee David Elleray's decision to give Denis Irwin a second yellow card which put him out of the FA Cup final.

Salt was rubbed into the wound when former Red Paul Ince bobbed up to grab the equaliser.

Manager's Report

❝ Going to Anfield is like a pilgrimage. It's the derby of all derbies. It always raises my hackles, more so this year because this is a major match.

We have mixed fortunes there, though I think we probably have as good a record as anyone. Mind you, you never get it easy. Whatever you get there you earn. I am sure they feel exactly the same about us.

In fact, it has been an absolute privilege over the years to play at Liverpool, and the interesting thing is that, despite the incredible intensity, the games are invariably entertaining. I can think of a couple of 3–3 draws that ran the whole gamut of emotions.

One year we were 3–1 down with 15 minutes to go and only ten men but we retrieved it for 3–3. In the Cantona era we were once three up and looking likely to cruise the final 20 minutes only to end up hanging on for dear life.

This game was obviously going to go a long way towards deciding the outcome of the championship and we really played exceptionally

Denis Irwin scores from the penalty spot, but he missed the FA Cup final after two yellow cards.

well. Dwight Yorke put us ahead in the first half after fantastic football up the right wing and a magnificent cross from David Beckham. The goal stunned Anfield, and I know why. The precision of the move and the accuracy of the centre were simply breathtaking.

The game may have been decided midway in the second half when Jamie Carragher almost cut Jesper Blomqvist in two to concede a penalty which Denis Irwin put away. It must have been an obvious penalty for it to have been given at Anfield by David Elleray!

So we were two up and cruising, though as I say it is always a mistake to make assumptions at Anfield, especially with Mr Elleray refereeing. I cannot understand how he came to give a penalty against Blomqvist for what to me was a fair challenge on Oyvind Leonhardsen. Maybe he was evening up the penalty score, but this wasn't in the same league as Carragher's offence. Anyway, Jamie Redknapp put the spot-kick away, and it wasn't long before Elleray compounded his penalty decision by dismissing Denis Irwin after booking him a second time.

The second card was presumably for kicking the ball away after the player had run it out of play. Yet TV later showed that there was one-sixth of a second between the whistle blowing and Denis striking the ball. I believe the player was simply in the act of playing the ball as the whistle went. Even Phil Thompson, as Liverpool as they come, was shaking his head in apologetic disbelief.

I don't see the Harrow schoolmaster as being anti-Manchester United, but it was at that point for me that his reputation sank. It was a cruel decision because of course it puts Denis out of the FA Cup final.

So now, with ten men, we were fighting for our lives, and as luck would have it, Paul Ince scrambled Liverpool a last-minute equaliser. The draw tightened up the top of the table with Arsenal back in front. The name of the game now is winning! ⟩

Liverpool 2
Manchester United 2

Liverpool: Friedel, Carragher, Matteo, Song (Berger 57), Staunton (Thompson 79), Babb, McManaman, Leonhardsen, Riedle, Ince, Redknapp

Manchester United: Schmeichel, G. Neville, Irwin, Keane, Johnsen, Stam, Beckham, Scholes, Cole (Butt 77), Yorke, Blomqvist (P. Neville 77)

Roy Keane

GOAL NO.1
Dwight Yorke 22 minutes
Roy Keane and David Beckham tied up the Liverpool defence on the right before Beckham skimmed over a great cross for Dwight Yorke to score with a header at the far post.

GOAL NO.2
Denis Irwin 57 minutes penalty
Jamie Carragher walloped Jesper Blomqvist to concede a penalty which United had no hesitation handing to Denis Irwin, despite his miss four days earlier. The Irishman confidently hit his spot-kick wide of the diving Brad Friedel.

9 May 1999

		P	W	D	L	F	A	Pts
1	Manchester Utd	36	21	12	3	78	36	75
2	Arsenal	36	21	12	3	58	16	75
3	Chelsea	36	19	14	3	53	27	71
4	Leeds Utd	36	17	12	7	59	32	63
5	Aston Villa	37	15	10	12	51	45	55
6	West Ham Utd	37	15	9	13	42	53	54
7	Derby County	37	13	13	11	39	43	52
8	Liverpool	37	14	9	14	65	49	51
9	Middlesbrough	37	12	15	10	48	50	51
10	Leicester City	37	12	13	12	40	45	49
11	Tottenham Hotspur	36	11	13	12	44	46	46
12	Newcastle Utd	37	11	12	14	47	53	45
13	Sheffield Wednesday	37	12	7	18	40	42	43
14	Everton	37	11	10	16	42	45	43
15	Wimbledon	37	10	12	15	40	60	42
16	Coventry City	37	11	8	18	37	49	41
17	Southampton	37	10	8	19	35	64	38
18	Charlton Athletic	37	8	12	17	41	55	36
19	Blackburn Rovers	36	7	12	17	37	51	33
20	Nottingham Forest	37	6	9	22	34	69	27

Match Report

United knew they had to win this one after letting two points slip at Liverpool in midweek and finding Arsenal putting the pressure on by climbing above them again.

This 2–1 win put the fierce rivals level on points with the same number of games played so it was a vital success which owed more to solid graft than flair.

United started with the urgency you would expect and appeared to have opened the scoring after half an hour when Roy Keane let fly with a rocket that proved too hot for Mark Schwarzer to hold. Teddy Sheringham, back in the team and playing an increasingly important role, pounced on the rebound and quickly had it in the net, but he was ruled offside. It was a close call and television later suggested that it should have been a goal.

Dwight Yorke raised United's hopes with a header but old boy Gary Pallister was displaying the kind of quality that had served United so well in his previous life at Old Trafford.

Jesper Blomqvist threatened as well, but United suffered a major blow in the 25th minute when Roy Keane limped off and had to be replaced by Nicky Butt.

Middlesbrough immediately came more into the game and Mark Summerbell was narrowly wide with a shot. United had the last word in the first half, though, when Butt lofted a ball into the opposition penalty area. Sheringham used his height to head across to Yorke for the striker to claim an injury-time goal, his 29th of the season and a typical strike. Boro claimed offside, and it was another close call, but this time the decision went in United's favour.

The manager obviously worked hard during the break to try to settle his nervous charges down, and for a spell they got their game together with strikes from Sheringham, Paul Scholes and Gary Neville.

Andy Cole was brought on to replace Blomqvist for the last 25

Paul Scholes strives for a key win at Middlesbrough.

minutes and tried hard to improve the goal difference, which at this stage looked as if it could decide the championship. He broke clear ten minutes from the end but he was forced wide and as he tried to lob the goalkeeper he lifted the ball over the bar as well. Middlesbrough came strongly at the end but United hung on for a scruffy and close but nevertheless key victory.

Manager's Report

❝ It was a scrappy game with no flow but we won 1–0 with another strike from Dwight Yorke.

We certainly needed the win after dropping points at Liverpool because it couldn't be closer at the top of the table. We are now level on points with Arsenal and share exactly the same goal difference. We have one small advantage. If it comes down to a tie-breaker we have scored 20 more goals than the Gunners and that would see us come out on top if we can't be separated by points or goal difference.

Incidentally, our superior scoring is an accurate reflection, I think, of our adventurous football, our determination to attack opponents both home and away and enter the risk zone in pursuit of our challenge. I believe it gives us the better right to win the Premiership and entitles us to consider that we would make worthy champions.

But I am running on ahead of myself. It's the points we are after, and though we got them at Middlesbrough I have to admit that we will need to play better if we are to hold off Arsenal. There was a lot of nervousness about our play, understandable of course as the tension builds. A lively pitch and a breeze of the kind you often get in the north east didn't help.

It was the kind of game you get on a run-in for the championship. We should have scored more than the one goal, but as I say it is the result that counts more than the performance at this stage. ❞

Dwight Yorke scored the winner with his 29th goal of the season.

Middlesbrough: Schwarzer, Stockdale, Gordon, Vickers, Gavin (Campbell 72), Pallister, Mustoe, Summerbell, Ricard, Deane, Townsend

Manchester United: Schmeichel, G. Neville, Irwin, May, Keane (Butt 25), Stam, Beckham, Scholes (P. Neville 89), Yorke, Sheringham, Blomqvist (Cole 66)

GOAL NO.1
Dwight Yorke 45 minutes

A cross from David Beckham was hoofed away by the Boro defence but Nicky Butt hit it back high into the danger area for Teddy Sheringham to nod across to Dwight Yorke. The striker finished off the simple move with a header for his 29th goal of the season.

9 May 1999							
	P	W	D	L	F	A	Pts
1 Manchester Utd	37	21	13	3	78	36	76
2 Arsenal	37	21	12	4	58	17	75
3 Chelsea	37	19	15	3	55	29	72
4 Leeds Utd	37	18	12	7	60	32	66
5 Aston Villa	37	15	10	12	51	45	55
6 West Ham Utd	37	15	9	13	42	53	54
7 Derby County	37	13	13	11	39	43	52
8 Liverpool	37	14	9	14	65	49	51
9 Middlesbrough	37	12	15	10	48	50	51
10 Leicester City	37	12	13	12	40	45	49
11 Tottenham Hotspur	37	11	14	12	46	48	47
12 Newcastle Utd	37	11	12	14	47	53	45
13 Sheffield Wednesday	37	12	7	18	40	42	43
14 Everton	37	11	10	16	42	45	43
15 Wimbledon	37	10	12	15	40	60	42
16 Coventry City	37	11	8	18	37	49	41
17 Southampton	37	10	8	19	35	64	38
18 Charlton Athletic	37	8	12	17	41	55	36
19 Blackburn Rovers	37	7	13	17	37	51	34
20 Nottingham Forest	37	6	9	22	34	69	27

Match Report

United seem to be running out of goals at just the wrong time, although Blackburn put up a more spirited display than you might associate with a club looking doomed to relegation. Perhaps Brian Kidd's savaging of his players' attitude in their previous match had got through to them because there was a brisk purpose about their play, especially towards the end when Peter Schmeichel was forced to make a series of important saves to keep the game goalless.

Overall, though, United were the more dominant side. Ryan Giggs hit a post with a header and Andy Cole had a good effort saved by John Filan.

Alex Ferguson kept Jaap Stam off at half-time to protect his Achilles and heel problem and later sent on Teddy Sheringham and Paul Scholes in an effort to break the deadlock. He was rewarded by a near thing from David May but had to rely on Schmeichel's excellence at the end to hang on to what may prove to be a title-winning point!

Arguably the most significant aspect of the match was the return to action of Giggs. After missing six matches with his recurring hamstring injury, he came through safely in time for the crucial games ahead.

Manager's Report

❛Aside from the title implications, this match brought me head to head with Brian Kidd, my former assistant, but what struck me more than anything was the way they decided to play. They had one striker, Ashley Ward, up front, two wide men and three in midfield. I got the feeling that their priority was to make sure that we didn't win the championship on their ground.

I wondered if anyone else had been influencing Brian because there was plenty at stake for him. Blackburn required a victory to avoid relegation and the way he had set his team out to play didn't suggest an attacking blitz! Anyway that was Brian's problem, and although he

Ryan Giggs tripping the light fantastic at Blackburn.

United were running out of goals, despite the best efforts of David Beckham (left) and Dwight Yorke (below).

had left Old Trafford in circumstances which had surprised me, I think we both had too much on our minds to worry about the split.

We had a new coach and we were in good heart because the night before, Leeds of all teams had done us a massive favour by beating Arsenal 1–0. This meant that a victory at Ewood Park would send us into our final game requiring nothing more than a draw to become champions.

So we certainly had plenty of incentive. We had some decent moments early in the game, but the way they were playing was hard to break down. I also had to leave Roy Keane out after he was crocked at Middlesbrough.

It was a scrambly sort of game. We should have done better. David May went close but overall we didn't really do enough to win the match. We couldn't complain at 0–0 and as things have turned out it isn't a bad result because it leaves us a point ahead of Arsenal with just the fixture against Spurs to come at Old Trafford. If anyone had given us the option at the start of the season of going into the final game in front of our own fans with a point advantage, I would have jumped at it!

So I was in good spirits when I went to Brian Kidd's office at the end of the match and was surprised to find him in a cheerful mood as well. Maybe he has been able to distance himself from the responsibility of the relegation that is now Blackburn's fate, or perhaps he feels he has to put on a front following his momentous decision to walk away from the success he enjoyed with us.

Our immediate aim now is to win at Old Trafford on our own ground, in front of our own fans and on the last day of the season. I have long cherished that ambition and now we have the chance of achieving it. All four of my previous championship wins have been finalised on someone else's ground, or before the end of the season courtesy of another result.

Again, there's everything to play for as I prepare for what amounts to three cup finals in ten days – a Premiership shoot-out with Spurs, Newcastle at Wembley and then Bayern Munich in Barcelona. I have asked the players to think only of the Tottenham game while I wrestle with the subtleties of team selection and all the other planning involved. ❯

Blackburn Rovers: Filan, Croft, Davidson, Carsley, Peacock, Henchoz, Gillespie, Dunn, Ward, Jansen (Johnson 81), Wilcox

Manchester United: Schmeichel, G. Neville, Irwin, P. Neville (Scholes 76), Johnsen, Stam (May 45), Beckham, Butt, Cole (Sheringham 71), Yorke, Giggs

		P	W	D	L	F	A	Pts
1	Manchester Utd	38	22	13	3	80	37	79
2	Arsenal	38	22	12	4	59	17	78
3	Chelsea	38	20	15	3	57	30	75
4	Leeds Utd	38	18	13	7	62	34	67
5	West Ham Utd	38	16	9	13	46	53	57
6	Aston Villa	38	15	10	13	51	46	55
7	Liverpool	38	15	9	14	68	49	54
8	Derby County	38	13	13	12	40	45	52
9	Middlesbrough	38	12	15	11	48	54	51
10	Leicester City	38	12	13	13	40	46	49
11	Tottenham Hotspur	38	11	14	13	47	50	47
12	Sheffield Wednesday	38	13	7	18	41	42	46
13	Newcastle Utd	38	11	13	14	48	54	46
14	Everton	38	11	10	17	42	47	43
15	Coventry City	38	11	9	18	39	51	42
16	Wimbledon	38	10	12	16	40	63	42
17	Southampton	38	11	8	19	37	64	41
18	Charlton Athletic	38	8	12	18	41	56	36
19	Blackburn Rovers	38	7	14	17	38	52	35
20	Nottingham Forest	38	7	9	22	35	69	30

Match Report

This was the fans' championship as Alex Ferguson achieved his dream of winning his fifth league title on his own ground in front of his home crowd.

The support rose to acclaim United's powerful finish, unbeaten in the League for 20 matches to pip Arsenal by a point for the title.

The final match was a heart-stopping occasion with Les Ferdinand shooting Spurs ahead in the 25th minute. United responded with characteristic flair. Goals from David Beckham and Andy Cole either side of the interval won them the championship for the twelfth time in their history.

Ryan Giggs was one of the main attacking players in United's championship success.

New coach Steve McClaren (centre) watches anxiously with Alex Ferguson (left) and assistant coach Jimmy Ryan.

Manchester United	2
Tottenham Hotspur	1

Manager's Report

It's in the nature of Manchester United to do things the hard way, and sure enough, we lose a goal.

We so often make a crisis out of a drama and true to form Les Ferdinand lobbed Peter Schmeichel from the narrowest of angles midway through the first half for the first goal of this scrap for the championship. Here we go again, I thought, but as usual we kept plugging away and you could see the character in the team emerging. Roy Keane was back after his ankle injury and he was at his growling best.

It wasn't an easy game for us, and it wasn't simple for Spurs either, knowing that if they beat us they would be handing the league title to Arsenal their deadly rivals; not that that influenced their performance which was honest and challenging.

We steadily improved our game and David Beckham got us an equaliser just before the interval. It was a crucial time, and it meant

Manchester United: Schmeichel, G. Neville, Irwin, May, Johnson, Keane, Beckham, Scholes (Butt 70), Yorke, Sheringham (Cole 45), Giggs (P. Neville 80)

Tottenham Hotspur: Walker, Carr, Edinburgh, Freund, Scales (Young 71), Campbell, Sherwood, Iverson, Anderton, Ferdinand, Ginola (Dominguez 10, Sinton 78)

GOAL NO.1
David Beckham 43 minutes
United produced a great build-up for their 43rd minute equaliser. Paul Scholes and Ryan Giggs exchanged passes to open up the Spurs defence for David Beckham to swerve in a glorious drive.

GOAL NO.2
Andy Cole 48 minutes
Andy Cole didn't start until the second half and then took just three minutes to pull down a high ball from Gary Neville and flick it up again, chipping Ian Walker with consummate cheek.

Alex Ferguson waves to family and friends after winning his fifth Premiership title in seven years.

that during the break, instead of worrying about getting back into the game, I could talk about how we were going to win it.

I also made one of those tough decisions that can come back to haunt you – I took Teddy Sheringham off in favour of Andy Cole. Teddy was visibly hurt and displeased and I had to take time out to sit him down and explain exactly why I was making the change. After we had won the game with a goal from Cole just three minutes after the

Two of the players who shot United to the trophy – Dwight Yorke and Andy Cole.

substitution, people asked me if I felt vindicated, but that was not part of my reaction at all. My main thought was that I just wished I had not felt it was the right thing to do because I knew how much it had hurt Sheringham. But given the same situation I would still make the same decision. I had to react to the situation and do something positive.

It was a great goal by Cole but coming when it did, it left us 42 agonising minutes to sweat. Every minute that ticked by was an eternity. Towards the end of every match I am always looking at my watch, and I was waiting for Graham Poll to blow when the whistle slipped out of his hand. Of all the matches for that to happen. I know we are only talking split seconds here, but it seemed a lot longer to me at the time.

When Graham finally got the whistle to his lips our celebrations started. Everyone was hugging and congratulating. I sprinted on to the field. This was the one that really mattered. This is going to open the door for the other two because it will put everyone in the right frame of mind. It is a great psychological boost knowing that whatever happens at Wembley and Barcelona we have already achieved something very special after a long, hard struggle. The fact that we have done it by just one point ahead of Arsenal, the champions, shows you just how close it has been.

My heart soared as I raced on to the pitch because I just feel we have a great chance now of landing the treble. We are in fantastic shape. This was our 60th game of the season but we are fit and fresh, and the whole place is alive. Training is easy for everyone concerned and the banter in the dressing-room is terrific. The players all have smiles on their faces and Manchester United is the place to be all right. As the manager, this makes all the struggle and pain worthwhile. This is a high that makes up for all the lows that the game inevitably brings.

Excitement is in the air as we prepare for the next two great challenges. ❥

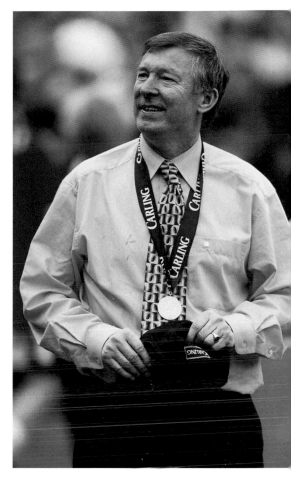

Alex Ferguson proudly wears his championship medal while his champions take their bow.

Match Report

Teddy Sheringham is starting to challenge Ole Gunnar Solskjaer as United's super sub! The Londoner came off the bench in the ninth minute to replace the injured Roy Keane and took only two minutes to shoot United in front.

David Beckham was a revelation after moving to take Keane's midfield role, and Paul Scholes confirmed United's superiority with a second-half goal that clinched the league and FA Cup double.

Manager's Report

‘I had to give a lot of careful consideration to my selection for the FA Cup final team, a game we obviously wanted to win, but which to a certain extent was being overshadowed by the European final against

Manchester United: Schmeichel, G. Neville, P. Neville, May, Johnsen, Keane (Sheringham 9), Beckham, Scholes (Stam 76), Cole (Yorke 60), Solskjaer, Giggs

Newcastle United: Harper, Griffin, Charvet, Domi, Dabizas, Hamann (Ferguson 45), Lee, Solano (Maric 68), Shearer, Ketsbaia (Glass 78), Speed

Paul Scholes has every reason to look pleased with himself after scoring the goal that made sure the FA Cup was on its way to Old Trafford.

Bayern Munich four days later. Did I trust my pool of players to the extent that I could afford to juggle them around and spread the load?

I knew I didn't have Denis Irwin for Wembley through suspension, and similarly Paul Scholes and Roy Keane will be missing from the team in Barcelona. But at least I knew that I would be able to play Phil Neville against Newcastle at Wembley and have Denis fresh for the Champions League final. Then it got more complicated. I decided to risk leaving Dwight Yorke and Teddy Sheringham on the bench for this match with Barcelona in mind, and with Jaap Stam still having problems with his Achilles I was not prepared to bring him back. I definitely want him for the European game, although I did put him on the bench because I felt he deserved an FA Cup final medal.

I left Nicky Butt out because I couldn't afford to risk him being injured. With Scholes and Keane out of the European final, I need Nicky fit and fresh. He will have a lot of work to do and responsibility

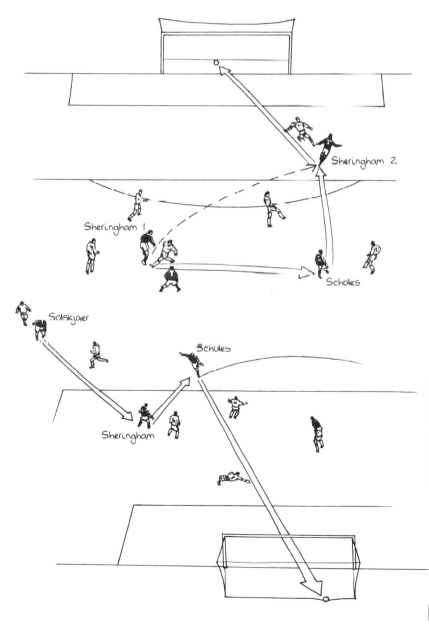

GOAL NO.1
Teddy Sheringham 11 minutes
Andy Cole got Teddy Sheringham away and the striker played a neat one-two with Paul Scholes to close in on goal and beat Steve Harper with a drive from just inside the box.

GOAL NO.2
Paul Scholes 52 minutes
Ole Gunnar Solskjaer snapped up a loose ball after pressure from Ryan Giggs, and brought Teddy Sheringham into play. With his back to goal, Sheringham simply laid the ball into the path of Paul Scholes for a well-taken goal.

The final whistle and United have won the FA Cup. Up go the arms on the bench (above) and up goes the Cup in the hands of skipper Roy Keane (below).

to carry. If he got himself injured I would have a serious problem in midfield.

I took the precaution of leaving Jesper Blomqvist out of the FA Cup final completely. The reasoning is that I intend to play Ryan Giggs in midfield against Bayern with Jesper on the wing. I told him before today's game that he would be playing on Wednesday because I knew it would buck him up after his initial disappointment.

Injuries change things, as we will see, but that was my plan at the time!

At least I knew that Scholes and Keane would be revved up for

Newcastle in what was in effect their last game of the season. That was a positive thing for me, though it lasted until only the sixth minute when Gary Speed clattered our captain. It was a terribly late tackle and it wrecked Keane's ankle.

I have got to say I was surprised at Newcastle's obvious intent. The tackles were flying in and it was amazing that they got through the first period without having anyone sent off.

Keane's departure gave me a dilemma. Should I have had Nicky Butt on the bench to cover this kind of eventuality? Too late now, so I brought on Teddy Sheringham and switched Ole Gunnar Solskjaer to wide right with David Beckham moving inside to play in the centre of the park with Paul Scholes.

Goals change games, but so can substitutes, and on this occasion Sheringham scored with his second touch of the ball to put us in front after only 11 minutes. From what had looked a catastrophic situation without Keane, we had gone in a flash to take the lead.

We were firmly in the driving seat and from then on it was an absolute stroll. I couldn't believe an FA Cup final could be so easy. Once again some of their players were shadows and we hardly saw Alan Shearer in the game. I am even more convinced that there is something amiss between him and his manager.

Paul Scholes made the game safe for us early in the second half when it became even more of a cruise. Scoring at Wembley in the Cup final is not a bad way to sign off. It was obviously bitterly disappointing for Roy to finish the season like that, on top of his suspension. At least he and Paul picked up an FA Cup winner's medal.

Now we must ready ourselves for the third leg of the treble, and I must get down to assessing the brilliant performance by David Beckham after his move to centre midfield. ❯

Manager's Report

'We moved from Wembley straight to Burnham Beeches outside London and trained at Bisham Abbey on Sunday morning preparatory to flying to Spain for the Champions League final.

Although we had just won the FA Cup and completed the double, there was a tremendous sense of purpose and dedication about the players, and of their own accord they were all in bed by midnight with hardly a drink to toast our success. No question, they intended going to Barcelona to beat Bayern Munich.

The Sunday training was great fun, but I had a pressing problem to sort out – where should I play David Beckham after his performance at Wembley?

My first intention had been to play Ryan Giggs in centre midfield so that his pace and penetration would give Lothar Matthaus a few problems. I wanted to search out the veteran German international star, but Beckham's display on Saturday was demanding that I played him centre midfield. He revelled in the role at Wembley and it kept coming back to me that the good pitch at the Nou Camp Stadium would suit him admirably. Nicky Butt could do his usual job in midfield and leave David to control the passing momentum.

So my mind was made up as we boarded Concorde for the flight to

Peter Schmeichel turns in dismay as Mario Basler's free kick hits the back of his net after just six minutes.

Andy Cole tried hard but, like the rest of the team, made little impact on Bayern until the game was almost over.

Barcelona, a touch designed to bring a sense of occasion to our preparations.

Our hotel at Sitges was perfect with a lovely outlook over the sea. I must admit I was taken aback by the number of our supporters staying in the hotel and eagerly waiting to greet us. I let my guard slip. In fact I did more than that, I lost my temper. I had been anticipating a secluded preparation and I shouted at them, why don't you give us a bit of peace, and went on to say that if we didn't win they would be the first to complain.

It was so much on my mind that this was our biggest game for 31 years, since United's only other European Cup success in 1968, and at times players need solitude – not to be cut off completely from the real world, but left to get on with their job without constant autographs and photographs.

In fact, it never became a problem – possibly because I had blown my top – but I regretted I had done it. I place great importance on supporters, and I was out of order. I later apologised to them. It was a difficult moment but we quickly put it behind us.

I organised three team-talks. At the first meeting I told the players who would start and why, and how we could win the game. At the second talk, we went through Bayern's tactics based on how they had played against Kiev, scoring an early goal and shutting up shop. We discussed their threat in the air because they are a big physical side, though not big enough to beat us I insisted. In the third team session, Steve McClaren went through our organisation at set-pieces for and against us.

We watched out for the little things, such as sunbathing. I had to chase David Beckham off his verandah a couple of times. I felt for Phil

GOAL NO.1

Teddy Sheringham 90 minutes

Teddy Sheringham repeated his Wembley heroics as a substitute when he came on to score an injury-time equaliser. David Beckham's corner kick was met by Ryan Giggs but the winger mishit his attempt on goal and the ball skewed to Sheringham who scored from close range with a shot just inside the post.

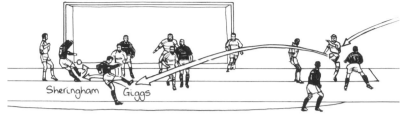

GOAL NO.2

Ole Gunnar Solskjaer 91 minutes

The second super-sub strike came from Ole Gunnar Solskjaer with a volley into the roof of the net at the far post after Teddy Sheringham had headed on another Beckham corner. The Bayern defence, still reeling from the first injury-time stunner, had no answer to the goal which completed a wondrous treble for Manchester United.

The two scoring heroes, Teddy Sheringham and Ole Gunnar Solskjaer, celebrate the treble with three-fingered salutes.

Neville, Teddy Sheringham and Ole Gunnar Solskjaer starting on the bench. There would have been even more heartbreak had Roy Keane and Paul Scholes been available.

We had a fright the night before in training – Beckham ended up sitting with an ice pack on his knee – but it passed and we were free of niggling injuries.

So on to the game itself. Mario Basler gave Bayern the lead in the sixth minute direct from a free kick for an innocuous challenge by Ronny Johnsen on Carsten Jancker. Once ahead, Bayern made it

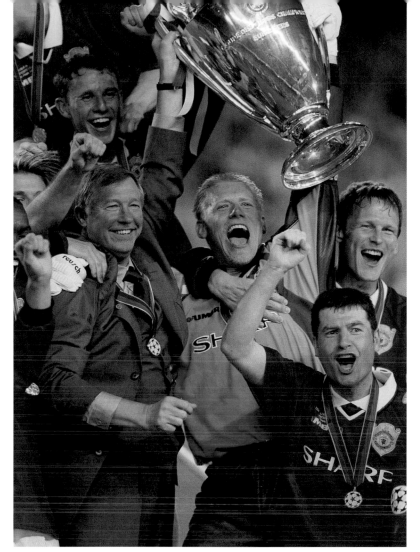

Left: A proud Alex Ferguson joins his joyful players, Nicky Butt, Peter Schmeichel, Teddy Sheringham and Denis Irwin.

Below: The squad line up after their incredible victory against Bayern Munich completed the unique treble.

difficult for us, as expected, and I honestly can't think of anything exciting or significant until those last three incredible minutes.

At half-time I urged the players to get more passing into their game in our usual style. I also told them something Steve Archibald mentioned when he came to watch us train the night before. He recalled his dismay after losing a European final when he said it had been agony looking at the Cup on the table waiting to be presented knowing that he couldn't touch it or hold it. I said to my players, remember that the only way you will get to put your hands on the European Cup is if you win it.

Certainly something seemed to come over them as we got nearly to the end of normal time, and the drama was produced by two David Beckham corners. Teddy Sheringham, on for the last 23 minutes, netted the equaliser and then Ole Gunnar Solskjaer, who didn't come on until the 81st minute, scored the winner.

I have since watched the match video, and although it can be argued we were lucky to score such late goals after the Germans had twice hit the woodwork, I thought we were the better side and deserved to win because we *tried* to win. Bayern relied on their old belief that what you have got you don't give away. They put their trust in their organisation and the machinery of performance, but at the end of the day it was not quite enough. We brought a greater adventure to the final and I think fate rewarded us.

Everyone will have their memory of those last few minutes. I know I have mine. When I close my eyes they flash into my mind. The unique treble has been achieved. **?**

The morning after at the team hotel allowed Alex Ferguson some quiet moments before the flight home and an ecstatic welcome in Manchester.